Working
Women
of Early Modern
Venice

THE JOHNS HOPKINS UNIVERSITY STUDIES
IN HISTORICAL AND POLITICAL SCIENCE

118th Series (2000)

1. Lu Ann Homza, *Religious Authority in the Spanish Renaissance*

2. Victoria E. Thompson, *The Virtuous Marketplace: Men and Women, Money and Politics in Paris, 1830–1870*

3. Monica Chojnacka, *Working Women of Early Modern Venice*

Working Women of Early Modern Venice

Monica Chojnacka

THE
JOHNS
HOPKINS
UNIVERSITY
PRESS
*Baltimore
and London*

This book has been brought to publication with the
generous assistance of the Gladys Krieble Delmas
Foundation.

The Johns Hopkins University Press
2715 North Charles Street
Baltimore, Maryland 21218-4363
www.press.jhu.edu

An earlier version of chapter 1 appeared as "Women,
Men, and Residential Patterns in Early Modern
Venice" in the January 2000 issue of *Journal of
Family History* 25:6–25.

ISBN 0-8018-6485-2

Library of Congress Cataloging-in-Publication Data
will be found at the end of this book.
A catalog record for this book is
available from the British Library.

For Pietro, Giulia, and Anna

Contents

Illustrations and Tables

Acknowledgments

T HIS book owes much to the advice and support of others. Grants have played an important role since I began the research that forms the foundation of the book: a Delmas grant and a Fulbright made that first period of research possible, and a Mabel McLeod Lewis fellowship gave me an uninterrupted year of writing. The Delmas Foundation has been crucial to my work ever since, making possible several trips to Venice to complete my research. I have also received travel help from the University of Georgia, in the form of a Junior Faculty Research Grant and a Sara Moss Grant.

All Venetian scholars know what a joy research in Venice's archives can be. I spent many productive months in three of these. The archive of the Istituzioni di Ricovero e di Educazione is a treasure trove of documents about the city's charitable institutions. The generosity of its archivist, Dottor Giuseppe Ellero, with his knowledge of the archive, made work there both pleasant and productive. I was also fortunate at the Archivio della Curia Patriarcale, where Dottor Youssri Boulos was similarly generous with his expertise. Finally, the majority of my work was conducted at the crown jewel of Venetian archives, the Archivio di Stato di Venezia. I particularly thank three of its archivists, Dottoresse Claudia Salmini, Alessandra Sambo, and Maria Pia Pedani for their excellent advice over the years.

The Department of History at the University of Georgia has been exemplary in making research and publication a priority for its junior faculty, both by arranging convenient teaching schedules and by allowing time off from on-campus duties to conduct research abroad. I wish particularly to acknowledge my departmental chairs, first David Roberts and then James Cobb, for their commitment to their junior faculty's scholarship.

Colleagues and friends, both stateside and overseas, have made the writing of this book bearable, and sometimes enjoyable. These include Katharine Swett, Muriel McLendon, Matteo Casini, Jutta Sperling, Maria Teresa Todesco, Anna Bellavitis, Richard Wetzell, and Alfredo Viggiano. Laura Mason, Bryant Simon, Joshua Cole, Michael Kwass, and Ann Marie Reardon have not only sustained me intellectually and socially, they also helped with babysitting emergencies. Judith C. Brown began as my doctoral advisor and has remained a colleague in the best sense of the word; I continue to value her friendship and counsel.

Barbara J. Harris played a central role in the final year of the manuscript's preparation. She heroically read several drafts and offered key suggestions and insightful criticism, not to mention unstinting support. I owe her a great deal.

Ingeborg Sterzinger Vidoni has been many things to me over the last decade: Venetian host, mother-in-law, and friend. My parents, Stanley Chojnacki and Maureen O'Higgins, in separate but equally crucial ways, have always encouraged and helped me along this journey. I hope they know how grateful I am. My husband, Pietro Vidoni, has not lived with this project for as long as they have, but he has endured its presence more intensely. He often helped me with obscure Venetian words, and that was the least of his contributions. I dedicate this book to him and our two young daughters.

Introduction

Toward the end of the sixteenth century, a young woman named Paolina visited her older sister at the Venetian *ospedale* of S. Giovanni e Paolo, also known as the Derelitti. This charitable institution had originally been founded to shelter orphans, but by the late sixteenth century the Derelitti's mission had expanded to include women in trouble. Paolina's sister, Pollonia, was one of those women: a *convertita,* or reformed prostitute, she had come to the hospital to escape a world of poverty, uncertainty, and danger.

Soon after arriving at the Derelitti, Paolina approached the priests of the house to beg tearfully that she, too, be permitted to remain under the Derelitti's protection. She explained that she was currently living in the home of her employer, a Madonna Faustina, who regularly sent her into the streets on errands, effectively locking her out of the house. The hospital officials interrogated Paolina to make sure that she had no written contract with Faustina; when the girl insisted that she had not, she was allowed to remain at the hospital with her sister.

Four days later Faustina appeared at the hospital searching for her servant. She came with a friend named Maria, who claimed to be Paolina's *ameda,* or aunt. The women demanded to see the girl and, when she was brought to them, Faustina angrily reproached her, saying, "You were wrong not to come back after I sent you to take a hat to my friend." The priest in charge defended Paolina, explaining that she had not run away deliberately, but rather had been convinced to stay by Pollonia, who was horrified that her younger sister had been shoved out of her employer's home to wander the streets. At this, Maria turned to Faustina and exclaimed, "You promised me that you would not send her onto the street anymore." Then Maria advised the priest to do nothing about the matter until Paolina's father came. The two women left, but not before Faustina, still enraged at losing the girl, hurled back at the priest that "I wouldn't take her back now if she shat gold *[non la toria se la mi chagasse oro]*."

But Faustina didn't mean it. Three days later she returned, this time demanding a kerchief of hers that was in Paolina's possession. Nervously, the priest again agreed to bring the girl down to the older woman. He then urged Faustina to meet with the Derelitti's governors and plead her case with them if she thought that Paolina had treated her unfairly. Faustina ignored him, snatched the kerchief from the girl in a brief struggle, and again left. She returned a third and final time, now with a male friend named Miro, who was apparently a friend of Paolina's father. The couple demanded to see the girl; shortly thereafter, Miro left and came back with some other men. Though the priest by now was urging Paolina to hurry back upstairs, before the girl could escape she was overpowered by the men and carried off.[1]

Paolina's story came to the Derelitti's board of governors by way of the priest who participated in these events. He reported the frightening encounter to impress upon the board the need for protection against a Venetian public that he considered increasingly dangerous and unruly. Because the priest's focus was the episode at the Derelitti, his account gives little contextual information about Paolina or the circumstances surrounding her desire to come to the Derelitti in the first place. What sort of work did Madonna Faustina do? What was the relationship between Faustina and Paolina's family? Faustina knew the girl's aunt, who knew or was related to Paolina's father. But where was Paolina's father, and why did he not appear? If Paolina's father was alive and in Venice, why was the girl living under Faustina's roof? The absence of answers is frustrating and, most frustrating of all, we cannot know what happened to Paolina after Faustina's cronies abducted her.

If the priest's account raises questions, it also throws into relief several aspects of women's lives in early modern Venice. First, Paolina and Pollonia appear to have been young women on their own. Paolina's father is mentioned by her aunt Maria (Pollonia may have had a different father), but he is otherwise absent from this story, apparently not a resource for his daughter. The girls' mother is even more conspicuously absent, perhaps dead. Maria defended Paolina briefly, but could not prevent her abduction. Clearly, the girls lacked an effective family network or friends on which they could depend for shelter and support. But they had one another, and they were also fortunate to be able to turn to the Derelitti.

Faustina is the villain of this story. Nevertheless, the little we know of her life illustrates several elements of Venetian popular-class, or *popolana,* society. She traveled to the Derelitti in her own right, to claim her errant servant. Significantly, we do not know if she was single, married, or widowed. For the priest who told his tale of woe to the Derelitti governors, Faustina's marital status was irrelevant. We do learn from his testimony, however, that she ran her own business and took full responsibility for it. Faustina emerges as a woman of action, fearless and aggressive in claiming what she considers rightfully hers.

Faustina was an independent businesswoman who did not hesitate to challenge the moral and civic authority of an institution like the Derelitti, though it was staffed by a priest and supervised by the city's elite. Yet she did not do so completely alone. She first came accompanied by a female friend, Maria. After failing to reclaim Paolina on that visit, she returned with first one and then several men, who functioned as her silent, obedient assistants.

This brief glimpse of the encounter between Paolina, Pollonia, Faustina, and the Derelitti displays in miniature some of the options and limitations that made up early modern women's lives. None of the three women fits our image of a typical female subject of sixteenth-century Venice. Certainly there were more illustrious Venetians in this period, from the noblewomen who exercised power from their *palazzi* to the writers Moderata Fonte and Lucrezia Marinella, and to the famed poet and courtesan Veronica Franco.[2] But Paolina, Pollonia, and Faustina were typical Venetian women in several respects. In their different ways all three negotiated their own destinies, displaying both the necessary initiative and resources to do so. Pollonia escaped a life of exploitation by seeking out the religious authorities at the Derelitti and proclaiming her conversion to a more moral life. Paolina sought her sister out and with her help temporarily succeeded in finding a safer situation than the one she had found as a young working woman. Finally, Faustina may have used some male muscle to spirit away her errant servant, but she was clearly in charge, to the point of bullying and frightening a priest.

This book is about the Paolinas, Pollonias, and Faustinas of early modern Venice. They came from Venice's humbler ranks, the *popolani.* I hope to create a multidimensional picture of such women by examining their lives, their limits, and possibilities, and by showing them as actors in their own right. Whether as bereft of resources as Paolina and Pollonia or as prosperous and well-connected to a network of friends as Faustina, Venetian women shaped their own destinies in a myriad of ways.

Of course, women never carved out their own destinies completely independently of the larger forces that directed their lives: the church, the secular government, and their male relatives. Numerous historians have shown us that premodern women always operated within a patriarchal context that found reinforcement in theology, judicial law and practice, and social custom.[3] But within the restrictions of patriarchal society, Venetian women occupied and moved among different social spaces. This book explores the ways in which women negotiated city spaces in early modern Venice and argues that women exercised more social power in early modern society than has traditionally been recognized. By *social power* I mean the ability to make independent decisions as well as influence the actions of other people. This social power stemmed from women's economic resources, their residential autonomy and partnership with others, and a physical mobility that permitted women to change homes, jobs, even cities when the need arose.

Most studies of early modern Italy focus on women within the context of private or limited spaces, specifically the convent, and especially the home. This choice is dictated by the realization that women in premodern times were most likely to exercise or express autonomy within those spaces.[4] Additionally, studies of female autonomy or power tend to focus on women from Venice's elite. The stories of such women are important, but, by virtue of the subjects' privileged status and small number, they can offer only limited insight into the experiences and options of most Venetian women.[5]

When Venetian public life is given a gendered dimension by historians, that dimension tends to be unequivocally masculine, starting with physical freedom. Not only did Venetian women tend to remain within enclosed spaces, assert some historians, they dared not even leave the safety of their homes and local squares. Customs conspired to keep respectable women close to their households, even to the point of terrorizing them should they venture beyond too far or too often.[6]

By contrast, this book argues that the early modern city belonged to its women as well as its men. The key is a particular definition of social power or agency. I use these terms to encompass a range of activity—occupational, familial, and social—that permitted and demanded that women function either as partners with or independently of the men around them. Key also is my investigation into the lives of all women, not just the city's elite. In fact, a secondary theme that runs through the book is that Venice's humbler women, its *popolane,* could sometimes profit from options (marital or occupational) that were closed to their more privileged counterparts. For example, I argue that a central component of Venetian women's agency was their movement out of the house—into the city and beyond. Elite women were restricted by custom, dynastic concerns about their honor, and even clothing fashions that made physical movement difficult. By contrast, the mobility of popolane increased in the early modern period. Two factors were central to this change: a rise in immigration, reflected in greater mobility on the part of both migrant and native women; and the establishment of the Inquisition and new charitable institutions, which created communities for women, communities that could develop independent of neighborhood alliances or familial loyalties.

I have eschewed the traditional structure of examining women's history along the stages of their life cycles. While the book pays attention to the varying ranges of possibility available to women depending on their stage of life, its focus is a community of women who shared a common identity as residents of a household, a neighborhood, or the entire city, an identity that sometimes superseded differences of marital status.

Certainly marital status affected women's actions and opportunities, and chapter 1 examines different living patterns among married, single, and widowed women. Transitions in marital status were pivotal moments in a woman's life, with marriage signaling for most women entry into adulthood and a new social respectability, widowhood marking a new possibility of financial independence or a descent into poverty.[7] But here I argue that women at all three of these stages acted independently in ways that have not been previously explored.[8] In effect, women's experiences were colored, but not always determined, by their marital status. The ability to hold property, to work and socialize with one's neighbors and other men and women across the city, and to select a living situation were not determined by marital status alone. Instead, these activities sometimes transcended such status.

Finally, this book is primarily about popular-class women, though not exclusively so. The last fifteen years have seen an explosion of research on Venetian women, so that now the body of literature on Venice is beginning to rival that of Florence. In contrast to Florence, however, most of the important work on Venice focuses on patrician women and female religious.[9] Although we have learned a great deal about marriage patterns, female agency within noble households, inheritance patterns, and enclosed communities, we still know relatively little about the majority of Venetian women, how their experiences mirrored those of patricians and nuns and how they differed from them.

While popolane have received attention in other towns in Italy and other parts of early modern Europe, such women have gotten little coverage in Venice, their experiences have been largely subsumed under those of popolani men or noble women.[10] Obviously, they shared experiences and characteristics with both groups. Popolane married popolani, and worked alongside them to achieve some modicum of security or simply to survive. They participated in the same festivals, shared the same music, lived within the political and social limits of the same world. Like noble women, popolane knew that they were expected to marry, produce and care for children, and contribute to their husband's honor and his household. Though the focus here is on the broad range of women below the nobility, women of privilege, including the nobility, do enter the picture in certain places. They are most prominent, not surprisingly, in chapter 2, which examines women and wealth.[11]

Another theme that runs throughout the book, especially chapters 3 through 6, is community. Here, I define community as shared interests, common goals or circumstances or experiences. I argue that women's social experience consisted of layers of community identity. Female identities were built around women's roles as daughters, wives, mothers, and widows, but not exclusively so. Women were also friends, neighbors, partners, clients, and employers, part of several different groups linked by common experiences of the city itself, within their households and across town.[12]

SOURCES

Most of the primary sources used extensively here are themselves products of sixteenth-century Venetian history. The late sixteenth century was a time of transition for Venice. In addition to battles with the Turks and other European powers, Venetians coped with considerable internal change. In the period from roughly 1540 to 1630, Venice underwent a number of developments that had a direct impact on the family and, in particular, on women. First, the growth of manufacturing meant new occupational opportunities for women as well as men.[13] Second, women were among the immigrants drawn to Venice by the new economic possibilities the city offered, and their presence affected the traditional neighborhood communities in which most Venetian women worked and socialized. Finally, the Counter Reformation introduced a series of institutional and intellectual developments that affected the lives of many Venetians, including popolane.[14]

The Counter Reformation led to the establishment of new controls over Venetians and other Italians. The Tridentine church was determined to remove ambiguity from its doctrines and superstition and magic from its popular practices. One such control was the Inquisition, which began hearing cases in Venice in 1547. The Inquisition served both to define unacceptable behavior and to punish it. Also known as the S. Uffizio, or Holy Office, the Inquisition tried women for witchcraft and, occasionally, for heresy from 1547 to 1720 (men were usually tried for heresy). The records, consisting of testimony by the accused and by the witnesses for and against her, provide a glimpse into daily neighborhood life with all of its alliances and enmities, as described by early modern Venetians themselves.[15]

Another, more benign way of measuring and enforcing faith in early modern Venice was by the *status animarum,* the "soul counts" or parish registers, designed to collect local records of residents' orthodoxy. In this way, the church defined the parameters of each parish, ensuring the inclusion of all of its members.[16] The parish priest or his assistant traveled street by street, from home to home, noting the names and number of people in the household, their relationship to one another, and above all the sacramental status of each parishioner; that is, whether the individual had received first communion and had been confirmed. Because property holding was irrelevant, even the humblest and most marginal people were entered onto the lists, from the aged to newborns. Thus, these registers provide a relatively complete snapshot of parish life across economic and social boundaries.

They are not perfect representations of a neighborhood population, however. The status animarum are more selective in some ways than a secular source would be because they focus on the members of a particular

Roman Catholic parish. This means that Jews, Turks, recent immigrants, and beggars without a residence do not appear on the census taker's list. Nevertheless, the registers provide a more comprehensive look at typical Venetian household and neighborhood structures than do some government surveys because all members of a given household were faithfully registered, including very young children; the Tridentine church was anxious to ensure that all Venetians, regardless of age, had been baptized.[17]

A third collection of sources comprises notarial and financial records and government tax indexes, all of which show women as actors in the financial world, who could and did manage their own economic affairs. A collection of wills at the Istituzioni di Ricovero e di Educazioni both indicate the sort of wealth a woman could control in the early modern period and highlight the variety of personal relationships that resulted in bequests. A final major source are the institutional records of several charitable institutions for women that were founded in the sixteenth century. These institutions signal new developments in both civic awareness of women "at risk" and in women's opportunities to build communities independent of family and neighborhood.

ORGANIZATION

The book is organized as a series of expanding frames within which popolane women moved. Chapter 1, "Residence, Sex, and Marriage," focuses on the household. Here, I challenge historiographical assumptions about residential patterns in early modern Europe, which have divided the continent into two dichotomous models: the North and the South. This chapter shows that the Venetian patterns resemble that northern model rather than that of Italy and the Iberian peninsula. Most significantly, the chapter demonstrates that there was no one living pattern for women in early modern Venice. Rather, women chose from a range of options, living with siblings, husbands, employers, and companions.

Chapter 2, "Women of Means: Property and Possessions," explores the kind of power women might wield within the household through their economic clout. Using tax and notarial documents, I show that women could own a considerable amount of property and wealth independently of their husbands or guardians. I also argue that even a woman's personal possessions gave her a localized power because of her ability to bequeath them.

Chapter 3, "Around the Neighborhood," takes us out of the household by analyzing the importance of neighborhood society for Venetian women. Neighborhood society played as central a role in a woman's life as did her home. In fact, neighborhood relationships sometimes served as substitutes for a familial community, particularly for single women. The census records show that within a neighborhood, pockets of community could develop around occupation, social status, marital status, or provenance. Thus, one street might be filled with immigrant weavers; another street, even the next one, might house a number of wealthy noble families. Relationships could also reach across groups: the Inquisition trials reveal the ways in which proximity sometimes bred familiarity and even friendship across occupation, ethnicity, and marital status. Even if widows sometimes clustered in one courtyard, for example, they still freely associated with single and married neighbors and built friendships with them.

Chapter 4, "Immigrant Women: Into the Neighborhood," assesses the impact of the growing immigrant population on Venetian neighborhoods. After establishing the importance of immigration to Venice in the early modern period and explaining its rise, chapter 4 goes on to evaluate the degree to which immigrant women managed to insert themselves into local networks and the effect of their arrival on native women. The chapter examines the nature of immigrant identity in early modern Venice and how that identity affected the creation of female professional and social networks. Immigrant women sometimes created their own pockets of community within a neighborhood. But immigrant and native women could also pool their resources to live and work together.

Chapter 5, "Beyond the Contrada: Women and Mobility," takes us out of the neighborhood and examines women's participation in a Venetian society that was intensely mobile. This chapter broadens the discussion of chapter 4 by arguing that immigrant women were only part of a larger mobile population of women moving into, out of, and around Venice. Recent articles on Venetian women have described them as confined to their neighborhoods.[18] Here, I argue that although women remained grounded in their household and neighborhood, they were by no means limited to these local communities. In fact, women traveled regularly across parish boundaries on a daily basis to meet friends, lovers, and clients. In addition, they often changed houses and parishes. Women also moved into and out of Venice itself; for example, court records from the Inquisition and Pien Collegio Appeals Court offer examples of women sent into temporary or permanent exile from the city. Finally, women's horizons could range far beyond their actual travels, as their relatives and spouses traveled abroad and as they encountered immigrants from other lands.

Chapter 6, "City of Women: Institutions and Communities," examines the impact of institutional intervention into the lives of Venetian women in the early modern period. A new type of institution that affected women's relationship to their communities was the charitable house (like the Derelitti that sheltered Pollonia and Paolina), institutions founded by counterreformist women and men. These *case di carità* were created to help women in moments of economic vulnerability and moral crisis. Not only did they offer poor women a second chance at a respectable life (and marriage), they also offered a few elite women the opportunity to renounce marriage without entering a convent and to find a challenging, rewarding profession. Filled with women, staffed by women, and administered by women, the *case* represented a new, citywide form of female community.

In sum, this book argues that women's lives were multidimensional, bound by a series of overlapping responsibilities and relationships that linked them to other households, other parishes, even other cities and towns. Such relationships created and reinforced the many communities, some exclusively female and some mixed, to which women belonged. The chapters that follow explore those experiences and relationships.

Working
Women
of Early Modern
Venice

CHAPTER ONE

Residence, Sex, and Marriage

The Structure of

Venetian Households

W HAT can we learn about women's agency from a study of parish censuses? The residential patterns that emerge from the *status animarum* taken in Venice at the close of the sixteenth century document that when a woman decided how or where she would live, she might choose from a surprising range of housing possibilities. While marital status clearly framed her options, other factors and relationships also played a role in her choice of a home.

In 1592, Chiara was living in the parish of S. Sofia (see map). A widow, she headed a household that included her two children and two male servants. The presence of servants identified her as relatively prosperous, particularly for a widow. A more modest example of Venetian widowhood lived just two houses down: Marina resided there alone, her children either nonexistent or grown. Several streets away, the widow Vittoria made ends meet by renting out a room to another woman, Virginia. Yet another widow, Antonia, boarded in the home of a *cestariol* (food porter), along with another tenant, a tailor named Bastiano.

Pasqueta headed a household in the nearby parish of SS. Apostoli. She lived with her sister-in-law and nephew, one male servant, and three adult boarders: Lugretia, an unmarried woman *("Lugretia sola")*; Giulio, a cobbler; Giulio's wife, Paula, and the couple's daughter. The widow Lucia lived alone a few streets away. Nearby was the stonemason Bortolo with his wife and two children, one of them a niece.

All of these households were typical of early modern Venice. Parish registers from the end of the sixteenth century show that the city boasted

I

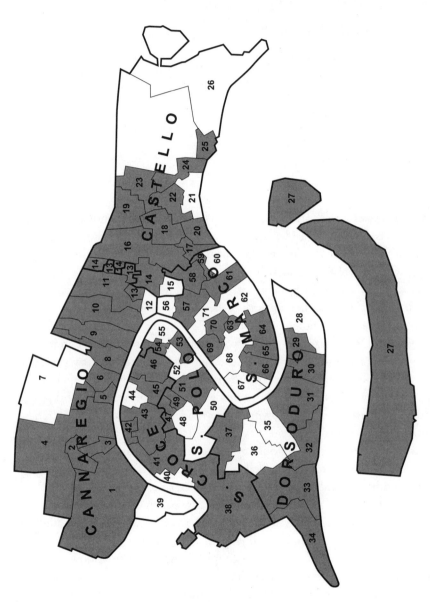

VENETIAN PARISHES

Shading indicates areas represented in the status animarum. Michael Feeney

Cannaregio

1. S. Geremia
2. Ghetto
3. S. Leonardo
4. S. Marcuola
5. S. Maria Maddalena
6. S. Fosca
7. S. Marcilian
8. S. Felice
9. S. Sofia
10. SS. Apostoli
11. S. Canciano
12. S. Giovanni Grisostomo
13. S. Maria Nova

Castello

14. S. Marina
15. S. Lio
16. S. Maria Formosa
17. S. Giovanni Novo
18. S. Severo
19. S. Giustina
20. S. Provolo
21. S. Giovanni in Bragora
22. S. Antonin
23. S. Ternità
24. S. Martino
25. S. Biagio
26. S. Pietro di Castello

Dorsoduro

27. S. Eufemia
28. S. Gregorio
29. S. Vio
30. S. Agnese
31. S. Trovaso
32. S. Basegio
33. S. Anzolo Raffael
34. S. Nicolò
35. S. Barnaba
36. S. Margherita
37. S. Pantalon

S. Croce

38. S. Croce
39. S. Lucia
40. S. Simeon Piccolo
41. S. Simeon Grande
42. S. Zuan Degolà
43. S. Giacomo dall Orio
44. S. Stae
45. S. Maria Mater Domini
46. S. Cassiano

S. Polo

47. S. Boldo
48. S. Stin
49. S. Agostin
50. S. Tomà
51. S. Polo
52. S. Aponal
53. S. Silvestro
54. S. Mattio
55. S. Giovanni Elemosinario

S. Marco

56. S. Bortolomio
57. S. Salvador
58. S. Zulian
59. S. Basso
60. S. Marco
61. S. Giminian
62. S. Moisè
63. S. Fantin
64. S. Maria Zobenigo
65. S. Maurizio
66. S. Vidal
67. S. Samuele
68. S. Angelo
69. S. Beneto
70. S. Paternian
71. S. Luca

a variety of household structures, not only in terms of size but also in kind. Some homes consisted of a single woman or man (most likely a woman), while others housed substantial numbers of relatives, boarders, and servants. Women's residential patterns reveal the ways in which women might exert authority or independence within their homes. For both married and single women, the range of living options also points to complicated networks of personal relationships that could exist within and beyond the household. Whether they lived alone or with husbands, kin, or companions, the residential choices that women made reveal the scope of their connections to a wider world.

COUPLES

Most Venetian households were headed by married couples, as shown in table 1.1. Out of the nearly twenty thousand homes studied here, more than twelve thousand (12,662) had a husband and wife at the head. In fact, it is rare to find couples elsewhere in the household structure. A very small number, 93, worked as servants and lived in the employer's home. Typical of this group were the servants Bortolo and his wife. They resided, along with their daughter, in the home of their employers, Paulo dalla Corona and his wife, in the parish of S. Zulian. The servant Bernardin and his wife also lived in the home of their employer, the nobleman Bartholomio Capello, in the parish of S. Giovanni Novo. That couple had five living children.[1] A larger number of couples, 358, rented or sublet a room or two in someone else's home. In the parish of SS. Apostoli, for example, the goldsmith Zuane and his wife Orseta rented rooms from Francesco, a spice dealer.

Most striking here is the substantial number of couples heading their own household. The censuses show that in early modern Venice, marriage virtually guaranteed a couple their own home. Put another way, couples usually did not marry until they could move directly into their own place. A marriage, then, did not usually bring a new woman into the home of a patriarch: a newlywed couple did not begin their life together under the roof of another authority. Instead, marriage signaled independence and physical autonomy, as husband and wife set up their new home together.

Age played a role in couples' ability to set up their own residence. Among the *popolani* (members of the popular classes), wives and husbands

TABLE 1.1

Living Arrangements for Married Couples, 1589–1607

Residence	All Couples (%)	
Own household	12,662	(92.7)
In parents' home	416	(3.0)
In sibling's home	128	(0.9)
In employer's home	93	(0.7)
Boarders in landlord's home	358	(2.7)
Total	13,657	(100.0)

Source: ASCP, Sezione Antica, Archivio Segreto, status animarum, B. 1–3.

were relatively close in age, with the women marrying in their late teens or early twenties, the men a few years later.[2] *Popolane* women married later than their elite counterparts because they were expected to accumulate their own dowry and skills that would make them materially appealing mates; this was easier to accomplish at nineteen than at fourteen. Conversely, popolani men may have married earlier than elite men because they were expected to provide for themselves as early as possible, rather than wait for a prestigious appointment within the family business or entry into political life through Venice's Maggior Consiglio, or Great Council.[3]

Apparently the cost of renting and furnishing an apartment was not prohibitive, even for young couples from humble families. Newlyweds received furnishings from their parents; brides often contributed useful household items to the marriage as part of their dowries. The trousseaux of popolane varied widely. At the very least, women could count on bringing many light, easily portable possessions, especially clothing and bedding, to their new homes. Some women possessed heavier items. Anzola Zanotta took great pride in itemizing her feather bed *(letto di piuma)*, with its sheets and many cushions. Another woman, the daughter of a spice merchant, counted four walnut chests among her belongings.[4]

In addition to material goods, brides made other contributions to their new households. At the time of marriage, the groom had probably been working since his early teens, perhaps as an apprentice in an artisanal craft

TABLE 1.2

Households Headed by Married Couples, 1589–1607

Type of Household	Number (%)
Couples alone	1,714 (14)
Couples living only with their children	6,492 (51)
Couples sharing their dwelling with others	
in addition to children	4,456 (35)
Total	12,662 (100)

Source: ASCP, Archivio Segreto, status animarum, B. 1–3.

or in the shipyards (the Arsenale).[5] But the bride, too, brought work experience to the marriage. She had trained with her mother in "women's" work such as sewing and spinning and might also have learned to assist her father in his trade. Or she might have worked as a domestic servant, an occupation overwhelmingly filled by single women.[6]

Because both bride and groom had been working, and accumulating wealth, for several years before marriage, they could likely afford to rent their own home. Only rarely could they afford to buy it: by the mid-seventeenth century, only 1,432 out of 25,240 homes were occupied by homeowners; the rest, 94 percent, were rentals.[7] A typical rent for a modest apartment in a working-class neighborhood (such as S. Marta) was 8 ducats a year. By contrast, a prosperous wool merchant rented comfortable lodgings in a nicer part of town for 76 ducats a year. An unskilled worker at the Arsenale shipyard earned 8 to 10 soldi per day, equal to an annual salary of 16 to 20 ducats. A skilled worker such as a carpenter or stonemason earned around 30 soldi per day, or around 60 ducats yearly. A skilled worker who paid 12 ducats a year in rent was spending about one-fifth of his wages for his lodgings.[8] If his wife brought in money as well, their combined income generally covered their ordinary expenses comfortably, though little was left over for leisure or luxury.[9]

With the home rented and furnished, a couple could begin building a life together, as well as a household. Half of all Venetian couples heading their own homes lived only with their children (see table 1.2). A small proportion—only 14 percent—of couples lived alone; that is, only with one another. About one-third shared their homes with their adult children and grandchildren, other family members, servants, and boarders.

THE IMPORTANCE OF KIN

Couples were especially likely to give shelter to their unmarried or widowed relations. A modest number of these kin were siblings, both female and male (see table 1.3). The total number of women identified by their relation to the household head (the husband) as sister or cousin *(zermana, sorella, cusina, cugina)* is 1,079. Such labels are ambiguous because they were used to denote any woman of lateral kinship, most likely a sister, but potentially a cousin, even a distant one. Of these "sisters," 127 married women (and their husbands) lived with their siblings. The other 952 consist of 818 unmarried women *(nubili)* and 134 widows.[10]

It is not surprising to find unmarried women in the homes of their brothers. But a small number of the women who lived in the home of a sibling may in fact have been living in the home of a married sister. Included in the group of unmarried sisters are some of the women identified in the census as *cognata,* or sister-in-law. When the cognata is listed in a household that includes a brother of the household head, then her place in the house is clear: she is that brother's wife and the household head's sister-in-law. In the parish of S. Maria Formosa, for example, the

TABLE 1.3

Men and Women Living with Siblings, by Marital Status and Sex, 1589–1607

Sex	Marital Status		
	Married (%)	Single (%)	Total (%)
Female	127 (12)	952 (88)	1,079 (100)
		(134 widowed)	
Male	126 (12)	915 (88)	1,041 (100)
Total	253 (12)	1,867 (88)	2,120 (100)

Source: ASCP, Archivio Segreto, status animarum, B. 1–3.

TABLE 1.4

Siblings-in-Law of the Head of Household, by Marital Status and Sex, 1589–1607

Sex	Marital Status		
	Married (%)	Single (%)	Total (%)
Sisters-in-law	138 (44)	176 (56)	314 (100)
Brothers-in-law	25 (23)	84 (77)	109 (100)
Total	163 (38)	260 (62)	423 (100)

Source: ASCP, Archivio Segreto, status animarum, B. 1–3.

noble Antonio Badoer's household consisted of himself and his wife, their two children, his mother, his brother, a sister-in-law, and three female servants. In this case, it is reasonable to assume that the sister-in-law listed is the wife of Antonio's brother.

But there were other types of *cognate* as well: Galeazzo Malatesta, who lived in the parish of S. Martino, presided over a home that included his wife, their four children, a cognata, and three *garzoni,* or male servants. Since relationships were described with reference to the male head of household, the cognata in question was indisputably the husband's, not his wife's. In the case of Galeazzo, then, his sister-in-law was probably his wife's sister. In a similar instance, when the census taker of S. Ternità entered the house of Alvise, a stevedore, he was careful to note in his register that Alvise's cognata was, in fact, "his wife's sister."[11] The censuses include a modest number of households, 176, with a cognata who had no husband (see table 1.4). Married women, then, sometimes took sisters into their homes.[12]

Wives occasionally took in their brothers as well. The number of Venetian men living in their married siblings' homes was close to that of women. There are 1,041 men listed as brothers, cousins, or brothers-in-law of the household head. Of these men, 915 appear to be unmarried.[13] The overwhelming majority of the cognati in households headed by married men (84 out of 109) were themselves single. Such a *cognato* was the widowed husband of the head of the household's sister and, thus, his brother-in-law, or else he was the wife's brother. This was likely the case for Lorenzo, a widowed boatman with one child who lived in the Corte Nova in the parish of SS. Apostoli. He shared his home with a cognato, the cognato's wife, and their two children. This second man was almost certainly the brother of Lorenzo's deceased wife.[14]

These small but suggestive numbers, displayed in tables 1.3 and 1.4, indicate that a married woman's contacts with both her brothers and sisters could remain strong, well into adulthood.[15] The presence of a wife's siblings in her home also indicates that she exercised enough influence within the household to offer shelter to her own relatives, both male and female. Such influence was bolstered by her economic contribution to household expenses through her work as a spinner, a market woman, or some other female occupation.

A *popolana* who supplemented her family's daily expenses with her own earnings could command a level of respect from her husband that allowed her to make decisions of importance within the home.[16] This may have been the case for Zorzi and his wife Lucieta, who it seems were not a wealthy couple. Zorzi had a position of some responsibility in the prison, but did not earn enough to keep servants. Yet their household included, along with two children, Lucieta's sister.[17] Another woman, the wife of a dry-goods retailer in the parish of SS. Apostoli, brought both her mother and a female cousin into the household.[18] Benvegnuda, the wife of a goldsmith named Paolo, welcomed both her sister and a female cousin into the couple's home.[19]

Of course, welcoming a sibling into one's home was not simply an act of charity. Brothers and sisters did not live on their more settled siblings' largess. Rather, they were valued for their contributions to the household economy. From this perspective, a brother would be more welcome than a sister because generally his earning power was higher. A brother could earn a decent living from a job at the Arsenale or in one of the manufacturing centers of the city. Sixteenth-century Venice was a manufacturing boom town; there was plenty of work for most men.[20] Brothers could also make a direct contribution to a family business. At the very least, a willing brother or cognato could contribute muscle and perhaps some experience to the business of his brother or brother-in-law. Iseppo Fustinoni, a spice dealer who lived with his wife and two young children in the parish of S. Giovanni Novo, also sheltered two brothers, one adult and one adolescent. The older brother, too, was a spice dealer, and the younger brother, 14-year-old Bortholo, "stays in the shop." Bortholo must have worked alongside Iseppo's 14-year-old shop assistant, who also lived with the family.[21]

By contrast, an unmarried sister's support for the household usually came in the form of helping around the house (and store, if there was one) and perhaps caring for the children. This was probably the case in the home of Ventura, a fruit vendor who lived in Campo S. Filippo e Giacomo, with his wife, five children, two boarders, and his sister-in-law.[22] It is unlikely that she went out to work as a domestic servant since the vast majority of domestic servants lived in the home of their employer.[23] In monetary terms, an unmarried sister's contribution to the family cannot often have been very large. Sometimes she could be a downright drain on resources: Jacomo, a goldsmith in the parish of S. Giovanni Novo, looked after his own three children as well as the four belonging to his widowed sister-in-law Vienna, who lived with Jacomo and his wife.[24] Although female relatives brought few financial assets to a household, almost ten times as many women as men were taken in by a sister and her husband. Economic assistance, then, was not always a primary factor in the decision to shelter a wife's siblings. Perhaps affection was.

More surprising than the presence of sisters-in-law in a man's home are the indications that brothers and sisters could maintain a level of contact that would enable a bachelor to find a home under his married sister's roof. When we think of brother/sister relationships in early modern Europe, it is usually in the context of a brother organizing his sister's dowry and arranging her marriage, particularly among the elite. Further down the social scale, the brother/sister relationship has also been viewed as a dependent, one-sided one, with the unfortunate *nubile,* or unmarried woman, finding shelter with her married brother, or a widow turning to her brother for financial counsel or sponsorship. But the presence of unmarried men in the homes of their married sisters shows that dependency could run in the opposite direction as well. For example, Battista, a dealer in herbs, lived with his wife and children at the foot of the Rialto bridge. His wife's brother, a widower, also lived with them, along with his two children.[25]

Because married couples provided the most stable households, siblings regularly sought their assistance over that of unmarried kin. That is, mar-

ried women might shelter their unmarried or widowed siblings, but unmarried or widowed women almost never did so. Only 99 of the 4,285
households headed by single or widowed women sheltered siblings of
either sex. A much larger percentage of single men with their own homes,
714 out of 2,772, housed brothers and sisters, in roughly equal numbers.
On average, single (unmarried or widowed) men had more resources than
single women, and so were better equipped to assist their siblings. This
means that single male household heads were also in a better position to
benefit from the economic contribution—or in the case of sisters, housekeeping and occasionally an additional source of income—and the companionship that siblings could offer in exchange for shelter. This may have
been the case for Domenego, a bachelor in the parish of S. Ternità who
lived with two sisters, one of whom was a widow.[26]

Even when siblings could not offer each other shelter, they could pool
resources to find it under the roof of a third party. In the parish of S. Giovanni Novo, the tailor Anzolo rented a room from Antonio, a basket
maker, and his family. Anzolo's sister, Madalena, also lodged with the
family.[27] In another part of town, the sisters Vicenza and Dionora de
Gilioli, tried before the Inquisition in 1608, lodged in the home of a
priest.[28]

PARENTS AND CHILDREN

While a Venetian household headed by a couple might include more
than one adult sibling, it was unlikely to shelter adult offspring. Those
who married, as we have seen, quickly set up households of their own.
Unmarried adults tended to leave their parents' home as well; most either
found shelter with other single men and women or moved in with their
married siblings. Table 1.5 suggests that single, adult Venetians rarely
turned to their parents for lodgings.[29]

The few Venetians we can positively identify as adults still living with
their parents were married. We have already observed the tendency of
young couples to strike out on their own. When couples did live under a
parent's roof, they were twice as likely to find shelter with the husband's
family as with the wife's. This is in keeping with our expectations of premodern families. The common wisdom has long been that a woman, once
married, cast off her natal loyalties, at least until widowhood. Sometimes

TABLE I.5

Adult Offspring Living with Parents, by Sex and Marital Status, 1589–1607

Marital Status	Men (%)	Women (%)	Total (%)
Unmarried	67 (13)	47 (8)	114 (11)
Married	277 (55)	139 (24)	416 (39)
In-law	139 (28)	277 (49)	416 (39)
Widowed	16 (3)	88 (16)	104 (9)
Widowed in-law	5 (1)	16 (3)	21 (2)
Total	504 (100)	567 (100)	1,071 (100)

Source: ASCP, Archivio Segreto, status animarum, B. 1–3.

such a shift in loyalties was concretely expressed by the physical transfer of the woman to her husband's home after marriage.[30]

But the censuses show that the frequency with which that move took place in Venice was closely tied to social status and wealth. In tables 1.6 and 1.7, we see how considerable the gap was between noble and commoner families when it came to a bride's residence in the home of her in-laws. Of the Venetian couples who made their homes with parents, one-third of them, 33 percent, lived with the bride's family. But when we focus exclusively on patrician families, we find that less than 10 percent of such couples lived with the parents of the woman. Noble and wealthy families had more invested in the marriages of their sons—the fate of the patriline—than did humbler families; it was crucial for these families to keep newlywed sons close by, even under the same roof.

Brides from humbler families, by contrast, may have found it easier to stay in close touch with their families after marriage. Certainly they had a better chance of continuing to live with them.[31] This was the case with the two daughters of Angela dal Zio, a widow. Her household included both women and their husbands.[32] Here we see a considerable difference between the patriciate's familial relations and those of the Venetian populace at large.[33]

If married women were unlikely to seek (or find) shelter with their parents, widowed women were even less likely to do so. A woman was almost as likely to be widowed as married in early modern Europe. Her husband might perish from an accident on the job, at sea, in war, or by a violent scuffle on a street or at a watering hole. For a young widow left with children to support, returning to her parents' home would seem an obvious option. When Iseppa was widowed and left with two children to support, for example, she was able to move in with her mother.[34] But Iseppa was the exception rather than the rule; most widows with children in early modern Venice could not count on finding shelter with a parent.

The reluctance or inability of widowed women to return to their parents' home did not stop them from providing shelter for their parents—particularly their mothers—when the need arose. This was not the case for married women, however. Just as they were unlikely to ask their parents for shelter, they were also unlikely to offer it. Only 26 couples hosted an elderly parent. While married couples clearly maintained contact with their parents, then, they almost never did so to the point of sheltering

TABLE 1.6

Patrician Adult Offspring Living with Parents, by Sex and Marital Status, 1589–1607

Marital Status of Offspring	Men (%)	Women (%)	Total (%)
Unmarried *(nubile)* or widowed	18 (21)	10 (13)	28 (16)
Married	63 (72)	6 (8)	69 (42)
In-law	6 (7)	63 (79)	69 (42)
Total	87 (100)	79 (100)	166 (100)

Source: ASCP, Archivio Segreto, status animarum, B. 1–3.

TABLE 1.7

Married Couples Living with Parents, 1589–1607

	Whole Population	Patrician
With wife's parents	139	6
With husband's parents	277	63
Total	416	69

Source: ASCP, Archivio Segreto, status animarum, B. 1–3.

TABLE 1.8

Parents Living in the Home of Their Offspring, 1589–1607

Marital Status of Offspring	Mothers (%)	Fathers (%)	Total (%)
Married	13 (1)	13 (18)	26 (2)
Unmarried (*nubile*) or widowed	1,038 (99)	60 (82)	1,098 (98)
Total	1,051 (100)*	73 (100)*	1,124 (100)

Source: ASCP, Archivio Segreto, status animarum, B. 1–3.

*The total for mothers includes thirty-six in-laws; the total for fathers includes two in-laws.

them, as they did with their brothers and sisters. Instead, the majority of widowed parents lived with unmarried or widowed offspring, usually daughters (see table 1.8).

SINGLE WOMEN

Just as married couples' households could be small or large, so too do we find variety in the living patterns of single women. Venice was filled with both unmarried and widowed women. Of the 94,862 Venetians (including children) registered in the censuses, 25,301 were single. Well over half of these were women. Furthermore, single women, a larger, more constant presence in Venetian neighborhoods than were single men, headed twice as many households as did their male counterparts. The difference is even more striking when we examine widowed Venetians specifically: three times as many widows as widowers headed their own households.

But when we leave aside raw numbers and focus on proportions, what is most impressive is the similarity rather than the difference between single women and single men. To consider first the *nubili* and *celibi,* the unmarried women and unmarried men: as table 1.9 shows, these categories had almost identical residential patterns. Sixteen percent of unmarried men and 15 percent of unmarried women headed their own homes. A tiny, almost negligible percentage (0.5 percent of women, 0.7 percent of men) lived with parents. Nine percent of *donne nubili* lived with siblings, 8 percent of *uomini celibi* did so.

The majority of both nubili and celibi worked as servants. A slightly larger percentage of the unmarried females than males lived as servants in their employer's home—67 percent compared with 57 percent. The reason was that a larger percentage of unmarried men could afford to board in someone else's house: just over 18 percent, as opposed to the 8 percent of unmarried women, did so. Thus, while nubili and celibi headed households or found shelter with their families with equal frequency, men had a better chance than women of avoiding domestic service and forging a career that would give them a measure of residential and occupational independence.

The differences are more striking than the similarities when we turn to widows and widowers (see table 1.10). Here, the comparisons must be treated with particular caution because widowers are hard to identify in the censuses. A woman's widowed status almost always accompanied her name; the same was not true for widowed men. The widowed status of a man can only be inferred by the presence of children with no mother in his home to claim them; that is, no wife, no sister, no female boarder. Thus, the number of widowers that appears here is almost certainly under-representative. Interpreted another way, however, the figure may be accurate. A widower with no children was, for all practical purposes, a free

TABLE 1.9

*Unmarried, Adult Venetians (*nubili *and* celibi*), by Sex and Position in Household, 1589–1607*

Household Position	Women (%) (nubili)		Men (%) (celibi)		Total (%)	
Head of household	1,371	(16)	1,745	(16)	3,116	(16)
Offspring	47	(1)	74	(1)	121	(1)
Sibling	818	(9)	856	(8)	1,674	(8)
Servant	5,745	(66)	6,180	(57)	11,925	(61)
Other	691	(8)	1,977	(18)	2,668	(14)
Total	8,672	(100)	10,832	(100)	19,504	(100)

Source: ASCP, Archivio Segreto, status animarum, B. 1–3.

TABLE 1.10

Widows and Widowers, by Position in Household, 1589–1607

Household Position	Widows (%)	Widowers (%)	Total (%)
Head of household	2,974 (60)	788 (84)	3,762 (64)
Parent	1,063 (21.5)	65 (7)	1,128 (19)
Offspring*	106 (2.5)	14 (1)	120 (2)
Sibling*	134 (3)	59 (7)	193 (3)
Servant	132 (3)	8 (0.9)	140 (2)
Other	515 (10)	1 (0.1)	516 (10)
Total	4,924 (100)	935 (100)	5,859 (100)

Source: ASCP, Archivio Segreto, status animarum, B. 1–3.

*Figures include in-laws.

man, equal in status and possibilities to any bachelor. By contrast, a widow found her life drastically changed by her spouse's death, even if she had no children, because her main source of financial and social security had vanished.

Although there were many more widows than widowers — almost five times more according to the parish registers [35] — they were less likely to head households. Sixty-one percent of widows presided over their own abode, no small figure, but a much greater percentage of widowers (84 percent) could make that boast. After the category of household head, the most common household position for widows was that of a mother who lived in the home of an adult child. A widowed father, however, almost never turned to his offspring for shelter. Neither widows nor widowers put much stake in parental help, nor did they often look to siblings for a roof over their heads. Nor did they return to a life of domestic service after the death of a spouse: only 3 percent of widows and less than 1 percent of widowers worked as servants. A few of them rented rooms. Ten percent of the widows listed in the censuses boarded with someone else. But only one boarder can confidently be identified as a widower.[36] In most cases, widows and widowers either did not need or could not find someone else to take them in.

Whether she lived alone or with others, a woman usually found herself plunged into financial difficulty after her husband's death.[37] But widowhood did not affect all women equally. Although the general population of widows must have found themselves plunged into difficult circumstances after the death of a husband, this may not have been the case for widows of the noble class. If we use the number of servants to measure wealth or general comfort in a household, we see that noble widows did not experience sharp reductions in affluence (table 1.11); instead, they employed servants at nearly the same rate as other categories in the noble population.

Because so many nubili and widows headed their own households, the structure of their residences merits examination. First, we have already seen that widowed women were more likely to head their own homes than nubili. This is not surprising: the widowed group was generally older than the spinster cohort. A widow usually had children to support and might continue to live in the dwelling she had once shared with her husband. Some widows may have had assistance from their families; Pietro Secco rented one of his apartments to his widowed sister for 10 ducats a year.[38] By contrast, most nubili, many of them relatively young, tended to live and work in domestic service. There was the occasional exception, of course: the highborn Laura Gritti, a *nubile,* headed a home composed of herself, three nephews, and six servants.[39] But most young women were not so privileged. Through domestic service, they hoped to accumulate

TABLE 1.11

Patrician Households in General Compared with Patrician Households Headed by Widows, by Number of Servants, 1589–1607

Number of Servants	All Patricians (%)	Patrician Widows (%)
0	98 (9)	15 (11)
1–2	341 (32)	42 (30)
3–4	314 (30)	46 (33)
5+	305 (29)	37 (26)
Total	1,058 (100)	140 (100)

Source: ASCP, Archivio Segreto, status animarum, B. 1–3.

TABLE 1.12

Households Headed by Nubili and Widows, showing Household Structure, 1589–1607

Type of Household	Households Headed by Unmarried Women (nubili) (%)		Households Headed by Widows (%)	
Women living alone	337	(25)	629	(21)
Women living only with children	343	(25)	1,472	(50)
Women living with relatives, servants, and others	691	(50)	873	(29)
Total	1,371	(100)	2,974	(100)

Source: ASCP, Archivio Segreto, status animarum, B. 1–3.

money and goods for a dowry with an eye toward marriage, though some would stay on with their employers into middle and old age.[40]

Both nubili and widows tended to share their homes with others, as we see in tables 1.12 and 1.13. Only 25 percent of nubili and 21 percent of widows appear in the registers as living completely alone. One-half of the widows heading their households lived with children, as did 25 percent of nubili. The nubili who managed to head their own households probably enjoyed more prosperity, and certainly had more companionship, than did widows in a similar situation. Half of them shared their homes with relatives, servants, or boarders, whereas less than 30 percent of head-of-household widows did so. Women who rented rooms to boarders were not among the most impoverished: they did, after all, have the space to do so in the first place. The decision to let a room was a pragmatic, and not always desperate, one. In a 1620 trial, the witness Caterina, a 25-year-old woman whose husband lived elsewhere, casually noted that shortly after moving to the parish of S. Aponal she found "the house was a little too big for just me, so I rented a room to ser. Vivian to hold classes."[41]

Single women, either nubili, separated, or widowed, often came to-

gether in a home to pool their resources and perhaps find companion-
ship as well: in the parish of SS. Apostoli, a widowed seamstress named
Anzola shared her home with the widowed Margarita, also a seamstress.
Both women had children: Anzola had one and Margarita had three.
Meneghina, a Slavic woman "who does not live with her husband *[non
sta col marido]*," presided over a houseful of women: Tomasina, Antonia
from the Friuli, and Lucrezia, daughter of Battista, all boarded with her
(Lucrezia, too, was separated from her husband).

In the Corte de Cha Trevisan we find Vendramina (herself from Treviso). She rented rooms to the Friulian widow Daniela and Daniela's 8-
year old son. There was also a male boarder, a printer named Biasio. In
addition, Vendramina took care of an orphaned baby *(orfana dalla pietà)*,
Anastasia, only 6 months old. In the same parish, in the Ruga giuffa, lived

TABLE 1.13

*Complex Households Headed by Nubili and Widows, showing Other
Household Members, 1589–1607*

Relationship to Head of Household	Headed by Nubili (%)		Headed by Widows (%)	
Parent	52	(8)	47	(5)
Sibling	101	(16)	101	(11)
Servant	336	(53)	364	(42)
Other	269	(43)	450	(52)
Total number of complex households*	691	(100)	873	(100)

Source: ASCP, Sezione Antica, Archivio Segreto, status animarum, B. 1–3.

Note: The numbers given here for parents, siblings, servants, and others living
with female and widowed heads of household do not add up to the total
number of complex households at the bottom of the table because the
categories overlap. That is, some of these households had parents and servants,
others had siblings and boarders, and so on. This table shows how many female-
headed households had siblings, how many had servants, and so forth; therefore,
the same house may appear in more than one category.

*A complex household here is one in which reside adults in addition to the
household head(s) and children.

another widow with no visible means of support, Antonia. The only other occupant of her home was her adopted daughter, 7 years old.[42]

The presence of children in the homes of 343 unmarried women requires some explanation. Since there were no other adults living in these homes (no servants, no boarders, no sisters), the unmarried woman is the only candidate for parenthood. The obvious question is, were some of these women in fact widows? The Friulian Maria Poselina was recorded in the parish of S. Ternità along with three children. Did the census taker forget to note that she was a widow, even though, just four houses away, he was careful to identify Madonna Camilla as a widow, and a few houses down in the other direction, the widow Chiara? Or were Maria's children illegitimate? We have no way of knowing. We do know that the census takers scrupulously recorded the widowed status of thousands of women, street by street, throughout the city. These 343 women who appear with children but without a husband or the label *widow* may have taken in nieces and nephews or had children out of wedlock. The latter explanation was explicit for some women, like Caterina, another Friulian, in the parish of S. Maria Formosa. She lived only with her young daughter and was identified in the register as a prostitute.

Some single women may have separated from their husbands, as did Elena de Pietro, who, according to the census taker in S. Ternità, "non sta con suo marito." Cattarina, who lived in the same parish, was less diplomatic (or else the census taker was): her full entry reads, "Cattarina the daughter of Iacomo, she does not want to live with her husband." Instead, she lived completely alone.[43] A similar case was that of Antonia, who boarded with Paulina of Vicenza. Antonia was identified as "the wife of Francesco . . . a Veronese man, who has by now been gone for 10 years."[44] In the same parish but several streets away lived Paula with her two children. She was registered as "the wife of Zuane, a caulker," but Zuane himself did not appear in the register as a resident of the home. A woman named Paula shared her home with two of her brothers as well as with three boarders, two women and a man from Germania. Finally, some of these women were nubili who would remain unmarried, a few by choice, others having failed to find a husband. These were women who had gotten pregnant but not married and who, increasingly poor and with children to support, were unlikely to find a husband when they had to compete with younger, unfettered women, or widows with property.[45]

From all of this data, some living patterns emerge. Widows, who might inherit goods or money from their husbands and often had children to support, headed their own households in overwhelming numbers. Nubili were less likely to run their own homes. They were usually younger, with fewer assets and responsibilities than widows. They tended to work as domestic servants and live with their employers. However, when nubili did manage to set up their own residences, they could enjoy a somewhat higher standard of living than their widowed counterparts, employing more servants and housing relatives and boarders.

Many such households were composed solely of women. The widow Anzola lived with her four children in an area described as "from the bridge by the church to the campo with two wells." In addition to the children, her home included a sister, a maid, and two boarders: Maddalena, who "does not live with her husband," and Marieta, a widow "who is taken care of here for the love of God."[46] Many streets away in the same parish, Corona, a woman from Vicenza, headed a household composed of Marieta, a young orphan, and two female boarders. The census taker noted that "all three women are married and living apart from their husbands."[47] Women sometimes lived and worked together in the same dwelling. In the parish of SS. Apostoli, on the Fondamenta de Crosechieri, lived four women "who look after little children": Polonia, Zaneta, Betta, and Betta's sister Lucrecia.[48]

LIVING IN THE WORKPLACE

A substantial number of Venetian women both lived and worked within the same walls. The vast majority of these were servants, most of them *nubile* (see table 1.14). Servants' ages are given rarely; those given tend to be for children, ranging in age from 7 to 16. The choice to list only the ages of the very young suggests that children who worked as servants were the exception rather than the rule. In the few cases where servants had children, we can speculate that these children labored for their parents' employer. Boys appear more often than girls (66 compared with 12) because they worked as apprentices for artisans. But most servants appear to have been adults.[49]

How did servants live? Many may have felt isolated: of the 3,336 homes with female domestics, 2,008, or almost two-thirds, were staffed by only

TABLE 1.14

Domestic Servants, by Sex and Marital Status, 1589–1607

	Sex	
Marital Status	Women (%)	Men (%)
Unmarried *(nubile)*	5,761 (98.0)	6,180 (97.3)
Widowed	11 (0.2)	8 (0.1)
Married	93 (1.6)	93 (1.5)
Child[50]	12 (0.2)	66 (1.1)
Total	5,877 (100)	6,347 (100)

Source: ASCP, Archivio Segreto, status animarum, B. 1–3.

one *serva*. Households with more servants promised more companionship and help with the housework, along with competition and tension. Even in the wealthiest homes, servants' quarters were close; female domestics almost always shared a bed. A typical situation was the household of the wealthy widow Maria Zane, in the Calle da cha Zane of S. Giovanni Novo. Her household included three women servants: Anzola; Margherita (a widow); and Betta, the wife of a cobbler who lived elsewhere, with her toddler son. But if drudgery, exploitation, and low wages were regular elements of domestic service, a *serva's* living situation, as this example shows, could also offer the young woman opportunities for friendship and intimacy.[50] This may have been especially true for foreign women, who often worked in service and were the least likely to have established family or friendship networks.[51]

Another category of women who worked where they lived were prostitutes *(meretrici)*. The prostitutes recorded in the censuses are clearly a minuscule number of the actual prostitute population in early modern Venice. The census takers, many of them priests of the parish being surveyed, were probably reluctant to list large numbers of "loose" women among their parishioners. Perhaps some prostitutes were equally diffident about declaring their occupation to the local priest or his representative. In any event, only 213 prostitutes appear in the censuses (see table 1.15). Unlike female domestics, prostitutes ran their own show, however modest. A few (63) lived as boarders, and 10 women lived with their mothers. But most prostitutes identified as such in the parish registers headed their own households.

Prostitutes who headed their own homes often shared them with other women (see table 1.16). Just over one-quarter lived alone; the majority sheltered relatives, boarders, and servants. About one-third had children to support, and 28 percent lived with other women, most of them fellow prostitutes. If poverty often forced women into prostitution, prostitutes were not always poor: almost one-fifth of those who headed their own homes had at least one servant. A small number lived with men. Sometimes the men were boarders; in other cases, the relationship was acknowledged as intimate. In the parish of S. Marcuola, the prostitute Cornelia Gritti's home included a nobleman who had probably fallen on hard times: the clarissimo signor Alvixe, described as Cornelia's *concubino*.

Prostitutes often shared their homes with one another. Giulia Vignona, a courtesan living in S. Sofia, shared her dwelling with another *cortegiana*, Isabella Badoera. In the same parish, two other prostitutes, Isabella and Caterina, were listed together as household head. Not far away was

TABLE 1.15

Venetian Prostitutes, by Household Status, 1589–1607

Position within Household	Prostitutes (%)	
Head of household	137	(64.0)
Daughter	10	(5.0)
Mother	1	(0.4)
Sister	1	(0.4)
Servant	1	(0.4)
Other Women*	63	(30.0)
Total	213	(100.00)

Source: ASCP, Archivio Segreto, status animarum, B. 1–3.

*The category *Other Women* refers to women living in the household who were neither servants nor relatives. In this case, the other women were prostitutes who shared a home with or rented a room from the head of the household, often another prostitute.

TABLE 1.16

Households Headed by Prostitutes, 1589–1607

Household Type	Number (%)
Alone	36 (26)
With children	47 (34)
With relatives	19 (14)
With servants	26 (19)
With other women	39 (28)
With men	8 (6)
Total	137 (100)

Source: ASCP, Archivio Segreto, status animarum, B. 1–3.

another household made up of prostitutes: Maria, Camilla, Iacoma, and Franceschina. Sometimes the number of prostitutes sharing lodgings suggested an informal brothel: on the street of Ca' Trivisan in the parish of S. Maria Formosa, thirteen prostitutes shared an apartment.

Sometimes occupational and familial ties intersected. In the parish of SS. Apostoli *(calle del occhialer),* the prostitute Viena rented a room out to a man, one Marcantonio, but her profession was given as "prostitute along with her sister *[meretrice con sua sorella].*" In the *calle dei volti* in the same parish, Veneranda headed a household composed of herself, her niece, and her mother: all three were meretrici.

But not all prostitutes lived with other prostitutes. In the parish of S. Raffaello, the prostitute Isabetta, originally from Treviso *(Isabetta trivisana, meretrice),* shared her home with another immigrant, Isabella from Vicenza, whose status was simply *in compagnia* (keeping Isabetta company). Some prostitutes also had families to look after: Catterina da Venetia lived with her mother and child. The Friulian Catterina had three children under her roof, but still found room for five of her colleagues.[52]

₡

IN EARLY modern Venice, marriage ensured an impressive degree of independence from the families of both bride and groom. This was especially true for the offspring of popolane families. The independence asserted by young married couples worked in both directions: they rarely sought shelter from their parents or gave shelter to their parents. When adult married children did live in a parental home, their choice of parents depended on their social class: upper-class young couples were most likely to dwell in the home of the groom's family; popolani were more evenly split between her parents and his.

Venetian couples seem to have maintained fewer ties to their natal families than is traditionally thought to be the case for most of southern Europe.[53] But Venetian couples did not sever all such ties. Some of them took in unmarried brothers and sisters. Wives as well as husbands made the decision to shelter their siblings (and, on rare occasions, parents), which suggests that women not only contributed to the household, but also had a say in its composition.

Single women chose from different housing options, depending on circumstances. Here, marital status was a larger factor than sex in determining residence; single men and women had surprisingly similar living patterns. A few lived with family, but most struck out on their own, either living in an employer's home, sharing lodgings with other women, or heading a household composed of boarders and servants. Those who became prostitutes were likely to find companionship with other women in the same occupation.

This array of living patterns suggest a more complex picture than earlier studies of Italian family structure have painted. It may be true that the extended family was prevalent in rural parts of southern Italy and Iberia, while the households of the more urban northern Europe tended to be small and primarily composed of nuclear families. In many respects, the Venetian example is much closer to that of northern Europe than the less-developed sections of the Italian peninsula. Venice may be an anomaly. Or, the range of living patterns found here, which show strong ties among natal family members as well as unrelated women, may be more typical of southern European cities than has previously been thought.[54] Clearest of all is the fact that there was no one single living pattern for Venetian women and men.

Within this range of residential choice, how did women run their daily lives and configure their personal and professional associations? The next chapter examines the economic power of women in early modern Venice, for clues about the kinds of social power they might wield, within the home and beyond it.

CHAPTER TWO

Women of Means
Property and Possessions

WHEN a young woman named Marta fled her place of employment in the mid-seventeenth century, she walked away with all her possessions: four plain shirts, one with embroidery, a fur cape or coat, assorted stockings and aprons (one decorated with lace), several pairs of shoes, a bodice, two dresses, and some bed linens.[1] Andriana, the wife of a prosperous tailor, was better off. She lived with her family in the parish of S. Stin, but owned another residence with her sister Gaspara some distance away, in the parish of SS. Apostoli. The rent they received from their tenant Stefano Tagiapietra yielded 10 ducats a year to each sister.[2] Lavinia Cernosa, like other widows, had a longer financial history and the possibility of greater wealth and responsibility for that wealth. For looking after her nephew, she received a payment of 720 ducats worth of capital, as well as an annual inheritance income from the Morosini family of 36 ducats.[3]

Marta, Andriana, and Lavinia represent the wide range of wealth and property that women controlled in early modern Venice. Young women like Marta were among the most vulnerable residents of the republic. They sustained themselves and their families, not by living off their property, but by working and saving when and where they could. But women like Andriana and Lavinia, with substantial or at least respectable liquid assets or real estate, made up a larger part of the population than we have been led to expect for early modern Italy.[4] Even more significantly, the wealth that these women possessed was often independent wealth. That is, women often declared, petitioned for, or paid taxes on property or goods independently of their male relatives.

Several different sources reveal women's roles as earners, possessors, protectors, and managers of wealth. Notarial documents demonstrate women's aggressive protection and assertion of their rights to family money and goods. Records of women who, as lessors, held *livelli,* or leases, show one type of property open to individual women. Tax rolls from 1582 give evidence of how widely different forms of property ownership were distributed across categories of class and marital status. These rolls, or *decime,* also document women who functioned as managers of their own wealth and that of others. Wills, too, confirm that the type and amount of women's wealth covered a broad spectrum but that, regardless of a woman's amount of money or type of goods, her possessions endowed her with some degree of social power. This was true across Venetian society, from the most privileged noblewoman *(patrizia)* to the humblest *serva.*

We already know that women could own property in early modern Venice. Widows, especially, could wield power through their wills (and testamentary intentions) to make themselves a political or social force.[5] But Venetian women's financial clout rested on more than their wills and intentions to distribute legacies in the future. Many were active financial agents who negotiated leases, challenged debts, and filed business proposals with the state. Even if women did not control large tracts of property or coffers of money, a variety of personal possessions helped them negotiate their relationships within their households and beyond. In small ways and large, then, both patrician and popolane women were financial actors in early modern Venice.

Especially significant is the presence of nubili and married women among propertied Venetians. Historians have come to expect that widows owned property more frequently and in larger amounts than their married and nubili counterparts. This is not surprising: widows, simply by being, on average, older than most nubili and matrons, and having survived their husbands, had more time and opportunity to purchase, inherit, or marry into financial assets. A wealthy widow was autonomous financially and often free from the control of her father or guardian after her husband's death. Nevertheless, there is also evidence that both nubili and married women controlled their own property, sometimes jointly with their siblings and husbands, sometimes alone.

LEASES

Many women appear in the early-seventeenth-century survey of lease-holders collected by the Dieci Savi Sopra le Decime, a government office that surveyed wealth in order to levy a property tax. Leases were common in early modern Venice. There were two types of livelli: the first was a *livello consegnativo,* which was effectively a mortgage, by which the lessor took possession of a property and assumed all of the expenses associated with it. The second was essentially a loan of money with the property in question "leased" by the borrower to the lender in order to avoid charges of usury. The loan was to be paid back in the form of lease payments, not to exceed 5.5 percent of the total value of the property.[6]

Gigi Corazzol has conducted a systematic study of leaseholding in Venice for 1591. In that year, women made up only a small portion of the lease market. But among the patrician class, which dominated the lease market, women lent almost half of all of the money disbursed in the form of livelli. They borrowed money less often than they lent it: of the 47,206 ducats borrowed by individuals in 1591, noblewomen borrowed only 4,800 ducats, or 10 percent.

Widows figured prominently as both lenders and borrowers, with many of the married women who lent money being widows on their second marriages.[7] But nubili made up some of the leaseholders (lenders) as well. In the 1617 livelli declarations, Cristina de Mezo acknowledged owning leases on four homes.[8] Another *nubile,* Helia di Raspi, daughter of Pasquin, reported that she was living in someone else's home, that of Marco de Fondi, in the parish of S. Aponal, but her own assets included a house in the parish of S. Felice, some distance away, from which she received a substantial rent of 100 ducats. She also held a lease for "certain mills and homes in Vicenza worth 120 ducats," which had been the source of some conflict, since the payments on the lease by the residents of her property had not always been prompt.[9] Women also made business agreements with one another. Anzola Beltrame held a lease worth 400 ducats, for which she received interest payments at 5.5 percent, or 22 ducats a year, from Fiorenza Golardo.[10]

The nubili sisters Caterina and Elisabetta shared not only a financial interest but also a religious conversion. Originally Jews, as girls they had entered the Casa de Catecumeni, a charitable institution that sponsored conversions to Roman Catholicism. Now adults, they filed a formal request with the house for money owed them on a lease they had deeded over to the casa. The livello paid 9 ducats annually; Caterina and Betta offered to relinquish all rights to the payment for a price: 100 ducats to Caterina, the eldest, and 50 ducats to Betta.[11]

Married women were active in the lease market as well. Giustina Panizzosa was among the married women who held a lease in 1617. She was the Padua-born wife of the Venetian notary Gieronimo Brinis. Her assets included a house inhabited by a cloth dealer who paid her an annual lease payment of 36 ducats. Giustina herself paid rent on a series of leases that had been placed on the house in earlier times. Her debts in turn were offset by the income from at least two other homes in Padua.[12] She noted that this property, or the leases on it, were part of her dowry *(mie raggioni Dotali)*. Even though she was currently married, the leases were presented in the declaration unambiguously as her own, not her husband's. She was careful to note not only the sum she received from her tenants, but her expenses as well. These included payments on old leases to hospitals from whom she had rented property in the past, and a "perpetual payment" to a convent where she had placed her daughter several years earlier.[13]

Giustina was not unusual in owning property independently of her husband. Marietta, the wife of Bastian, a furrier, owned several houses in Venice in her own right. Sometimes wives also assumed control of their husband's property when he was unavailable.[14] Marcella Lippomano filed a tax declaration in 1582 on behalf of her husband Agustin, who was listed simply as "absent."[15]

Giustina's property was part of her dowry. She clearly controlled it even while her husband was alive. Another woman, Orsetta Gyuran, revealed her control over her dotal properties in her will, made while her husband, Antonio Querini, was still living. She requested that he be her executor and explicitly left him one-third of her dowry, "the third that is plainly his, that it not be touched by anyone else, neither my children, nor my family." Orsetta owed him this, the *corredo,* or one-third of her dowry to which he was legally entitled. The rest of her wealth she divided among her children, who included a daughter, Zanetta, who had run away from home four years earlier: "nevertheless, if she is alive I leave her one hundred ducats of my goods." To her son Benetto she left another hundred ducats, plus the 126 ducats "in credit" she expected to receive from the will of the nobleman Benetto Tiepolo.[16]

Some women wanted to control their wealth not only after their own demise but after the death of their heirs as well. Elisabetta de Bossi gave her husband the balance of her dowry, but only the usufruct of it. In her will she wrote: "The rest of my dowry I leave to Rugir my husband . . . he is obligated to give the twelfth each year to the Reverend brother Francesco my confessor. . . . After the death of my husband I want the remainder of my dowry to go to the scuola of the Carmini."[17]

In addition to owning property themselves and managing that of their husbands, women managed the property of others, usually that of their daughters. Marina Basto, a twice-married noblewoman, wrote to the Pien Collegio, an appeals court, on her daughter's behalf. The girl's marriage contract was in jeopardy because too much time had elapsed between the initial agreement and the final one. This was because the men in charge of the negotiations, including Marina's husband, had left town. Marina, who had been left in charge, explained that she had been unable to complete the negotiations without the men's assistance. She called attention to her vulnerable state, referring to herself as "only a woman, a poor widow," incapable of meeting the deadlines, and asked the court for a delay.[18] Despite her claim of incompetence, Marina showed herself to be anything but: by playing on ideas of female weakness, Marina could gain further time to negotiate a favorable deal for her daughter and family.[19]

Widows, of course, were most likely of all women to manage assets independently of men. Laura, the daughter of a cobbler and the widow of a spice dealer, made a will in 1610 that demonstrated how she had come into her own financially by surviving both husband and father. In addition to her furniture, Laura also bequeathed her and her husband's spice shop, part of which she had inherited, part of which was hers as "payment of dowry." Laura was also in possession of two livelli, each worth 100 ducats. Finally, Laura claimed an interest in the many livelli held by her husband's brother Piero.[20]

TAXES

The examples above show women holding leases and land in their own names, whether spinsters, married, or widowed. But do these cases truly reveal a significant number of propertied Venetian women? A tax survey from 1582 suggests that they do. Like men, women who owned property had not only to pay debts, but taxes as well. In 1582, when the Dieci

TABLE 2.1

Women Principals in Decime Hearings, 1582, by Marital Status and Who Was Corespondent

	Nubili (%)	Married Women (%)	Widows (%)
Alone	327 (74)	260 (95)	667 (91.5)
With sister(s)	45 (10)	1 (0.3)	08 (1.1)
With brother(s)	29 (7)	1 (0.3)	04 (0.5)
With sister(s) and brother(s)	26 (5.8)	0	0
With husband	0	6 (2)	0
With son(s)	0	0	18 (2.5)
With daughter(s)	0	0	08 (1.1)
With son(s) and daughter(s)	0	0	23 (3.2)
With friend(s)	13 (3)	03 (1)	01 (0.1)
With mother	1 (0.2)	1 (0.3)	0
Total	441 (100)	272 (100)	729 (100)

Source: ASV, Dieci Savi Sopra le Decime, indice delle condizioni delle decime, Indice 446.

Savi Sopra le Decime collected tax statements from Venice's residents, approximately one-third of the declarations were filed by women. A recently compiled index of this survey, located at the Venetian State Archives' study room, permits a preliminary quantitative analysis of the entire source (see table 2.1).[21] The headings for each index entry, taken from the titles of the individual declarations, list the name and marital status of the female respondents. The entry also notes if the women were acting on behalf of someone else, if they themselves were being represented, or if they owned the property jointly with another person. Sometimes the profession of a woman's husband or father was also included.

A breakdown by marital status shows that the majority of women holding property in their own name were widowed, some more than once. Fifty percent of the women whose names appear on these rolls as principal declarants of wealth were widows, 30 percent were nubili, and 20 percent were married women. Virtually all of the married and widowed women who appeared on the lists did so alone, with a few widows (forty-nine, or 6 percent) filing jointly with their children. A tiny number of married women (six, or 2 percent) declared property held in common with their husbands. This suggests that women either ceded their wealth to their husbands upon marriage or else kept it exclusively for themselves. In the tax declarations to the decime, only four married women filed with their husbands or had their property declared for them by their husbands. In broad terms, husbands and wives might unite their family interests, but they often maintained separate finances.

Property in this context can mean many things and indicate a wide range of wealth. Many of the women who filed with the decime were noble, possessors of substantial dowries and legacies from their husbands and other relatives. But some came from more modest backgrounds, and some from downright humble ones. Most women's entries do not include information on the occupation of a husband or father, but those that do give us an idea of the range in professional status that was represented in the decime declarations.

Table 2.2 shows, not surprisingly, that a number of the professions associated with the women who declared property were high-status, high-paying occupations. The most widely represented occupation for nubili, married women, and widows alike is doctor, apparently a high-paying profession then as now. Doctors' widows are especially well represented in the survey: there are eighteen of them. Some of the other women were wives and widows of clearly powerful, influential men: several had married men who became secretaries to the republic's most powerful government institutions, like the Council of Ten, the Avogaria de Comun court (state attorney's office), and the ducal palace bureaucracy. There were also military wives and widows. And of course the majority of women, for whom no associative profession was listed (and who are excluded from table 2.2), were likely the daughters and wives of nobles or wealthy commoners who lived off their investments and sinecures, rather than an occupation.

But, as table 2.2 shows, a variety of occupational backgrounds permitted women to own property on their own. Women with property included daughters of a boatman, a baker, and a carpenter. Wives held property independently of husbands who might be booksellers, tailors,

TABLE 2.2

Professions Attached to Husbands or Fathers of Female, Nonpatrician Respondents to the Decime, 1582

Nubili	Married Women	Widows
doctor (6)	doctor (3), spice dealer (2)	doctor (18), spice dealer (3)
(dottor/medico/fisico)	state lawyer (2)	dyer, sculptor, barber
cloth retailer	pots-and-pans dealer	turner, metalworker
spice dealer (3)	tailor (3)	painter, boatbuilder
flour seller	glassworker, caulker (2)	caulker
carpenter	goldsmith (4), carpenter	milliner, cobbler, notary
lawyer	sailor (4), fisherman	state lawyer,
tailor	silk merchant (2)	ducal secretary (3)
bookseller	ship navigator	lantern seller, lawyer
weaver	governor, Corfu cavalry	cloth merchant
boatman	spinner, wine porter	secretary for the council of
boatbuilder	stonecutter, wool beater (2)	Ten, cloth retailer
engineer	jeweler, butcher	poultry seller, fruit seller
baker	appraiser	fried-food seller (2)
linen worker	commander (military) (2)	secretary (2)
goldsmith (3)	boatman, mason	potter (2), legal clerk
	secretary of the council of	notary of the Avogaria
	Ten, mask maker	court
	fabric stretcher, cooper	
	stationer	

Source: ASV, Dieci Savi Sopra le Decime, indice delle condizioni delle decime, Indice 445.

or fishermen. One was married to a pots-and-pans dealer, another to a mason. At least two widows had married spice dealers, two had married potters, one married a barber, and one married a metalworker. Poultry sellers and a man with a fruit stand had also left wives with property to declare.

What the women in the survey actually declared varied widely. We of course expect the poultry seller's widow to have fewer and less lucrative assets than the widow of a nobleman or a ducal secretary. Nevertheless, all these women clearly possessed more than the average Venetian popolana, which is why they made it on to the survey at all. Thus, they were not typical, yet their numbers and the variety of their backgrounds point to greater possibility for exercising economic power than historians have traditionally assumed for early modern Venetian women.[22]

Many women, including nubili, found that their property in reality consisted of a complex web of debt and obligation as well as revenue. Paola Fieramonte explained that she lived in the parish of S. Aponal, dividing her time between two residences, one belonging to the noble Jacopo Barbaro, the other belonging to Zuanne Malipiero. For these, she paid 9 ducats a year. Her property in fact consisted of an overlapping series of obligations and leases, those due to her and those she was paying on other properties. She received rents from at least two apartments, which totaled 27 ducats annually, but paid the leases on those homes as well, which cost her 7 ducats a year. Her net real-estate income thus came to 20 ducats a year.[23]

Nubili were more likely than married women or widows to hold property jointly with others, especially siblings. Nearly one-quarter of them filed declarations with brothers and sisters, particularly sisters. The four sisters Giulia, Anna, Isabetta, and Veniera held several assets jointly, including leases and the ownership of terrain near the city of Vicenza.[24] In another case, where two sisters were in joint ownership, a husband played a secondary role in handling the family fortune: Alba and Isabetta, daughters of the nobleman Zuan Nadal, pursued a case against one Giulio Vignon for a false accusation against their good name. Isabetta's husband, Aurelio, was also mentioned as a complainant, but the two sisters were clearly the main actors in the affair.[25] The tendency of nubili sisters to hold property in common is surprising. In general, property shared among three or four women could not have presented a very attractive dowry to a prospective husband. Unless it was a vast property that would still present an impressive asset when reduced to one-quarter or one-third of its original size, it was unlikely to bring his family much wealth. Did the parents of such nubili give them this land with the intention that it remain within the family, that their daughters might have some financial security independent of dowries and husbands?[26]

SIBLINGS AND WEALTH

Whatever the intent of parents who gave their daughters (and sons) property in common, the effect was to strengthen the blood ties among unmarried siblings, at least as far as common financial interest was concerned. Chapter 1 noted that lateral kinship played a relatively small role in women's residential patterns: women usually found alternatives to living with their brothers and sisters. Family ties, then, were not always manifested by co-residence. But even siblings who did not live together could maintain a relationship of shared goals or property. Lateral kinship could still be reinforced by common economic interests.

Sisters and brothers often banded together to protect property they held or hoped to inherit. Sisters especially may have found safety in numbers when appealing a tax or fine or asking the courts to expedite testamentary procedures. The four sisters Margarita, Lucia, Cattarina, and Vicenza Boscolon, "along with our only brother Andrea," asked the court for assistance in resolving the debts they had been forced to assume upon the death of their father. Like other women who made such supplications, the Boscolon sisters called attention to their special vulnerability as women. They began their appeal with the formulaic observation that "it was never the intention of Your Serenity . . . that any of your citizens should be forced to labor under conditions more difficult than he can sustain, and this is particularly true for poor women." [27] The Boscolons went on to explain that their father had had tax problems in the past and had struggled to keep his businesses in "industry and commerce [*industria et mercantie*]" alive. When he died, he left his five children with no property or goods *(non havendo lassato . . . beni alcuni stabeli, ne mobeli)*, only a mountain of debt, totaling 1,900 ducats—a discouragingly high sum when we recall that a worker might earn 60 ducats a year. The four sisters and their brother argued that any hope of earning that much money had died with the father's death and they should be relieved of the burden.

The sisters Orsa and Borthola di Zanchi filed a petition with the Pien Collegio (appeals court) in 1564 on behalf of themselves and a mentally incapacitated brother. The women were protesting a tax originally levied on a woman from whom their father had purchased property for them. The woman, Franceschina Tuviani, had owned several dilapidated homes *(alcune casette vecchie et ruinose poste in contra' de santo Antonin)*. Since Franceschina had died the preceding year, collectors were now, in 1564, trying to collect both back taxes and multiple fines from the new owners. Borthola and Orsa asked the court to right this wrong, "as has been done in similar cases."[28]

Even when they lived apart, there was nothing like debt to bring siblings together. In a case similar to the di Zanchi's, Vicenzo, ZuanGiacomo, and Paula Cavazza protested that they had been set upon by creditors after their father's death. The problem had been aggravated, they explained, because their mother had managed her husband's affairs badly, without providing for the future. Her mismanagement was not initially obvious: "Our mother . . . was completely ignorant of our father's activities: so that until now we lived far from any problem or worry, contenting ourselves with our small fortune." The axe fell when the creditors swooped down on the children, taking advantage of their innocence, or so the Cavazza siblings claimed.[29]

We have already seen two cases in which sisters spoke for themselves as well as for a brother, who for one reason or another was incapable of acting on his own or as an equal participant. Sisters could also intercede on behalf of brothers in financial trouble. Isabetta, a widow, asked the Pien Collegio for justice. Her brother Luca faced taxes for real estate that he had sold or otherwise lost. Isabetta had a vested interest in the property under discussion; she had already given one of the houses to her oldest daughter as a dowry.[30]

Such collective interests among siblings, especially popolani, may have complemented and enlarged women's financial resources. Nor did collective financial investments stop with siblings. Just as the terms *sorella, zermana,* and *cusina* could connote a general lateral kinship among women rather than a specifically defined bond like cousin or sister, so too did financial ties spill over into a broader kinship realm. For example, in 1585 the sisters and niece of Baldissere Balbi filed a joint petition with the Pien Collegio asking that a tax be lifted from some property Baldissere had bequeathed them. No husbands were mentioned; they either did not exist or, in this matter, were irrelevant.[31]

NUBILI AND FAMILY INTERESTS

Debts could be related to a shared business concern rather than to a legacy of land. In 1581, a brother-and-sister team, Nicolo and the *nubile* Regina da Mosto, filed a complaint with the Pien Collegio. They claimed that after their father's death in 1576, they had been left with nothing but the ownership of two bakeries, one of which paid nothing, the other of which was saddled with debt that the collectors were trying to squeeze out of the recently orphaned siblings.[32]

Siblings came together for financial reasons other than debt. A group of four siblings—the brothers Giovanni Battista and Nicolo and their sisters Lodovica and Faustina, both of whom appear to be unmarried—asked for government help to take possession of land and goods they had jointly inherited.[33] Another family of sisters and a brother wrote the Pien Collegio to obtain a patent for an invention they had recently developed, a sort of submarine. The petitioners began their appeal by noting the republic's customary encouragement of "ingenuity" in its citizens. They then introduced themselves: Salvador de Gradi, the only brother, with his sisters Laura, Isabetta, Simona, and Christina. A second man, Francesco Cavanei, was listed last. The de Gradis and their partner described in detail the device they had invented:

> Considering how great the damage is to ships, both armed and un-armed, when they sink under water, and how useful it would be to recover the goods and weapons and all the other things [in the ships]. . . . After great effort and expense we have discovered two important secrets and inventions, the first something that allows a man or men . . . to go underwater . . . and remain able to breathe, without these men needing to enclose themselves in anything, the other to give them light so that they can see, and remain under said water for the space of approximately three hours.[34]

This invention, asserted the de Gradis and Cavanei, would bring great profit to the Serenissima. The siblings and their partner asked for the rights to their invention for a fifty-year period.

Who were the de Gradi women? Adults, they appear to have been un-married—otherwise their husbands would have appeared alongside them in the petition, if not in their stead. Instead, brother and sisters are all identified by their father, Marcantonio, a member of the citizen class. One of the sisters, Simona, made a will in 1607. She left the bulk of her estate to four nieces (she was particularly attached to one niece, Gabriella) and one nephew, all children of a fifth sister, Paola.[35] Simona's will does not mention a husband or children; presumably she was unmarried at the time of its composition. Her holdings were substantial enough to necessitate elaborate arrangements for their distribution among her nieces and nephew.

Simona's holdings consisted primarily of one *palazzo,* or building, divided into several apartments. Her distribution of the apartments was complicated: her favorite nieces, Gabriella and Eugenia, inherited the lion's share of the property. Since Eugenia was already in possession of at least one apartment, she was ordered to pay Gabriella a sum of 550 ducats, a substantial sum. In addition, Eugenia was also responsible for making a much smaller payment to all three of her sisters, Gabriella, Virginia, and Maria, in return for the annual profit she would receive from the rent of an apartment. Finally, Simona also considered her nephew, Ludovico, brother of the four sisters. While she referred only vaguely to the dowries of Gabriella and Eugenia, Simona was very concerned with Ludovico's marriage plans, threatening to cut his heirs out of the will if he chose the wrong partner:

> The rest of all of my goods that I currently possess . . . I leave to Lodovico my nephew, son of the above-named Paula my sister and of m. Marco Armano . . . and after his death I want said goods of mine to go to his legitimate children . . . born of a legitimate marriage, that they must not be sons of the daughter of that nut *[folera]* Antea, but of another woman that he chose for wife, because I don't want the children of said Antea to have any goods from my testament, with the obligation to Gabriella . . . and should Lodovico die without legitimate children . . . I want said goods of mine to go to the children of the above-named nieces Maria, Virginia, Eugenia, and Gabriella divided among them in equal parts.[36]

Nubili, of course, were not the only women without husbands to remember their siblings' children in their wills. Maria da Spin, the widow of a pots-and-pans seller, left 30 ducats to her brother Zanetto's family: 10 ducats each to her nephews Pietro and Hieronimo, and another 10 to her sister-in-law Isabetta, also a widow. To her sister, also named Isabetta, she left 5 ducats.[37]

Nubili sometimes found business partners outside of the family. In 1585, three men and one woman, all apparently unrelated, presented a *supplica,* or petition to the Pien Collegio. Rocco de Benetto, Iseppo da Canal, Anzola Verde from Corfu, and Zuane de Bastian were all elderly by the time they filed the petition. Some thirty or forty years earlier, one or all of them had purchased property near the Fontego dei Tedeschi, the clearinghouse for German merchants. Rocco, Iseppo, Anzola, and Zuane complained that they could not live on the meager rent they received on the building, especially when the rent was weighed against the taxes they paid. The group respectfully asked permission to raise the rent.[38]

Anzola was a Greek immigrant, apparently unmarried, who as a young woman had entered into a business venture with three men. Often these *suppliche* included what we might today call human-interest material—information about the supplicant's family and living circumstances to humanize the plaintiffs and point to the exceptional circumstances that made this request especially compelling. Yet this supplica contains no explanation for the partnership, nor for Anzola's membership, because there was nothing remarkable about it.

MARRIED WOMEN AND SIBLINGS

We have seen that married women could hold property independently of husbands, and that nubili could control their own assets—insofar as paying taxes and challenging debts indicates control—as well as hold property jointly with their siblings. Married women, however, do not appear to have held property in common with siblings. Paola de Gradi did not participate in her siblings' inventive endeavors, according to the supplica, and she was the only sister we know of who married. Did women relinquish jointly held assets upon marriage? The record is silent on this. In any event, most of the nubili registered in the list (75 percent) held property on their own, like Giulia Marchesini, a *nubile* with substantial, independently held real estate on the mainland.[39] Women with property in their name alone had a better chance of controlling that property after marriage than those who shared holdings with siblings.

Even if married women rarely held property in common with siblings, they might still look after them financially. The wealthy Anzola Rizzo's will also reveals a world that extended beyond the traditional boundaries of familial or dynastic strategy. Anzola was married to Zuane Rizzo, a lawyer's son, when she made her will in 1576. She left the bulk of her estate to him and any future children, but she wanted to look after other relatives as well. Her first concern was her sister Helena, to whom she left 300 ducats. Helena also stood to inherit bolts of cloth and further wealth upon her marriage. The women were apparently orphaned: Anzola explained her generosity to Helena by noting that "I must be a father to her *[facendo al modo de suo Padre]*." Anzola's generosity only went so far, however: she added that, "if I have children, I don't want my sister to get anything but the linen cloth."[40]

Married women also managed their own property. Felicità Molino petitioned the Pien Collegio for help in 1587. She was married to Iulio Preguerra, but Iulio took no part in her appeal. Her ancestors had acquired land in Dalmatia in the fifteenth century; in 1498 they also acquired property near Treviso. Felicità was asking for recognition of her legal right to these properties, independent of relatives and her husband.[41]

To what extent did women actually control their assets? The lists do give some indication of this. Most women made these declarations on their own, though some did so through a guardian or trustee, a *commissario*. For example, Martin Maffetti represented his wife, Julia di Passi, to the tax office; the widow Cecilia Saler was "presented by her children."[42] But the number of women who had men officially represent them to the Dieci Savi was relatively small, according to the archival index: fewer than ten women out of more than two hundred explicitly declared their holdings with or through a male proxy.

Some women chose other women to help them. More women functioned as *commissarie* than were represented by men in that capacity. Twenty-eight nubili appear in the index as commissarie. Often they performed this service for other women. Blood ties were important: Filomena Contarina served as *commissaria* for her sister Contarina, while the sisters Orsa and Marina Balbi filed a declaration on behalf of their aunt Elisabetta Contarini.[43] When Cattarina and Betta, the Jewish converts mentioned above, filed their petition with the Casa di Catecumeni, Cattarina noted that she was acting as *procuratrice,* or representative, for her younger sister.[44]

Married women acted as commissarie less often. Their children either ran their affairs independently or turned to their fathers for assistance or direction. There were exceptions: Isabetta dalla Vecchia, married to Zuane Surian, appeared as a *tutrice,* or guardian, in the rolls when she acted on behalf of Nicolosa, her daughter by her first marriage.[45] Husbands also trusted their wives to manage their affairs after their death. When Vittorio Trasontin made his will in 1562, he asked that his wife Maria be his commissaria. In addition, "I wish that the said Madonna Maria be the commissaria of my godson Vittorio, and that she govern all of my present and future properties."[46]

WIDOWS

Once widowed, women maintained or perhaps reestablished economic relations with their siblings. Bianca Vitturi, a widow, noted in her declaration to the Dieci Savi that she was currently sharing a home and expenses in the parish of S. Maurizio with her brother Bortolomio and her sister Elena.[47] Barbara, another widow, filed a petition with the Pien Collegio with her brother Zorzi. The siblings asked the court to reconsider a tax levied on a house that they owned jointly that they had inherited from their father, Magno.[48] Widows also maintained an interest in their natal family's affairs without the support of sisters and brothers. Perina, the widow of nobleman Zuanne Contarini, asked the Pien Collegio for aid in reclaiming lost property that had been mismanaged by her parents since 1506.[49]

When widows acted as commissarie, it was usually for their children. Cecilia Basadona served as commissaria for her daughter. Elena Davanzo filed a declaration "for herself and as guardian of her children."[50] Fausta Corner also served as the tutrice for her son and daughter, Camillo and Orsetta.[51] Sometimes widows were in need of commissarie, and they had a number of options. Catterina Bergamasca asked that her estate be managed by three people: her adult son, a priest, and two sisters, Andriana Contarini and Chiara Duodo, powerful noblewomen who could ensure that her wishes were carried out.[52]

WOMEN AS MANAGERS

We have seen that women could own and manage goods and property themselves, independently of their fathers, husbands, brothers, or sons. This was true for nubili as well as for married women and widows. Table 2.3 shows a sample of transactions supervised by Venetian notaries from 1565 to 1625. The transactions include wills, lease agreements, and business contracts. How these transactions were distributed across the

TABLE 2.3

Women Conducting Business with Notaries, by Marital Status, 1565–1625

Year	Nubili (%)	Married Women (%)	Widows (%)
1565	20 (36)	18 (32)	18 (32)
1575	45 (25)	45 (25)	86 (50)
1585	43 (26)	58 (36)	62 (38)
1595	12 (31)	9 (23)	18 (46)
1605	58 (27)	75 (35)	83 (38)
1615	73 (31)	61 (26)	103 (43)
1625	24 (32)	22 (29)	30 (39)

Source: ASV, Atti Notarile, B. 2573 (Contarini, P, 1565); B. 2583 (Contarini, P, 1575); B. 452 (Brinis, A, 1575); B. 462 (Brinis, A, 1585); B. 2627 (Crivelli, Z, 1575); B. 2637 (Crivelli, Z, 1585); B. 2647 (Crivelli, Z, 1595); B. 2696 and 2697 (Crivelli, Z.F, 1595); B. 2656 (Crivelli, Z, 1605); B. 2703 (Crivelli, Z.F, 1605); B. 765 (Brinis, G, 1605); B. 2667 (Crivelli, Z, 1615); B. 2713 (Crivelli, Z.F, 1615); B. 775 (Brinis, G, 1615); B. 4992 (Doglioni, F, 1615); B. 2723 (Crivelli, Z.F, 1625); B. 5004 (Doglioni, F, 1625).

female population varies somewhat from one period to the next: in 1575, nearly one-half of all of the women engaging in business dealings were widows (many of them no doubt recently widowed by the plague that swept Venice that year). In general, however, nubili, matrons, and widows dealt with notaries in roughly equal numbers—nubili without the direct supervision of a father or guardian, and married women independently of their husbands.

WOMEN AND THE COURTS

Women regularly approached the Pien Collegio for satisfaction of a grievance that threatened their assets, whether those assets were small or large. Anna, a washerwoman *(lavandera)* fought for money she claimed to have inherited from her cousin Maria. As she explained, Maria "did not want to die without ordering her things." In front of three witnesses, Maria, who was herself illiterate, had drafted a will in the summer of 1550, leaving the balance *(residuo)* to Anna. This will, written by the only literate witness, was then given to Anna for safekeeping. After Maria died Anna presented the will, only to be told that it was invalid. She thus presented her case to the appeals court, asking for justice.[53]

In 1573 Paulina Capodevin (her father may have been a wine merchant) brought charges against the men who had been appointed as her guardians after her father's death. Her mother, too, may have been dead, since Paulina did not mention her. These guardians, "as too often happens in this city," squandered her wealth, "the wealth that my father acquired with sweat and hard work." Now that Paulina had come of age she had begun to examine her portfolio and found "nothing but lists and confusion and the appropriation of my goods by these commissari who, rather than alert me to their bad management, have fled."[54]

Many female supplicants to the Pien Collegio were trying to cope after the death of a father or a husband. Widows figured prominently in the appeals. Like daughters, they frequently asked the court to recognize their rights as heirs, but also to absolve them of their responsibilities to cover the deceased's debts. The key argument, made over and over, was that the widow or daughters in question lacked the skills or opportunity to earn the necessary money to pay off the debts. Whether true or not, for so many women to employ it such a claim must have been an effective strategy. Justina, the widow of a dyer, found herself saddled with his business debts after his death. She asserted more than once that "I, a poor widow, have never made use of the [failing business], nor engaged in any other sort of commerce." Rather, she had dedicated herself to her large family.[55] Sometimes women received unexpected sources of income, like Laura di Mazi, who won a lawsuit against the nobleman Andrea Gradenigo. Gradenigo was ordered to pay her 180 ducats in damages, plus interest at 8 percent, as compensation. Laura's case, in fact, is less revealing of women's income than it is of women's effective access to institutions that sustained their property rights.[56]

SOURCES OF WEALTH

Inheritance was the principal source of wealth for women. Some women inherited money and goods from their parents, sometimes as dowries, and sometimes as simple legacies. This was the case for Orsa and

Borthola di Zanchi, mentioned above, whose father had left them several homes to rent. Gratiosa, Pulisena, Borthola, and Caterina, daughters of the citizen Marcantonio Bon, received property upon their father's death that included his legacy to them, their mother's dowry, and a legacy from their maternal grandfather "to sustain our miserable lives." [57]

Fathers sometimes left their daughters possessions or sources of income that they could exploit independently of a marriage dowry. In 1580 Isabella Vendramin petitioned the Pien Collegio regarding her claim to a government job. Isabella (apparently unmarried; no husband is mentioned in the supplica) had received from her father the title to a senatorial bureaucratic post in the customs-duty office. "He put said office in my name in order to sustain me and my [future] children." The petition went on to explain that the man chosen by Isabella to fill that office was now required to share his office (and presumably the stipend) with another man, as a result of a new law. At stake were both the men's stipends and the share of the sinecure the women who owned the titles could expect to receive. Isabella asked that her appointee be allowed to continue to do his job alone.[58] Another woman, Philippa, also inherited an office, an infantry unit. She received this directly from the state after her husband and sons died defending Venetian interests against the Turks. Her greatest wish was to pass the unit on, after her death, to her niece and nephew for a period of ten years (after which it would presumably revert to the state).[59]

Parents, then, along with husbands, were the principal sources of women's wealth. But they were not the only ones. More distant relatives, too, looked out for women. The nobleman Tomaso Mocenigo left his palace (Ca' Mocenigo) and the furnishings within it to his niece Elena and her unnamed (perhaps future) husband.[60] Female relatives were an especially important source. Orsetta Moro, the highborn wife of Vicenzo Barocci, left a large number of bequests when she drafted her will in 1602. The first went to Bettina, her brother's daughter. Bettina was to inherit, upon her marriage, a legacy of 3,000 ducats, truly a princely sum. Another wealthy woman, Marietta, also thought about her nieces when drafting her will in 1597. She left the younger women, Cecilia and Marieta, a property to share in Carrara. Other women, friends or distant relatives, were promised legacies upon marriage (though Marieta noted in some cases that she owed these heirs the money: they were already married).[61] People making wills also remembered poorer women, especially servants. For example, Orsetta Moro's servants received bequests, as did their female children. The servant Polonia received 10 ducats "for her daughter."[62]

Women did, of course, earn some of their wealth on their own, albeit a modest portion of it. We have already seen, in passing, the mention of several women's trades. Women not only sold food and other goods on the streets and offered domestic services as laundresses, they worked as second-hand clothes dealers *(strazzaruola)*, linen makers *(linaruola)*, and bakers *(fornera)*. Among other occupations listed for widows and other single women in the parish censuses are fruit vendor *(fruttaruola)*, spice vendor *(spiciera)*, and traditionally male trades like boatwoman *(barcaruola)*, cobbler *(zavatera, cassellera)*, and sail maker *(vellera)*, although we find only one of the latter.[63] Such occupations enabled women to support themselves in the absence of inherited wealth, often independently of husbands or fathers. Participation in business ventures provided another source of income.[64]

WOMEN IN BUSINESS

Not all widows found themselves plunged into difficult straits because they had to contend with old debts. Pulissena Tiepolo asked the court to consider her claim on a cavalry unit *(cavalleria)* (twenty regiments, she specified), that had been awarded to her husband Giambattista Bollani because of his valor in battle.[65] And unlike Justina, the dyer's widow mentioned above, some widows did try to continue a husband's business. Cristina was the widow of Francesco Tirabosco, an almond dealer with a shop in the prime commercial area of Rialto. She complained to the Pien Collegio that she had been struggling to keep the business afloat and feed her three children, but was being thwarted by two obstacles: she claimed that, one, she had to pay unreasonable taxes on her profits and property; and, two, that two men with the same name as her husband and in the same line of work *(traficavano parimente)* were trying to steal her hard-earned clients. To make matters worse, Cristina was being taxed for the imposters' profits.[66]

We also learn of another widow who coped with her husband's death by embarking on a business venture: Anzola Mafei used her dowry money to invest in a building at the foot of the Rialto bridge. The property encompassed a shop and a small home for Anzola and her children, "an expensive investment." She owned one-third of the building; thus she was understandably distressed when the edifice was confiscated by the city authorities (her petition does not explain why). Now, in August of 1588, Anzola was requesting appropriate reimbursement. Other women created or supplemented income by the more usual method of renting rooms. Orsetta Piriotta's lengthy Inquisition trial was caused in part by some disgruntled tenants whom she had pressured for overdue rent.[67]

MODEST WEALTH

These tax rolls and lease records thus establish that many Venetian women owned wealth or property in their own right, independently of husbands, fathers, and brothers. Such wealth surely gave them some economic power, both within their homes and in the wider community of urban Venice. But, of course, the records refer to a minority. The majority of Venetian women did not appear on the rolls as significant property holders; nor did they count land tracts, leases, or government offices among their assets (nor, of course, did the majority of men). Most women did, however, control a modest set of possessions, personal items that could also affect how they interacted with other members of their households. As Marta's careful list of her possessions at the beginning of this chapter shows, at the humblest levels of society (as well as at the highest), clothing was valued property. In fact, the most common items found in women's wills and inventories were clothes and useful, domestic items that would last for generations. These items, though less valuable than land tracts, buildings, or large sums of money, gave poorer women some financial security beyond their modest wages.

When she composed her will in 1551, Prudentia Calafado was a *nubile* living under the roof of the wealthy Alvise Zorzi—"healthy in mind and intellect, but infirm in body."[68] She left almost all of her goods to her mother and sister and attached an inventory detailing what they would inherit. Prudentia's possessions included a picture frame made of walnut, a walnut bed frame with columns and canopy, a rug, several chests, some large and some small chairs, a table painted pale blue, bedding (including "cushions made with good feathers"), leather cushions, a mattress and mattress pad, a pillow, various bolts of fabric, bowls, dishes, pans, and a window screen of wood.[69]

Similar in type if not in quantity was the inventory of Caterina Berga-masca, a sailor's widow. Her goods included a number of large chests, pots and pans, a candelabra, and several aprons.[70] At her death, she possessed several cloths made of linen and wool, various housewares *(massarie)*, and wooden chests. Her clothes included a fur throw, a dress, two pairs of stockings, and several shirts, several veils, several aprons, and at least 50 ducats, 100 lire, and some soldi di piccoli.[71]

One popolana woman's will illustrated not only a network of relation-ships but also a collection of material goods and liquid wealth so exten-sive that she must have lived very comfortably. Antonia, a barber's widow whose will was read in 1574, was prosperous by any standard. An inven-tory attached to her will[72] included four heavy chests, a quilt, a bed frame made of walnut, a bedsack,[73] two mattresses, a woolen bed covering, a walnut chest of drawers, two candelabras, a walnut chair, and three old, small paintings with some images of the Madonna. Money found in two of the chests totaled 365 ducats and 10 piccoli.[74] Since 8 to 10 ducats was a typical annual rent for a modest home, it is clear that Antonia had enjoyed a secure widowhood.[75]

ℭ

WOMEN'S POLITICAL and legal subordination to men has historically been linked to their economic dependence on men, and rightly so. But many of the Venetian women described here could be economically indepen-dent if necessary, and possessed at least sufficient property and wealth to make them financial collaborators within the household economy. Most striking is the variety of ways in which women acquired property. They owned land, buildings, and, occasionally, government offices.

Equally striking is the prominence of propertied women across marital and social strata. Women held property in their own right before, dur-ing, and after marriage. Such wealth was not the exclusive purview of the nobility: women from humbler families also controlled assets themselves, albeit in more modest amounts.

If women at all stages of their lives owned and ran property, their mari-tal status played a larger role in shaping their response when they had to defend or fight to regain that property before the Pien Collegio. In the appeal files, nubili and widows abound; married women are scarce. This may be because nubili and widows were more likely to control property than matrons (although the decime and notarial records do not indicate such a stark contrast between married and unmarried women's holdings); the absence of married women from the Pien Collegio files may, however, reveal the particular vulnerability of unmarried women in this period. Even though they might own and control real estate, nubili and widows lacking the economic and legal protection of a husband and his family may have been easier targets for those seeking payments of old debts, or those refusing to pay debts owed to them. Alternatively, widowed and nubili may have protested financial disputes more vigorously before the Pien Collegio because they anticipated a favorable ruling based in part on that perceived vulnerability.[76]

Most of the women who brought their requests to the Pien Collegio did so with tales of woe. It was in their interest to portray themselves as desperate, helpless women in order to obtain government assistance or leniency. In fact, by taking the initiative to file the petition, by employing a notary and developing a strategy for obtaining money or tax relief, these women revealed themselves to be resourceful and competent owners and managers of property.

The information in these records invites speculation. For married women, ownership of property or valuable goods could permit a more egalitarian relationship within the home.[77] For nubili or widows, possessions, wages, and wealth served crucial functions, from keeping destitution at bay to preserving their independence. Property and wealth might make a woman attractive to a potential groom and his family, but this discussion shows that they could also bind her to her natal family by fostering their common financial interest. Such bonds could encourage a woman's investment in her natal family through her will, independent of marital ties and obligations. But property could give women more choices in the marriage market, especially once we descend below the level of the wealthy patriciate, whose marriage strategies were carefully planned out by the families involved. A woman of means was particularly desirable as a prospective wife; at the same time, a woman so placed did not have to marry for security.

Finally, many women, even those without land or business interests, had property of value to disburse. The different types of wealth described here suggest a distinction between two kinds of property, or two kinds of value that defined women's property. The first was absolute value: the value of land or coins, or the interest rate on a lease. This value gave possessors of it, both women and men, a clear income. The other sort of value was not income-producing and refers to the goods that might be passed on to others in a will—in the case of a woman, especially to other women. Goods such as wardrobe chests, beds, and aprons that were transferred from household to household, helped daughters, sisters, and neighbors create their own households, as wives but also as *nubili* and widows. The possession and transmission of these objects endowed women with a localized power—a social power vis-à-vis those who might hope to inherit their belongings. The possessions owned and controlled by the humblest women were valuable items whose worth would endure after their owner died. This power could help other women form households and begin their adult lives.

Women's lives in earlier times appear to us so constricted, limited as they were by the myriad of legal, economic, and religious restrictions that worked to keep women under the control of men. But the Venetian records show that the reality was often different. Instead, women could exercise varying degrees of initiative and control financial goods at all stages of their lives.

Whether or not they owned property, women's lives were defined by more than the dynamics of their households. Although the crux of their world was the home, women as well as men spent a large part of their day outside of those protective walls. When we leave a Venetian woman's home and step out onto the street, moving into the nearby *campo,* or square, we find a world of work, tension, and sociability in which most Venetians participated, and where a range of power relationships was explored and expressed. The next chapter examines how women moved between the home and neighborhood in early modern Venice.

CHAPTER THREE

Around the
Neighborhood

VENETIAN women often wielded power within their homes, as household heads and owners of property; when they stepped out of their homes, they entered a chaotic, growing city full of merchants, beggars, and visiting dignitaries. Between the home and the larger city lay the neighborhood, within which most women spent much of their days. Within the interconnecting alleys and embankments bordering the canals that snaked their way from one end of town to the other, neighborhoods housed the economic bustle and mix of classes and nations for which Venice was famous.

The term *contrada* is a vague one, difficult to define precisely. *Parrochia* and *contrada* both take their essential meaning from their ecclesiastical function, as the boundaries of a parish. But both came to mean, more broadly, the neighborhood. The Italian dictionary Zingarelli offers this definition of *contrada*: "The nearby area, the street of a residential area. . . . Older usage: neighborhood."[1] To understand the multiple meanings and functions of Venetian neighborhoods,[2] we must focus on the parish, which formed the heart of neighborhood life for many Venetians. This was also the defining district for Venetian authorities.

It is when we move beyond civic and ecclesiastical definitions of neighborhood that the flavor and features of particular local communities begin to emerge. First, the dominant presence of women is clear; they could populate entire sections of a neighborhood almost exclusively. Second, Inquisition records show the layers of identity by which women knew one another in this context. Third, men played a decidedly secondary role in neighborhood society, though they mixed easily, even intimately, with their female neighbors. Fourth, though social interaction within the neighborhood formed a tissue of obligation and reciprocity in local community life, economic ties and exchanges played an equally central role. Women, largely based in the neighborhood (though by no means confined to it, as we shall see in chapter 5),[3] thus ran what was often a largely local female economy. They conducted much of that business within their homes—activity that gives us one example of the porous boundaries that separated the home from wider parish life. Finally, the role of privileged women within the neighborhood was usually limited to patronage through bequests: neighborhood society was, by and large, a popolana affair.

OFFICIAL DEFINITIONS

In both ecclesiastical and government documents from this period, Venetians from the popular classes regularly identified themselves, relatives, and friends by parish.[4] Parishes traditionally conducted their own religious festivals and rituals. Although these had been largely taken over by citywide celebrations, by the sixteenth century an awareness of traditional festivals and the persistence of activities associated with them continued to contribute to a common identity among the residents of a parish.[5] Such identity was reinforced by the parish's official role. The Venetian contrade functioned as an administrative unit for the city as well as for the church, headed both by a priest who had been selected by the parish's homeowners and a "parish chief" who answered to the doge.[6] The parish, then, functioned as both a secular and ecclesiastical unit. People regularly identified themselves by their parishes, for example when they appeared before tribunals, declared their wealth to the Dieci Savi Sopra le Decime, or filed petitions with the Pien Collegio. In official terms, the parish was in effect the community within the city, within which Venetians created a civic and religious identity.

Certain parishes were more distinctive than others. The Arsenale neighborhood—which in fact encompassed several parishes, S. Pietro of Castello being the largest—was the heart of the city's shipbuilding industry and has been described as a prototype of the company town. It had a strong worker-identity and a relatively uniform and low standard of living.[7] More significantly, the *arsenalotti,* those who lived and worked at the Arsenale, felt themselves to be possessors of a particular identity, which was reinforced by occupational and social rituals.[8] Another area clearly defined by a single occupation was the parish of S. Nicolò dei Tolentini, linked to the large number of fishermen who called it home.[9]

But if the church and civic authorities alike saw the parish neighborhood as distinctly bordered and clearly defined, the reality for Venetians was more ambiguous. Venetians, both women and men, moved easily among parishes as they went about their daily business (see chapter 5). They did not work, shop, and socialize only in their contrada but moved into the web of streets that spread out from their homes, even if that meant leaving their home parish—for example, leaving S. Stefano and entering the adjacent S. Angelo. This chapter's examination of the ways in which Venetians created and expressed their local identities demonstrates that the neighborhood was a well-defined yet porous community, largely though not exclusively female, that bridged the gap between household and the city at large.

VENETIAN STREETS

Venetians used parish names to identify themselves to the formal civic and ecclesiastical authorities. But within the parish, how did they distinguish among their neighbors? The censuses reveal that some of Venice's twisting, narrow streets and city squares boasted qualities that marked the more specific identities of their inhabitants. Chiara, the wife of the nobleman Francesco Molin, lived with her husband and their staff on a prosperous street in the parish of S. Maddalena. She lived next door to her brother-in-law Zacharia, his wife, and their servants. Chiara lived on an elite, privileged section of the street. After Zacharia's place came the noble home of Stefano Viaro, and after that a branch of the noble house of Marcello. Next to the Marcellos and their retinue lived the wellborn Marco Morosini, with his wife, mother, and servants. But after the Morosini household, the character of the street began to change. The next neighbor was the physician Annibale Bonbiolo, who could place the honorific *Eccelente* before his name but lived only with his wife and five children, employing no servants. The five couples who followed Annibale also lived modestly and included a cobbler and a fruit vendor.

Chiara Molin's street *(calle)* turns out to have been an unusual one for S. Maddalena, both because it was fairly prosperous and because it was populated by couples and their children. Around the corner at the end of the street we find alleys and courtyards that were increasingly modest and dotted with single women, living alone or with family members and friends. Also notable here is the scarcity of servants. In fact, S. Maddalena, near the Jewish ghetto and far from the commercial districts, emerges as a relatively humble area. It was a contrada characterized by smallish dwellings with few servants or even boarders, compared with parishes in other parts of town. The few nobles clustered together on Chiara Molin's street made that street exceptional in S. Maddalena.[10] For the most part, then, identifying oneself as a resident of this parish conveyed a relatively humble social position.

But S. Maddalena's segregation of nobles to one street did not make it an unusual parish. Within many Venetian neighborhoods, entire streets were defined by a particular characteristic, such as the presence of nobles or the density of women residents. In the parish of S. Giovanni Novo, on the Calle da Cha Briani, a Friulian widow named Maddalena lived with a small boy described as "Bastian, orphan, 4 years old." Maddalena and Bastian had only each other; no servants, boarders, or relatives shared their home. But Maddalena may have turned to the women who lived nearby when she needed help caring for her orphaned charge. Next door was Paulina Viscardi, herself a widow with two children. Paulina had one boarder, the widow Elena. Next door to them lived Menega from Padua, along with two other women, and one house down from Menega was Anzola, another Paduan. Like Paulina, Anzola shared her home with a widow.[11]

The Calle da Cha Briani, filled with women, was not an unusual street. Women dominated many alleys and courtyards throughout the city. One such thoroughfare in the parish of S. Ternità was called the street "from the bridge at the church to the campo with two wells." Anzola de Valerio lived on that street with her boarder Catarina, from Treviso. Next door was another Anzola, a widowed mother of four. This Anzola shared lodgings with a sister, a maid, and two other women. Alessandra, yet another widow, lived on the other side, and after her came first Cornelia, a *nubile,* and then the widow Marina with her child. On the other side of Marina lived the noble Laura Badoer, with a child, a sister, two maids, and a manservant.[12]

While unmarried women sometimes clustered together in Venetian neighborhoods, unmarried men did not. The censuses show no correlation between street address and unmarried status for men. Men without wives were sprinkled throughout the city. Sometimes they might share lodgings, but they were more likely to live alone, rent a room, or stay with relatives. They rarely sought each other out when choosing a neighborhood. Whether women consciously sought to live near one another or simply were more likely than men to be thrown together by circumstance is unclear. More certain is the effect of such proximity. Living next door to someone in early modern Venice meant seeing that person daily and often. For people with few personal, immediate resources of money or family, neighborliness surely formed a crucial barrier between the individual and disaster in moments of personal difficulty. That unmarried women gravitated toward one another when they chose their dwellings was almost certainly therefore not sheer coincidence. A small community born of necessity and need, it was a community nonetheless.

Women were sometimes drawn together in a neighborhood not only by their single status but also by a shared profession. One of the occupations that brought women together was prostitution. In the parish of SS. Apostoli, the Corte Caravela was a prime location for *meretrici*. The prostitute Cassandra, for example, who lived alone, was right next door to two other *meretrici*, Osana and Laura. The next apartment housed Paulina, a prostitute who lived with her mother, and just after them came the *meretrici* Madalena, with her child, and then another in the same trade, Elena.

Circumstances may have dictated the choice of these *meretrici* to live close to one another, at least in part: either formally or informally, prostitutes were segregated by neighbors and officials who wanted to contain the *mala vita* in one location, avoidable by decent folk. Living near one another could also be good for business; potential clients knew where prostitutes clustered, and where to seek them out. But prostitutes were hardly segregated from daily neighborhood life. Though they sometimes clustered together, they might also live among other women and men with more respectable professions.[13] The *meretrice* Faustina shared her home with two other prostitutes. But her sister and nephew lived there, too, and her dwelling was surrounded by "decent folk" who were sustained by a variety of professions: on one side of her home lived the family of Cristofolo, a stevedore, and on the other side was Zuane, a basket maker, with his wife, child, and brother.[14]

Prostitutes, then, lived among men and women who practiced other trades. Though prostitution is the female occupation most often listed in the census,[15] as we saw in chapter 2 women practiced a wide variety of occupations, some of them registered sporadically by a few of the census takers. Even if a woman's principal, defining, occupation differed from her neighbors', however, women who lived near each other shared a common set of economic activities through their domestic skills. Simply put, women often practiced more than one occupation. Cooking, cleaning, and laundering could provide multiple, if meager, sources of income. Orsetta Frolade, a witness in an Inquisition trial, explained, for example, that "my profession is working, sewing, and spinning."[16]

Streets full of women were streets full of female work. As we saw in chapter 2, the censuses listed a number of trades that women worked in, including traditionally male occupations. In the cases of a boatwoman and a sail maker, it may well be that the women were the wives or widows of men who practiced these trades, though there is no explicit mention or even suggestion of this in the records. Since the standard designations "daughter of the sail maker" or "wife of the sail maker" are missing, we are entitled to speculate that they practiced these trades themselves. Even if such terms as *barcaruola* and *vellera* did refer to the occupational identity of the woman's husband or father, it appears that the woman, by association and perhaps also by her contribution to the trade, had assumed her own identity in it. Thus the description was feminized, with the male connection left out.

The censuses list women's occupations so rarely that there is no way to know whether women who practiced the same occupation lived near one another. We do, however, find cases of women living near men who practiced the same trade. Such was the case of Franceschina, a *sartora,* or seamstress, in S. Sofia. She was flanked by the widow Orelia on one side, and Zorzi, a *sartor,* on the other.

It is not surprising, of course, that streets were at least as likely to be dominated by male professions as by female ones. In S. Giovanni Novo, several men shared both a profession and an address. Antonio, a boatman, lived in the Corte de Cha Cessi. Next to him was Marco, another boatman. Two doors down lived Battista, and after him Giacomo, both of them boatmen. Boatmen also clustered together in the parish of S. Sofia. S. Sofia was home to bunches of food vendors as well.

The censuses thus show that some Venetians lived in areas with particular, defining characteristics, like the nobles of S. Maddalena, the widows and nubili of S. Ternità, and the prostitutes of SS. Apostoli. Social class, marital status, or occupation sometimes (though not always) drew Venetians to a particular street. These were defining qualities, for women as well as men. But beyond streets with particular identities, how else did Venetians mark their place within their neighborhood? Were there other characteristics, in addition to the character of certain streets, that dominated the way in which women specifically achieved or were assigned an identity and a place in their world? The Inquisition trials give us a closer look at the meaning of neighborhood for Venice's residents.

THE TEXTURE OF NEIGHBORHOOD LIFE: VOICES FROM THE INQUISITION

The Inquisition trial records, consisting of testimony before the inquisitor by both the accused and witnesses, have been used extensively to chart the exceptional, the unusual, the exotic.[17] But they also provide us with a glimpse into the normal, often prosaic relationships that existed within the neighborhood. If the women accused of maleficent magic *(maleficia)* or witchcraft *(strigaria)* were by definition exceptional, the witnesses who testified for and against them were less so. As both accused and witnesses answered the inquisitor's questions and defended themselves, they described the world of their contrada, explaining friendships and enmities and the ways in which these played out, sometimes in public. They revealed a world that was simultaneously cohesive and porous, and increasingly under threat from outside forces.

Much of the testimony of the S. Uffizio trials for witchcraft was based on public threats or bad, "unneighborly," behavior. Older women, especially, were often accused of desiring or resenting young men in their midst. Marina Chioggia had to confront one such accusation; so did Libera di Rossi. Excitement and a change of pace no doubt made many of these witnesses to public confrontations willing to appear before the inquisitor to give testimony about what they had seen. But the line between amused bystander and uneasy participant could easily blur when an angry neighbor vented her emotions. One witness to Marina Chioggia's first public display, Oliva, later found herself too closely involved for comfort. This time it was she who was the object of neighborly gawking as she tried to flee Marina's wrath. Marina, believing Oliva to be the mother of

Marieta, whom she hated, went to the older woman's home to threaten the daughter's marriage. Their encounter, reported Oliva, was witnessed by neighborhood women who crowded into her doorway; there were so many of them that she could not remember everyone who was present.[18]

As they testified, witnesses revealed how much they knew about their neighbors. For example, when one S. Uffizio witness was asked for names of other potential witnesses for or against the accused, she blithely rattled off a list of both men and women, giving along the way their professions and locations: "You could talk to a woman called Matthia, the wife of Giovanni the boatman who lives by the nuns in Sant'Alvise . . . and another Giovanni who is a German jeweler and who [also] lives in the nun's house at Sant'Alvise. Right [next door to] him you could speak to the maid of Guglielmo, and his [Guglielmo's] mother Isabetta."[19] The list of neighbors summoned to testify at another trial shows how heterogeneous this group of Venetians could be. In the trial of Orsetta Piriotta, held from 1618 to 1626 and discussed in greater detail at the end of this chapter, virtually the entire parish of S. Moisè was called. The witnesses included

> Elena, a widow
> Lucieta, wife of Alexander Shidelli, a tailor, aged 40
> Francesco Coatini from Vicenza, a scribe, aged 64
> Orsetta herself, widow of Gasparo the boatman, aged 46
> Thomasina, daughter of a baker, wife of a boatman, from the parish
>   of S. Martino, aged 21
> Sabina, daughter of the widow Betta, aged 25
> Domenico, aged 30
> Ambrosius, aged 30
> Helena Azalina, aged 60
> Bernardo, a carpenter from the Arsenal, aged 38
> Paulina, wife of Francesco Ceci, aged 28
> Orsetta, daughter of Giovanni, aged 30
> Isabella (this Orsetta's sister), aged 14
> Meneghina, daughter of Antonio the weaver, aged 24
> Aloysius, tailor, aged 33 [20]

The six cases discussed extensively below illustrate particularly telling aspects of neighborhood society; several others are used to provide supporting evidence. These cases show the layers of malice, affection, and indifference that built up among neighbors over years of interaction. They also make clear how profoundly economic relationships were connected to social ones in a neighborhood setting. And they reveal the degree to which the border between household and neighborhood could become thin almost to the point of invisibility.[21]

LAYERS OF IDENTITY

Marina Chioggia was tried for witchcraft in 1625 on the basis of threats and actions she had allegedly leveled against a young matron of her parish, Marietta. Marina, originally from Chioggia, was married to the son of the neighborhood cobbler. She was estranged from her husband, reported one witness, "because she is an evil woman."[22] Another witness, 49-year-old Maria, described the accused woman's behavior one afternoon in one of the public squares, when Marina made her intentions plain regarding the young couple Girolamo and Marieta Battagia: she wanted to break them up. The most damning testimony by the witness was her assertion that Marina had said publicly that "she did not want Marietta . . . to live through the year." This curse, reported Maria, "was heard by everyone and particularly Oliva the boatwoman, Angesina, Betta *furlana,* Valeria *formagiera,* the cheese seller, and other women. . . . And she said it also in other places, like the street where she was heard by Fiordelise, the wife of Salvator." At another point she added, "You can ask Zuann Masteller, and Francesco the husband of Livia, Pasqualin the tailor, [the sisters] Lugretia and Agnesina, Oliva the boatwoman, Zuane Verzin, and Andriana the Greek."[23]

Maria's testimony revealed the layers of identity by which local women knew each other. In her testimony, only one woman, Fiordelise, was identified by use of a husband's name. The other four women who allegedly witnessed Marina's public display were distinguished in Maria's account neither by their marital status nor their relationship to a man. Instead, Maria identified them by their provenance, their professional association, or their name alone. Oliva was a barcaruola, a woman with some occupational connection to boats (she may have worked on a boat, or for a boat builder, or she may have been married to a boatman); Betta was originally from the Friuli; Valeria sold cheese; Lugretia and Agnesina were sisters, not wives or daughters; and Andriana was Greek. As far as Maria was concerned, these were the most salient characteristics of her neighbors. Marital status, in this account, was largely irrelevant, except in the case of one man: Maria described a male neighbor, Francesco, as Livia's husband.[24]

Other trials also show the multifaceted ways in which women identified themselves and one another. Orseta Frolade, the defendant in a 1591 trial, was most forthright in her description of herself. She began by giving her own last name, though the Inquisition called her by that of her husband, then went on to offer additional important information about her identity: "My name is Orseta Frolade Santo, I come from the Friuli. My husband is named Batista Garzolo; I live in [the parish of] San Rocco in the campiello [a small square] next to the potter, and my occupation is to do piecework, to cook and to spin *[la mia profession è di lavorar, de cuser, de filar]*."[25] In another case, a witness named Olivia described the two women she believed had witnessed the accused engaging in witchcraft, identifying them as "Menega, the wife of Jacomo, who has been ill, and Paola, my friend."[26] Husbands also described their wives in ways that recognized an identity beyond simple marital status. When Jacopo de Sagis told the inquisitorial tribunal the story of his wife's death, he made it a point to describe her as "my wife Menega, schoolteacher *[maestra di schola]*."[27]

Marital status was also irrelevant for a witness in another case, that of Andriana Schiavona. Caterina, a Greek woman, was called to testify against her neighbor. She claimed to know the accused only slightly, but admitted that the two had run into each other in their parish of S. Martino. Caterina added that other women had been present at the moment that Andriana casually admitted to using magic to locate a missing ring. "The whole courtyard was there, in a manner of speaking," Caterina testified. "In particular there was Donna Lucieta, whom you have just examined, along with her sister; there was also a Greek woman, Oliva, as well as her mother Laura, and finally Marietta, who lives near me."[28]

Marital status might not be mentioned because it was irrelevant in the context in which one woman met up with or knew another. Andriana, the accused woman in this case, admitted to learning some magical arts from a Greek woman named Oliva. Oliva had been in her home, teaching her how to read signs in a jug of water, yet Andriana, when describing Oliva, pointed out, "I do not know if she is married or not."[29] Evidently

Oliva had been there for professional reasons, not to discuss her personal life.

MEN AND THE NEIGHBORHOOD

Antonio Pretegiani, a merchant from the parish of S. Marcuola, was 50 when called to testify in a 1620 trial. When questioned about his neighbors Angela and Zanetta, he replied, "I know no one, neither men nor women [engaged in evil deeds]. I concentrate on my market work, and whoever referred me to you has made a mistake."[30] In the case of Marina Chioggia, a male witness apologized for offering little information of substance because he left the parish daily to work, returning only at night.[31] And 21-year-old Girolamo—the hapless object of Marina Chioggia's affections—testified hardly at all, and then only to verify that he had signed a written accusation against the accused. It was Marietta, his wife, who took his affidavit to court to support her case.[32] In many witchcraft cases, in fact, men were little more than tangential witnesses. Occasionally, like Girolamo, they played a nearly silent, starring role as objects of desire. Girolamo was not in fact the first husband to catch Marina's eye, at least according to another witness who explained, "I don't know why she is a witch, but I have heard that she is a witch, because I heard [this from] the matron Livia . . . who complained that said Marina had bewitched her husband Andrea."[33]

In many cases, men (and boys) functioned as pawns in the conflict. The trial of the sisters Andriana and Paola Ludovici had at its core two male victims. Their accuser, Fiametta, produced a lengthy affidavit explaining that the sisters had duped her husband and poisoned and cursed her son. Fiametta's detailed testimony listed the names of all of the women involved, except for one of the two maids connected with the case. The only two characters who remain unnamed are the two males, her husband and son. They were at the center of the women's battle, but they were not real actors, only passive victims.[34]

The one man who could command authority and a central place in the conflicts among women was the parish priest. In Libera di Rossi's case, the priest was credited by witnesses with averting greater disaster by persuading the parties involved to make peace. The case involved a young couple whose lives were threatened by a vicious older woman with a history of cruel acts against happily married couples. This at least was the version of Maria, the young wife victimized by Libera's curse on her husband Iseppo. The parish priest, aware of past conflicts between Libera and Iseppo, counseled the sick man to make peace with the older woman. After he did so, Libera brought him a plate of grapes, which he obediently ate. Soon after, his health markedly improved.[35]

Men frequently denied knowing much about the cases for which they were called as witnesses. In the case of Libera di Rossi, one man said he knew that she had many enemies, but protested that he knew nothing in particular. Another was reluctant to place much faith on what he had heard, since the island of Burano was thick with unsubstantiated gossip. On the island, he explained, "if one person says it, everyone says it."[36]

Men as well as women became enmeshed in neighborhood conflicts, but they occupied less space, both as witnesses to and participants in confrontations and suspicious behavior. One of the male witnesses in Marina's case could report only hearsay that he had gleaned from his female neighbors, and another man, a fisherman named Angelo, protested that he knew little of such events because he was busy looking after his family.[37] Men were less involved in parish society mainly because they were more likely than women to spend the balance of their days away from their homes and local communities. Women made up a majority of the witnesses in witchcraft trials, and they referred almost always to their female rather than their male neighbors as trustworthy sources of further information.[38]

If men were generally less active participants in parish life, they nonetheless took an interest in local events, as we learn from the testimony of Angelo, mentioned above. Angelo claimed that he could offer little original testimony for or against Marina because he worked outside of the parish; what little he did know, he could report, not from local women, but from another man who had passed the story on to him: "It is 14 or 15 years that I have known her [Marina]. Andrea Calderiola, the glassmaker in the Calle dei Frati of San Stefano, four or six years ago by now, told me many times that he had seen said Marina practicing witchcraft."[39] A male witness in another case was unwilling at first to admit having much knowledge of the accused woman, Diana, but when pressed he appeared to know quite a bit about her life: "I know that there lives a woman in San Trovaso, and that this woman is called Diana, and I know her somewhat, because she lives near my relatives . . . but I am not close friends with her [*ma Io no prattico in casa sua*] and this woman Diana is 36 years of age and is married to a man who I believe is called Valerio, and I believe he is a broker . . . she had children, I do not know how many, one of which is still alive, with the name of Dionisio. Diana has two sisters."[40]

Thus men could and did form part of the gossip network that kept the society of the neighborhood alive, though they clearly played a secondary role in it. They could also benefit from the ties of obligation that a shared neighborhood residence sometimes created. When Andriana, a 40-year-old married woman accused of heresy, was asked about people who regularly visited her home, she named a sister and one young man: "Then there is one Zago of Santo Appolinar, who's called Fazzin, he is around 18 years old and is my neighbor, and he doesn't come for any other reason than friendship."[41] When called to testify, Zago offered more information: he explained that he knew Andriana well because "her home is close to mine" and "I go to her home sometimes to ask for help or for things like oil and vinegar, because I'm poor. And sometimes I have gone to her house for consolation over the deaths of my mother and father."[42] Clearly, the network of information and support must have both strengthened and strained the bonds among neighbors.[43]

A COMMUNITY OF WOMEN

Female neighbors could draw on the kinds of networks that surface in Inquisition trials in times of trouble. In the trial of Cristina Collarina, her former neighbor Paola testified that she had been in Cristina's home on only a few occasions, when Cristina was ill and she had taken her some food.[44] Women also came together to socialize and pass the time as they performed their daily chores or services for one another. Contarina, a 27-year-old single woman, admitted to the Inquisition in a 1618 trial that she knew the accused woman Orsetta but pointed out that they had associated under the most innocent of circumstances: "She has been my neighbor for five or six years and that is why I was in her house many times, visiting as women do together."[45]

If neighbors knew one another with varying degrees of intimacy, a constant of neighborhood life was the sense of community that predominated, with all of the support and conflict that entailed. The comfort by female neighbors of one of their own was in fact the catalyst for a par-

ticularly lengthy trial in 1588. The trouble began when a group of neighborhood women from the parish of S. Zulian accompanied the casket
of a dead little girl to the burial site at S. Francesco della Vigna, on the
northern edge of the city. Diana and Andriana were among those who
accompanied the child's grieving mother. Diana was, at 36, a little older
than Andriana, and certainly more prosperous. Her husband Benedetto
was a notary, whereas Andriana, 30 years old, had married a man currently
in prison. Diana testified that she attended the little girl's funeral as one
of a large group of mourners: "There were many women there." Diana
witnessed the burial and then turned to leave. As she departed, she was
stopped by another woman, Lugretia, who told her that she had seen Andriana, "who lives in the same courtyard as me," scoop up some earth from
the burial site. When Diana confronted Andriana, the younger woman
confessed everything: "She told me that she had taken the earth for a
woman named Cristina, who lives in the same courtyard [as we do]."[46]

Andriana, called next to testify, continued the story. "I ran into Cristina, who lives in my neighborhood, and she asked me where I was going.
When I told her I was going to help bury the little girl who had died,
Cristina said to me 'bring me a little bit [*picego—pizzico*] of the earth from
the dead.' . . . So I took some earth from the burial site and put it in my
apron, and I took it [back to the neighborhood], and I wanted to go to
Cristina's house, but there were a lot of women around, and Cristina saw
me and put her finger to her mouth [telling me to keep quiet] . . . so I
took it to my house, which Cristina rents to me. . . . Isabella, my friend
who lives with me, took it down and gave it to Cristina." When Cristina learned that Andriana had been summoned to testify against her, she
asked her to lie: "Cristina begged me to say that I had taken the earth
to put on my baby son. But earlier she had told me that she used it for
planting herbs, and so I wanted to tell the truth." Later, again hoping to
avoid a trial, Cristina came to Andriana and Isabella and suggested that
they leave town for a while: "She offered us three or four lire."[47]

Around the burial of the child swirled a community of women, bound
together by a web of ties and obligations. Diana, Andriana, Lugretia, Cristina, and Isabella all lived in the same courtyard. Diana, Andriana, and
Lugretia helped to comfort a grieving mother on her way to the burial
site. Cristina and Isabella remained anxiously at home, waiting for Andriana's return with the holy earth. Cristina's relationship to Isabella and

Andriana (a young woman with a husband in prison) was complex. Her control over them as their landlady may have forced Andriana to steal the earth for her. Cristina displayed her economic power again when she tried to bribe Andriana and Isabella to leave town. We return to this aspect of the case in the section below.

THE ECONOMY OF THE NEIGHBORHOOD

In 1620, Angela di Rossi and Zanetta Loschame of S. Marcuola were tried together for heretical and blasphemous acts. The first document in the record of their trial lists the accusations in full: "They do not go to confession, nor to mass; they disrespect the Faith by blaspheming; they perform witchcraft on others so that they too avoid attending mass; and in particular Zanetta once tried to obtain a dead man's head from Silvio, who worked at the church of S. Marcuola, with the hair still attached, in order to perform witchcraft." Silvio attested that Zanetta asked him for hair from a dead man's head but said he did not know what she wanted to do with it.[48]

More information about Zanetta and Angela and their neighbors emerged along with the testimony. Both women were married but lived together, apart from their husbands. One witness, a young tailor named Tobias, was a font of information for the Inquisition. When asked if he knew the reason for this summons before the court, he replied, "I imagine it's because of a woman who lives near me called Angela."[49] He went on to describe her: "Another woman was living with her, who's called Zanetta, she works as a furrier. I heard this morning that Zanetta has been taken away [by the authorities]." Tobias asserted that the women were known to practice witchcraft, at least according to another male neighbor, Zanetto Zorzi.

But while Tobias clearly knew the women and was aware of a sinister side to them, he was quick to emphasize that his own direct contact with both women had been limited and strictly related to business. His testimony highlights a crucial aspect of neighborhood relations: the economic base. "I was in their house for work," he explained, "to exchange some gold for them *[a farli qualche servitio di cambiarli qualche oro]*." It was not in fact unusual for men to enter women's homes for reasons of commerce. In addition to his work as a tailor, Tobias was apparently a money changer, or a go-between for one. Without a shop of his own, he conducted business in the homes of his clients, whether they were men or women.[50]

Giovanna was more willing than Tobias to admit knowing Angela well. She was the wife of a fruit vendor and lived in the same building, below the accused.[51] Like Tobias, Giovanna's relationship with Angela was at least partly an economic one. When Angela owed rent money, their mutual landlord asked Giovanna to go to the other woman's home and confiscate her mattress, as a form of credit. The encounter could not have been pleasant, but Giovanna did not recall Angela practicing any sort of magic to prevent her from doing as instructed.

In the trial of Cristina, the woman accused of acquiring soil from a burial site, economic motives muddied the accusations of witchcraft. Isabella, a principal player in the case, revealed to the court that Cristina, her landlady, had tried to get rid of her and her housemate Andriana so that the two could not testify against her: "She asked Andriana and me to go away for two or three months, and did not want my husband to know, and after that she became angry with us, and told us to leave, since the house where we stay is hers."[52]

Cristina told a different story. She insisted that she had never asked anyone to procure earth from a burial site for her. The testimony that preceded hers, she explained, was due to the fact that Isabella and Andriana were corrupt women, *donne di mala vita,* who were so unruly that their former landlord had tried to evict them. Cristina, out of the kindness of her heart, had taken their apartment for herself (one flight above hers), and then sublet it to them. But their behavior was so bad that she too had been forced to ask them to leave, and so they had become her enemies.[53]

Economic relationships lay at the heart of Cristina's case, and she clearly assumed that such an explanation would form the basis of a reasonable defense. The testimony of many witchcraft trials show that fears and accusations about magical, maleficent activity usually had little to do with the real conflict. In many cases, as with Cristina's, the accusers had a financial interest in ruining the accused. This at least was Cristina's contention. We do not know if her version was the true one, only that she believed such an explanation to be reasonable and believable. Certainly she was not alone in renting rooms to generate income, as we saw earlier in tax rolls and petition documents. The Inquisition records underscore the point. In the trial of Orsetta Piriotta, one witness described her neighbor Virginia: "She lives near me, and she is old and rents rooms."[54] A witness in a different case explained that she had begun to rent rooms when she moved to a new home, because it was a little too big for her alone.[55] In the case of Felicità Greca (the Greek), the witness Hieronimo explained how he knew the accused: "I have spent time in her house, and she rented me a room."[56]

Renting out rooms was one of the many ways that the wider world entered Venetian homes. Economic concerns combined with personal agendas and simple architecture to blur the border between home and neighborhood.

Porous Boundaries

In 1620, Maria was 18 years old and about to marry her boyfriend, the young fisherman Iseppo. Both lived on the island of Burano. Shortly before her marriage, Maria testified, she learned that her neighbor Libera had predicted that Iseppo would not be around much longer. "I went [to her home] to find her and said, 'Dear lady Libera, why should Iseppo my fiancé no longer come to me?' She answered 'Shut up; if I wanted, with three words I could turn him into a beast.'" This threat notwithstanding, Maria and Iseppo wed shortly thereafter and settled into their married life.

Not long thereafter, the new couple received a disturbing visit. It was evening. Iseppo was already asleep and Maria was working in the kitchen. While the young woman was cooking, Libera walked in. She asked Maria where her husband was and Maria replied that he was in bed. Libera then went directly to the bedroom where Iseppo lay. She watched him and pulled the covers off of him as he slept. Maria did not know exactly what Libera did to Iseppo, but the visitor did not stay long. "When I then went to the bed I saw that she had taken the covers off my husband and that he was fast asleep." The results became evident immediately. "From then on," the young woman testified, "for eight or ten days, my husband got sicker, and remained ill for about three months, and the doctor did not know what illness this was, [only that] he was on the verge of death." A desperate search of the bedroom turned up a basket filled with witchcraft tools, which a friend of Maria's took to the priest to examine. "Among the witchery there were diverse things, like pens, plum pits, a small head made of wood, and other things." The priest concluded that Iseppo had been cursed.[57]

As Iseppo languished, Maria ran into Libera on the street. "She asked me how my husband was doing. I told her that he was ill and that those who had cursed him should watch out. She answered that God would decide who should watch out."[58]

Catherina, the 45-year-old wife of a fisherman, was a witness in Libera's trial. She supported Maria's story with the account of an earlier episode involving Libera: one day Libera's niece Felicità had visited Catherina's home. The women began to speak of their neighbor Lazaro, who had fallen gravely ill. Felicità admitted that she had quarreled with Lazaro and told Catherina and another guest that Libera had cursed Lazaro and caused his malady. "[Libera] knew how to do such things," asserted Felicità, "and if she could do it as a young woman, imagine how strong her powers must be now that she's old." In the case of Lazaro, like that of Iseppo, witching materials were found in the bed, and Lazaro's wife reported having seen Libera making her husband's bed.[59]

How did Libera, apparently a known witch, enter these homes with impunity?[60] How did she get to Iseppo so easily, reaching his bed where he lay sleeping, oblivious and vulnerable? Of course, we have only Maria's word that Libera did in fact invade the couple's home to wreak disaster on the couple. What is striking about her testimony is the lack of explanation attached to it. Maria did not say, "Libera entered when my back was turned, when the door was unlocked for a moment or she managed to open the door with witchcraft." She offered no explanation at all. Perhaps none was needed because neighbors regularly entered one anothers' homes.

It was apparently easy to enter a neighbor's home, even a bedroom. Most Venetian apartments were small and subject to continuous traffic. Women especially used their homes as workplaces, to receive clients, to exchange services, and to drop off products, such as wool to be used for knitting. Friends, family, clients, and collaborators regularly entered private residences for social reasons as well, thinning further the boundaries between neighborhood and home.[61]

The boundaries were permeable even when Venetians did not cross the threshold of a neighbor's home. When Clara Schiacaris testified against a woman named Margherita, who was accused of being a witch, she claimed to have seen Margherita practicing her maleficent deeds in her home. But Clara had not set foot in Margherita's home; instead, she had watched her telling fortunes and casting spells with other women from a safe distance away, standing under the archway *(sottoportego)* outside, near the accused woman's window.[62] In a different case, another witness named Clara testified that she knew the accused, a Friulian woman named Angela, "because I have a balcony that looks into half of her house, and I have also sent my manservant *(garzon)* to get water from her."[63]

Andriana was accused in 1571 of heresy for being in possession of a collection of blasphemous pictures. As she described the circumstances by which she came into possession of the offending book, the ease with which people moved in and out of her home became apparent. When asked if she knew the reason she was summoned to the inquisitor's tribunal, she responded nervously: "I know nothing except that two days ago a priest came [to my home] and asked me to allow them to look in my drawers, which I diligently did." But then Andriana went on to explain and defend herself by telling her story of how friendship and heresy, trust and treachery had mixed together to bring her before the Inquisition that January. In April of the previous year, she told the court, a friend of hers named Giacomo stopped by her home. Andriana had known Giacomo for a long time; he was a haberdasher who for the last twenty years had run a hat shop in the *mercerie* (an important commercial district). Because of their long acquaintance, she explained, Andriana agreed to keep a book for him for a while. She recalled the book vividly: "[it was] covered in cloth with knots of silken cord of two colors."

Andriana took the book and tossed it casually onto her bed, thinking little of the favor. But soon after Giacomo stopped by, some other people came to her house, "whose names I don't recall." These guests saw the colorful book lying on Andriana's bed and began leafing through it. Andriana reported to the Inquisition her shock when she saw "many shameful and filthy pictures." Horrified, Andriana snatched the book from her visitors and shoved it into a drawer. The next day, when Giacomo came to claim his book, she hurriedly returned it to him; "I told him that I could not believe that he would bring such a shameful book into my house and that he must never again bring me such a thing."[64]

Andriana's testimony revealed that her neighborhood society included a wide circle of male and female acquaintances with access to her home.

Although she was a respectable married woman, Andriana's relationship with Giacomo was comfortable enough for him to come to her home informally and ask a favor of her. There is no hint of sexual scandal in their relationship, just neighborliness. Giacomo did not ask Andriana's husband, Austin, to keep the book for him, perhaps because Austin, who worked on a boat, was often away at sea.[65] Probably it was this easy familiarity, based on at least twenty years of contact, that led Andriana to welcome the hatmaker into her home and agree to help him. When he returned later for the book, her reaction (according to her testimony) was outrage and a sense of betrayal. She wondered how he could have abused her kindness by giving her such a dangerous and "shameful" book to keep. The naturalness with which she described her relationship with Giacomo, as well as her later encounter with other guests in her home, illustrates the steady traffic in and out of women's homes.[66]

In the above-mentioned case against Marina Chioggia, Marietta Battagia was asked how she knew that Marina was responsible for the misfortunes she had endured. Her response, recorded by the court, showed the contours of neighborhood society. "Because said Marina told Andriana the herb seller that she desired my husband Girolamo, and since I had married him, I would not live out the year." Girolamo had been in prison and, as soon as he was released and returned to his wife, she fell ill "and am still ill today." Despite Marina's curse, the woman accused of being a witch enjoyed easy access to both her victim's home and her husband: "Before I got sick, my husband was going to her house, because she was calling him to her to give him things to eat, which he then gave to me, now polenta, now fish, and other things." Later, evidence of Marina's evil deeds was found in Marieta and Girolamo's home; when Marina learned this, she became conciliatory: "When she learned that we had found her witchery in the kitchen and entryway she said that now that I'd found it I would no longer die. And she told Maria and Andriana the Greek that I would get better by using incense and other herbs boiled in oil, a remedy that I prepared but never used."[67]

Porous boundaries between neighbors played a role in other trials, too. The couple Margherita and Raffaele Marangon, from the parish of S. Aponal, were accused of relying on incantations and holy objects to heal their sick young son.[68] Their neighbor Antonia was called to testify about them. Antonia, 45, was the wife of Tranquilo, a diamond merchant.[69] She reported that Margherita had alerted her to the upcoming trial, engaging her in conversation while the two women stood on their respective balconies: "It was during the last jubilee that Margarita told me, while I was at my balcony, that she was afraid that she had been denounced to the Holy Office . . . she then asked me to come over to my little balcony nearer to her own." After talking with Antonia for a while, Margherita's husband Raffaele came home and Margherita went back inside. Later, Antonia observed that Margherita and Raffaele left their house under cover of night, for fear of being taken in by the authorities. The couple slept that night in the home of Vicenza, another neighbor, and remained underground for several more days.

Boundaries between home and neighborhood were also crossed in a case involving Andriana and Paola Ludovici, two sisters who lived in separate dwellings but allegedly conspired to wreak havoc on their neighbors.[70] There was a history of enmity between a young mother named Fiametta and the Ludovici sisters, at least according to the accusation Fiametta presented to the Inquisition. She said that the conflict had escalated when Andriana, accompanied by her servant, came to Fiametta's building. The two women then allegedly greased the stairs leading Fiametta to her apartment.[71] Fiametta's husband went down to confront the women, yelling at them because of the grease. Shortly thereafter, Fiametta was warned by Paola's neighbor Francesca to make peace with the sisters, and quickly: "She said 'Fiametta my dear, you had better make peace with Andriana, otherwise bad things will happen to you.'" Fiametta reported that Andriana confirmed the threat herself, returning to Fiametta's home to yell at her "that I would never be happy again, and that I'd regret having had anything to do with her and her family."

Here the story took a bizarre twist. According to Fiametta's testimony, some time after this confrontation between her and Andriana, Fiametta's husband and son were invited to dinner at Paola's home. "To my son they gave a stuffed bird to eat, among other things. . . . I believe that they gave him something bad; afterwards he became ill and things poured out of his mouth and also out of the other end." Francesca, the meddling neighbor who may also have been a healer, came to Fiametta and confirmed that the boy would not heal. More proof of the sisters' misdeeds came when Francesca's maid was carrying the sick boy outside and encountered the Ludovicis. She reported that when the sisters saw the sick child they burst into laughter. The little boy subsequently died.[72]

It may seem foolish for Fiametta's husband to have taken his son into this den of dangerous women, but in fact neighbors regularly entered one another's homes, even when that home might present a danger of some kind. A sailor's wife, Maria, testified in a different case that she had met the accused in the home of her daughter's neighbor, a prostitute. She described one such encounter in this way: "I have known her for twenty-four or twenty-five years by sight and because she brought me work, and the first time that I saw her I saw her in the home of Cattarina the prostitute because they lived near one another on the same street where my daughter Fabia lives, whom I had gone to visit."[73] Prostitutes and other threats, both physical and moral, were impossible to avoid completely on the streets of Venice. When the home was treated as an extension of the street, they seem to have been unavoidable there as well.

Felicità Greca

The 1612 case of Felicità Greca highlights several key elements of neighborhood life: the way economic and social bonds intertwined; the porous boundaries between neighborhood and home; and the complex nature of female social identity. Felicità's chief accuser was a neighbor and former friend, a *nubile* named Angela Scalogna. Angela was a particularly damaging witness because she knew Felicità well; the two women had lived together for four years. In her testimony, Angela described the change in their relationship that took place long after they had separated. Although Angela had moved out four years earlier, she maintained an amicable relationship with her former housemate, continuing to visit Felicità to help with the housework (probably in exchange for money). Angela insisted that during that time she had never witnessed any maleficia on Felicità's part. "It is true," she conceded, "that once a gypsy woman came, and [Felicità] had the gypsy toss some fava beans." *Buttar fave,* or tossing dried fava beans, was commonly believed to be one of the principal ways to foretell the future. Typically, the practitioner tossed the beans and read the future in the pattern they created. But Angela clearly did not regard this practice damning enough to condemn Felicità. In general, as far as Angela was concerned, Felicità's use of the fava beans was benign: "She kept the beans under the headboard of her bed and had them tossed because a young furnace owner whom she liked was angry at her."

The first indication Angela received that Felicità might be associated with maleficia affected her directly. The proof was a series of events that, in Angela's mind, were too closely linked to be coincidence. It happened, she explained, one day when Felicità was at home, having the gypsy toss beans for her. At the time this was happening, Angela was in her own home, taking care of the dog of another neighbor, the butcher. Suddenly, the dog burst into an inexplicable frenzy, running about the house and knocking over Angela's mother as she sat in her chair. The old woman was "forced to bed, crippled"; she had yet to walk normally again. Angela reported that "everyone" in the neighborhood was convinced that Felicità had been up to no good with her bean tossing and that Angela's mother's misfortune was the result. "People suspected this because they had seen the gypsy at her [Felicità's] house," Angela explained.

Armed with this suspicion and righteous anger, Angela went to Felicità's house to confront her. She did not go alone: Hieronima, "the daughter of the Slavic woman," accompanied her. Arriving at Felicità's house, the two women saw that the gypsy was still tossing beans and Angela exploded with rage. "I began to scream that it was wrong to do such things because I suspected that the bad magic had been put upon my mother, who has still not healed."[74]

We can learn quite a lot from Angela's testimony. First, that she and Felicità had been companions and housemates. Two single women, they shared lodgings even though Angela's mother lived nearby. Angela had changed homes more than once as an adult; eventually she left Felicità to move back in with her mother. She maintained good relations with Felicità after moving out, either working for or with her, or simply visiting occasionally. Angela also had at least one male friend in the neighborhood, the butcher. She knew him well enough to keep his dog for him. Angela's circle suggests that not only did women and men mix easily on Venetian streets, but so did immigrants with natives. Angela was Venetian, but she had shared lodgings with a Greek woman. And when she confronted Felicità, she did so supported by Hieronima, whose primary identity in this case stemmed from her mother's homeland. But Hieronima was not Angela's only ally; she claimed to draw righteous strength from the knowledge and support of the entire neighborhood. "Everyone" in the neighborhood knew of Felicità's activities, and Angela's mother's misfortune, and they all, according to Angela, suspected the Greek woman of evildoing.[75]

Felicità's trial also reveals the ambivalence that some Venetians felt about being part of a tightly knit neighborhood. Women could be as reluctant as men to participate in parish society, or (understandably) as eager to deny knowledge or involvement when summoned before an inquisitorial tribunal. One female witness in Felicità's case insisted on her distance from neighborhood gossip and social interaction, protesting that "I stay in my own home and I do not pay attention to the doings of others, and I know nothing of this."[76] But she acknowledged having known the defendant for years. She even admitted to having visited the Greek woman's home often to offer help when the accused was ill—thus indicating that despite her protestations to the contrary, she was indeed involved in the reciprocal community of women that characterized parish life.[77]

Felicità Greca's case illustrates the sorts of relationships that female neighbors forged with one another. They could be bound by companionship (like Felicità and Angela, for a time), economic bonds (Felicità and Angela either collaborated on work or performed services for each other), or simply kindness—the goodwill often called neighborliness, demonstrated by the witness who ministered to Felicità when the Greek woman was ill. The parish community, made up primarily of women, provided a network of economic and emotional support, by offering opportunities for socializing, work, and offering comfort in times of distress.

Orsetta Volpini detta Piriotta

Friendship, envy, economic concerns—all came together in the last of our six cases, that of Orsetta. Her trial began in 1618. One of the first witnesses was Lucieta, 40 years old and married to the tailor Alexander Shidelli, in the parish of S. Moisè. She told the court about Caterina Bressana (from Brescia), one of Orsetta's alleged victims. Caterina had been in the possession of a mysterious card, which Lucieta mentioned then hastily denied knowing much about. The inquisitor asked her "if she had ever heard this card read, where, when, in whose presence, and by whom?" She responded, "Yes, sir, once I heard it read in my home. Caterina was there, as was I, and a certain older man read it, his name is Francesco, I don't know his last name, but he works as a copier in San Moisè in those shops near the baker, on the street that goes towards Santa Maria Zobenigo." What did the card contain? Lucieta remembered seeing "some letters," but added, "I did not pay much attention while it was being read, so I don't remember much *[quando si legeva io mi attendeva poco, ne mi ricordo quello che contenesse]."* To drive home her point, she told the court that she could neither read nor write. When asked who had given Caterina the mysterious card, Lucieta replied that it had been Orsetta, a woman she had known for fourteen years.[78]

Francesco, the copier-scribe, was called next. The 65-year-old man said he had known Orsetta for many years; they lived near one another. Orsetta had asked him once to write a letter on her behalf to her son who was living in Zara, on the Dalmatian coast. In addition, Francesco recalled Orsetta asking him to write a *carta bergamina,* "but that was over a year ago." This card had a mix of letters on it, he remembered, both in Latin and Italian. "It seemed to me," he explained, "that that card was one of those that women call love cards." He expanded on this: "I think these are women's frivolities *[legierezze di donne]."*[79]

Orsetta explained everything to the judges when she was called before the court. The widow of a boatman, she was 46 when she began to stand trial; she would be 56 before the trial ended. The inquisitor began by asking her what she did for a living. She responded, "I spin, and I have a room for rent—I never rent more than one room." Orsetta hotly denied accusations that she had commissioned or designed so-called love cards. Instead, she pointed the finger at Caterina Bressana, "a young woman who boarded with me." Caterina had given Orsetta the famous card, asking her to find someone to copy it. "I did not know what the card was, since I don't know how to read or write, so I gave it to the man who writes letters to my son for me."[80]

But the court believed otherwise: they reprimanded Orsetta sternly, admonishing her not to lie. "It appears that you sold the said card to Caterina for 5 ducats, having persuaded her that men who touched that card would then come to her." Orsetta vigorously denied this. "No, sirs, that is absolutely not true. Let me explain how things were." Orsetta claimed that she had borrowed 50 lire from Caterina to buy some bedsheets. She intended to deduct that money from Caterina's rent. Any money that had changed hands between the two women had been either rent or repayment of the loan.[81] As far as she and Caterina were concerned, an economic dispute lay at the heart of the case. Although Caterina claimed that Orsetta had cheated her out of money, Orsetta would only admit to borrowing from the other woman. The witness Paulina confirmed at least part of Orsetta's story by reporting that she had heard Orsetta arguing outside her door with another woman over rent that was past due.[82]

But Orsetta's relationship with her neighbors had not been based on economic exchanges alone. Paolina had known Orsetta for eight years "because she has been my neighbor, and she also participated in the baptism of one of my mother's children, and she is my godmother *[santola]*."[83] Orsetta had also formed a friendship of kindness and reciprocity with at least one woman. Many years earlier, she had sheltered three young sisters for a time after their parents died. One of the girls, now grown, explained that "when my parents died and we three sisters were left, [Orsetta] took us into her house . . . because my mother had delivered a child of hers, and I stayed in her house for a while."[84] We do not know the result of the case; the extant transcripts rarely include judgments.

ELITE WOMEN AND NEIGHBORHOOD LIFE

The connections described among neighborhood women in the cases above, whether they involve economic interests, personal ties, enmity, or a sense of mutual obligation, existed primarily among popolane women. But, as we have seen, noble and wealthy women lived in these neighborhoods, too. What was their role in neighborhood life?

Elite women are largely absent from Inquisition trials. They rarely appear as witnesses, almost never as defendants. Their position undoubtedly protected them from accusations and prosecutions. Still, their absence from the lists of witnesses is telling. While the inquisitor (and the Venetian nobles flanking him) may have balked at summoning numbers of women from influential families on matters concerning the poor and other commoners, the absence of elite women from the witness lists of witchcraft trials indicates something more. Wealthy and noble women are not simply absent from the lists; they are absent from the testimony itself. In such testimony, where witnesses inadvertently described their social and professional networks, women of high and middling rank get nary a mention. It is as if such women did not exist.

But such women did of course exist. Another source, wills, offers some insight into the sorts of relationships they had with their humbler neighbors. If the Inquisition trials describe a world of horizontal networks among women and men of the popular classes, women's wills—as we have already noted briefly—reveal the presence of vertical networks between women, cross-class relationships that were primarily financial in nature. The degree and range of financial investment by upper-class women in these networks varied according to their level of privilege.

Like the records of Inquisition trials, wills reveal the important economic dimension of neighborhood life. Women engaged in a spectrum of economic endeavors and transactions daily, mostly in their neighborhoods. Because of this, many of the relationships they forged with their neighbors had an economic foundation. Women rented rooms to one another and exchanged goods and services. They hired and worked for other women as servants. Women also exchanged services, trading food for laundering or sewing. Women bartered, bought, and sold goods with their neighbors, creating complicated networks of economic interdependency. If it is true that men increasingly left their neighborhoods and homes to practice their trades in central, "public" city spaces,[85] then we may think of the local economics of the neighborhood as particularly female, since this was the locus of so much female economic activity.

Economic patronage of women by women formed an important component of female social networks. Women of privilege did not or could not participate in everyday neighborhood society, but some of them could still form ties with their neighbors and offer those women support at key moments in their lives, such as marriages or funerals. A small survey of wills suggests a pattern of testamentary legacy that breaks down along levels of wealth. Women of middling means were likely to demonstrate a commitment to their neighbors, whereas wealthy women devoted themselves almost exclusively to their relatives and the servants dwelling in their households.

Women who fell between the categories of poor and wealthy demonstrated through their testaments a real investment in their neighborhoods and in their relations with their humbler neighbors. If such women do not appear often in Inquisition trials as direct participants in the public society and conflicts of the neighborhood, they nevertheless knew and cared about their neighbors in ways that wealthier women did not. They expressed their commitment to the women who lived around them by providing for them in their wills.

Caterina Zambellotto, a Bergamese woman, was the widow of a sailor. Her 1574 will remembered the women of her neighborhood as well as her family. Her fur, a dress, shirts, and stockings all went to Lucia, who worked in an eyeglass shop.[86] If Lucia did not survive her, Caterina asked that Lucia's daughters inherit the goods in her stead. Caterina also left clothing to "the women who serve in this house," the house where she boarded. Finally, she remembered the little daughter of a man, Matthia Trivisana, leaving the girl 15 ducats "for her marriage."[87]

Laura, a widow who had inherited her husband's spice business, also looked after the women in her neighborhood when she drafted her will. She promised her servant Fiorina a legacy of 10 ducats. Laura also left 5 ducats for the good of the parish *(al capitolo della contrada)*. Her other bequests were more specific. She remembered two young women from the neighborhood in particular: the daughter of the eyeglass dealer was to get two of her shirts, as was the boatman's daughter, "who lives below me." Another pair of shirts went to Antonia, her washing woman. She also entrusted Antonia with taking an offering to the Trinity church on her behalf.[88]

Fourteen years earlier, another Laura remembered her social superiors as well as her social inferiors in her will. The widow of Iseppo, a linen worker *(linariol)*, Laura was living in the home of a noble family, Alvise and Lugretia, when she composed her will in 1596. She was humbly grateful to them for taking her in and left them her 1,000 ducats, requesting that anything remaining after the couple's deaths go to charitable institutions. Laura also left Lugretia the bolts of linen she had acquired through her husband's business. She asked that her other possessions be sold and that the profits (Laura estimated them to be about 25 ducats) be shared by her godmother Barbara's daughters, "who are good girls." To Barbara herself Laura bequeathed her widow's weeds plus 20 ducats. Laura's godfather *(compare)* was a linen worker, just as Iseppo had been; Laura left him 10 ducats. She left her fur throw and two shirts to Anna, "who is a maid in the home of the noble Pisani family, and who has been taking care of me." Finally, any extra monies were to go to Lugretia Pisani, "for the love and loyalty she has shown me."[89]

In May 1600, Elisabeta de Bossi made her last will and testament. Her assets were modest, but she distributed them with care. Among her bequests was one to a widow named Santina, "who visits with me [*che mi pratica per casa].*" She left Santina four shirts, and a dress (to be chosen by her husband and executor) that was "as good as new." For another, presumably younger woman, the daughter of a launderer, Elisabeta left money to be used toward the girl's dowry.[90]

Another woman, the daughter of an artisan, likewise favored female friends in her will, one of whom appears to have been her boarder.[91] Women who made such bequests were mostly the daughters and wives of well-off artisans and merchants. But in addition to revealing their sense of solidarity with other women, some wills suggest a male presence in women's lives that did not fit traditional familial roles. Laura, the daughter of a cobbler and wife of a spice dealer, left money to both men and women who were not her kin. In two cases Laura stipulated that the money was to be used for the legatees' dowries. Two other recipients of Laura's generosity were unnamed, described only as "the daughter of the glasses maker and the daughter of the boatman who lives below me."[92] Men were put in charge of insuring that the girls received the money. Another beneficiary was a laundress named Antonia. She was to receive two woven shirts and money in return for going to the Church of the Trinity to pray for Laura's dead husband in Laura's stead, suggesting that Laura trusted and liked Antonia enough to assign her such an important charge.[93]

The wills of wealthy women, by contrast, reveal the elite's enclosure within their homes and their isolation from quotidian neighborhood life. Their testaments consist largely of legacies to an extended family of nieces and nephews and to their servants. That was their world. Rarely did they display commitment to or acquaintance with the poorer women on their street, unless those women had served them in some direct way. Their wills also demonstrate that elite women could feel responsibility, even affection, for their domestics, especially female ones.

The noble Orsetta Moro, for example, remembered three female servants in her will—Polonia, Maria, and Daria. She also made a point of remembering Polonia's and Maria's daughters. In addition to these legacies, Maria's daughter and Daria (apparently still young and a *nubile*) would each receive a "furnished bed *[letto fornito]*."[94] Orsetta also remembered Caterina, a wet-nurse *(nena)*. Caterina was probably the wet-nurse for Orsetta's children, since she received a salary from Orsetta's husband. Orsetta asked that she be given 30 ducats in addition to that salary.[95] Orsetta was behaving like other privileged women in thinking exclusively about her family and household. Another elite Venetian, Chiara Torresan, left money to a number of servants, male and female, and set aside a future dowry for "Benetta, the little girl who lives in the house."[96]

Anzola Rizzo, the wealthy wife of a lawyer's son, followed the bequest pattern of the nobility when she made her will in 1576. She left the bulk of her estate to Zuanne, her husband, and any children that she might bear in the future. But she wanted to look after others as well and in doing so revealed the expanding circles of her world. Her sister Helena stood to inherit both liquid wealth and material goods.[97] After her family, Anzola's next thought was of her servants Zuan'Antonio and his wife Pelegrina; together they were to inherit 80 ducats. Anzola then turned to her nena, bequeathing to each of the wet-nurse's daughters 30 ducats upon marriage; to the nena herself and her husband, she left 40 ducats. To Margherita, her maid, she left a small financial bequest plus four of her shirts. Finally, Anzola's thoughts moved out into her neighborhood, with a single, generous bequest. To the young daughter of a neighbor, she bequeathed 100 ducats upon marriage.[98] We do not know what sort of relationship Anzola had with this young woman, only that she became her patron by enhancing the girl's marriage prospects.

༄

Vicenza Murera, Valeria Formagiera, Oliva Barcaruol. Felicità Greca, Andriana Schiavona. To the authorities, whether civic or ecclesiastical, what was important about these women was their marital status. When the officials or priests heard a petition, compiled a soul count, or recorded a witness's name, they made sure—or were expected to make sure—a woman's status as *nubile,* wife, or widow was duly noted. Ancillary information might be registered: age, profession, birthplace, last name. But the message of the authorities was clear: the most important thing to know about a woman—the most significant part of her identity—was her marital status. Popolani Venetians, however, both women and men, did not always agree with this perspective. When witnesses in the Inquisition spoke about their female neighbors, they did not uniformly categorize women by their marital status. Some women were described in this way, but many others were identified (and identified themselves) by their occupation or ethnic origin. What made a woman who she was, what clarified her identity, was only sometimes linked to her marital status, at least for those who saw her every day. Equally important were her occupational affiliation and her ethnic or geographic background.

The women described in these varied ways composed the neighborhoods and mutually dependant households we have seen described in the records of the Inquisition. This mutual dependency expressed itself through interest in and awareness of each other's activities. The cases discussed above also illustrate several other aspects of early modern neighborhood life. Neighborhoods could be distinctive, and within the neighborhood there might live distinct pockets of widows, fishermen, or elites. But neighborhoods were also microcosms of a wider world, with a mix of professions and classes. The interactions between elite women and popolane were relatively limited, however; their relationships were often confined to that of employer/employee. Among themselves, popolane women built connections that stemmed from their seeing each other daily on the street and in one another's home. The boundary between neighborhood and home was not always clear. Friendship, finance, and malice took Venetians into neighborhood homes.

Containing both the traditional and the new, the familiar and the strange, the neighborhood—a link between the household and the outside world—functioned as a linchpin in creating Venetian urban society. On the one hand, the borders between home, neighborhood, and the wider city were discrete, demarcated by walls, bridges, and economic and juridical boundaries. On the other hand, those borders were fragile, porous—allowing for a fluid shifting of work, friendship, family, and enmity. The bonds among neighbors sometimes created tensions; they could erupt into hostility and lead to accusations of witchcraft.

One aspect of parish life that could increase these tensions was the entry of immigrants into the local community. The neighborhood was a constantly changing community that responded to and participated in developments that affected the city as a whole, and one of the most important of these developments in early modern Venice was immigration. The entry of immigrants into the parishes and the lives of native Venetians contributed to a fluid and expansive urban space, where a wide range of languages, customs, and possibilities extended. Sometimes immigrants formed their own communities, such as the Jews (who were confined to a ghetto in 1516), most of the Greeks, and the Turks. Others, however, as will be seen in chapter 4, lived among ordinary Venetians and had a significant impact on traditional neighborhoods.

FIGURE 1. Women practiced a wide variety of occupations that required them to travel throughout the city. Grevembroch portrays two women in entertainment professions—a musician and a dancer. The musician is playing with a male partner. *Museo Correr*

FIGURE 2. Gabriele Bella's *Dance Party in the Square* (1779?) shows a scene typical of celebrations in early modern Venice. Men and women mixed easily in their

Within the image: *Fera De' Soldo In Campiffo*

neighborhoods. At left, women are chatting with one another; at right, women
patronize a tavern. *Museo Querini Stampalia*

FIGURE 3. "Wise women" like the one portrayed by Giovanni Battista Piazzetta in *The Fortune Teller* could exercise social power through supposed ability to divine the future or to heal; they thus could counterbalance their inherent vulnerability as popolana women. Here a young fortune-teller tells her very pregnant customer something she is pleased to hear. *The Accademia Gallery*

FIGURE 4. PietroPaolo di Santacroce's painting shows two women clearing dishes from a table after a meal. Women, whether members of the family, roommates, or servants, often worked together on domestic duties within a household. *The Accademia Gallery*

FIGURE 5. In *The Presentation of the Virgin,* Titian places an elderly woman eggseller hawking her basket of eggs front and center. She is typical of those he would have seen on the streets of Venice. *The Accademia Gallery*

FIGURE 6. The artist Vecellio describes this figure as a market woman from Chioggia or Pellestrina, two rural islands close to the main cluster of islands that make up the city of Venice. Such women traveled regularly to Venice to sell their goods. This woman proudly displays her basket of produce, her knife at the ready to cut into a fruit or vegetable to show its ripeness. Cesare Vecellio, *Habiti Antichi*

FIGURE 7. This may be a zitella like those discussed in chapter 6 (Vecellio describes her as a "girl from one of the Venetian female orphanages"). She is both pious and educated: she holds her rosary as she reads, possibly from a prayer book. But her piety and modest garb do not mean that she is enclosed. Instead, she has dressed for walking: her short dress and flat shoes allow easy movement, while she can use the broad-brimmed hat on her back for protection from the sun. Cesare Vecellio, *Habiti Antichi*

FIGURE 8 *(left)*. This *pizzochera* is a member of a religious community of women that lived throughout the city rather than in a cloistered environment. Such women often shared lodgings and lived humbly. As female religious who did not belong to a convent, they provided an alternative to women who did not wish to or could not marry (widows were among these) and women who did not wish to or could not enter an enclosed community. This woman's piety is evident: she clutches a candle with one hand, a rosary dangling from the other. But her vulnerability—the typical vulnerability of an elderly woman in an early modern city—is also clear: her face and hands are old, she seems barely able to hold onto the rosary, and she is hunched over with the weight of her age and her poverty. Cesare Vecellio, *Habiti Antichi*

FIGURE 9 *(right)*. Vecellio describes this woman as a Venetian domestic servant. Her clothing and demeanor suggest that even female *serve,* among the humblest residents of Venice, could attain some status and responsibility within a household. The woman depicted here exudes dignity, her expression is serene, and she demonstrates her literacy by holding a book in her hand. Cesare Vecellio, *Habiti Antichi*

CHAPTER FOUR

Immigrant Women
Into the Neighborhood

IMMIGRANT women filled the streets of Venice. Sometimes they and their male compatriots created neighborhoods of their own, but at least as often they settled among native Venetians and other foreigners. Vulnerable yet resourceful, such women participated in community life and affected neighborhood dynamics. As the sixteenth century drew to a close, one such migrant, Laura Alioni, was living in Venice and working as a servant there. Although she originally hailed from Italy (she did not specify from where), she had previously lived and worked in Switzerland. "I lived for two years in the valley of the Huguenots, in a place called the Tower of Luzerne," she explained in a statement to the Inquisition.

While in Switzerland, Laura had come under the influence of Huguenot practices, but this, she asserted, had happened for entirely innocent and comprehensible reasons: her Huguenot neighbor, Claudio Iamasi, was also a relative. Because Laura spent a lot of time with Claudio and his family, she explained, it was natural that she embrace their rituals as well. However, she insisted that although she had adopted their customs, she had never adopted their beliefs: "I went to their prayer services and in these two years never went to mass, nor to confession, nor did I take communion, [yet] my soul, even if I was among Lutherans for this time, was always of a good and Catholic Christianity, nor did I ever do or think what they do and think."[1] To strengthen her case, Laura also pointed out that the services she attended in Switzerland had always been either in French or German, neither of which she understood.

Laura told her story to the Inquisition when she was brought before the tribunal on charges of Lutheranism in 1591. Her account was in many ways typical of migrant women in this period. For Laura, as for many early modern women, traveling across regions and countries was a necessity for economic survival. Some arrived in Venice to take part in the expanding manufacturing economy, a preview of the larger numbers of women who would migrate to European cities three centuries later.[2] Traveling demanded a mental as well as physical mobility, as Laura's example shows. She readily admitted to the city and church authorities that she had adopted the religious customs of her Swiss hosts, but explained that she had done so in order to get along with them, rather than out of a deeply felt religious conversion. Once she found herself again on Roman Catholic soil, she insisted that she was only too happy to return to the true faith, in deed as well as in thought. She expected the tribunal before which she appeared to understand this: such doctrinal or ritual flexibility was part of the landscape of Counter Reformation Europe.

Laura was part of a community of migrant women who traveled across regions and countries, sometimes more than once, and along the way acquired the flexibility and resilience that such travel demanded. Historians have explored the topic of female migration for later periods in European history,[3] but we still know relatively little about it for the sixteenth and seventeenth centuries, especially on the Continent itself.[4] The goal here is not to offer demographic data but rather to demonstrate that immigrant women were a significant presence in local Venetian life and that they carried with them new ideas and customs, for which they sometimes became objects of suspicion even as they settled into their new homes. Female immigrants faced hardships both during their journeys and upon their arrival in the busy Venetian city; to survive, they had to be self-reliant. As a result, they may have been more independent after marriage than Venetian-born wives. Such women formed part of a larger population of mobile Venetians. Their stories highlight the heterogeneity and dynamism of Venetian society.

Upon arrival, the foremost challenge facing immigrant women was survival. Many turned to prostitution. In the smallish parish of San Matteo, for example, three of the five prostitutes identified by the census taker were foreign women: the Cypriot Andriana and the Paduans Marina and Benetta.[5] But immigrant women also managed to build and contribute to the local communities where they settled in more respectable ways. By the sixteenth century, they formed an integral part of many Venetian neighborhood communities, where they encountered both acceptance and rejection.

IMMIGRATION AND VENICE

Premodern Europeans were frequent migrants,[6] and Venice was an increasingly important magnet for many of them in the sixteenth century.[7] Immigrants traveled to Venice in the sixteenth century to seek shelter from the wars raging on the European continent as well as to participate in the city's growing industrial economy. After the 1575–76 plague, men and women from the mainland fled their decimated villages in even greater numbers to seek a better life in the city.[8]

Such waves of immigration helped make Venice the most densely populated city on the Italian peninsula.[9] Immigrants were crucial contributors to the economic dynamism that the city enjoyed throughout the century.[10] The effects of immigration on Venice's demographic growth were easily visible; the areas of the city that underwent the most population growth were centers of immigration: the parishes around Rialto (the commercial heart of the city), and the Jewish ghetto.[11]

Adding further to Venice's heterogeneous population was the large number of visitors in the city. In addition to the immigrants who set up home and shop permanently among native Venetians, Venice was filled with temporary visitors who walked its streets and paused in its squares to admire the architectural splendor or hunt for a hospitable tavern. Diplomats and their retinues, merchants and their servants, and the first real tourists (for example, Thomas Coryat) all contributed to Venice's energy and exoticism. Many merchants lived in Venice on a temporary basis or used the city as a base from which to travel on business. Such was the case of Don Enfrin Bonforno. A Jewish merchant from Ferrara, he lived in the ghetto with his brother when in Venice on business, usually managing to visit his Christian mistress Cristina Collari when he was in town.[12] All Venetians, whether or not involved in a personal relationship with an immigrant or visitor, would be accustomed to the babble of foreign tongues, the presence of people different from themselves. If the church and the civic authorities strove to maintain strict standards regarding orthodoxy and morality, they could not prevent the exposure of Venetians to alternative standards.

Because the authorities were keenly aware of the dangers such familiarity might pose, their attitude toward the newcomers was complicated. On the one hand, the government encouraged certain types of immigration in times of need. As early as 1543, they relaxed certain rules regarding artisanal labor on Saturday, for example, explicitly to accommodate the needs of the city's growing population.[13] After the 1575–76 plague, the government offered incentives to artisans on the mainland to make a new home in Venice to rebuild the decimated labor force.[14] On the other hand, the different languages and styles of dress that foreigners displayed were expressions of deeper differences and potential threats. Newcomers, both temporary and permanent, threatened civic security — or at least harmony — in several ways. First, the ideas espoused by foreign visitors and immigrants might create too much curiosity and critical thought. Proof, if necessary, could be found in the number of northern Europeans brought before the Inquisition on heresy charges.

Immigrants also presented a potential physical threat, in two ways. First, foreigners brought with them the dangers of contagion. For this reason the Provveditori alla Sanità, the city's board of health, was vigilant in monitoring the entry and quarantine of visitors who might be contagious. Second, immigrants added to the danger of increased crime. Those who came with few resources and little money might join this early modern city's lawless underclass, robbing, attacking, even murdering respectable people. Male immigrants posed the biggest threat. Venice was a dangerous city even without additional, violence-prone men roaming the streets. The city's commercial vitality ensured the presence of large numbers of single men, often a recipe for violence. The Bravi — thugs who hired themselves out to wealthy Venetians as bodyguards — were only an extreme example of a large, unruly male population in the city.[15] In 1578, The Council of Ten issued a ban threatening exile for any foreigners engaging in brawls.[16] The same body passed a series of orders, apparently unsuccessful, regarding the possession and transport of firearms within Venice. In 1596, the council forbade the use or public transport of "pistols and harquebuses" throughout the republic. They again issued bans in 1608, 1612, 1616, and several more times up to 1648. Such repetition of the same law suggests that the measure either was not enforced or was unenforceable. Earlier laws had spelled out the circumstances under which certain types of weapons could be carried around in public.[17]

Morally, too, the arrival of foreigners was thought to threaten the social fabric. Immigrants could be sources of dangerous ideas, especially in the era of the Counter Reformation. This belief was expressed in the number of foreigners brought before the Inquisition on heresy charges.[18] And immigrants, both men and women, presented sexual threats. In addition to increasing the population of potential violent offenders and rapists,[19] in the eyes of the authorities immigrant men were also potential bigamists. Bigamy became a problem when men immigrated to Venice without their families and married a second time there.[20] The danger posed by women immigrants was different. They were likely to join the substantial population of prostitutes, further fraying the city's moral fabric. To combat this threat specifically, in 1539 and again in 1572 legislators attempted to expel prostitutes who were recent immigrants.[21]

Monitoring entry into the city was crucial to controlling the flow of immigrants and visitors. Venetian law mandated that newcomers to the city register with the authorities, giving name and country of origin; they had to appear before the appropriate magistracy within a day of arrival.[22] The government also required innkeepers to keep a record of their guests and provide a copy for the authorities.[23]

The increase in Venice's population, then, although partially accomplished by design as a response to the growing needs and opportunities of a burgeoning urban society, created many problems.[24] In the period following the plague, immigration may have saved the city's manufacturing industry, but as a cluster of islands, Venice was incapable of expanding beyond the traditional city confines; as a result, sixteenth-century Venice was the most densely populated city in Italy.[25] Such crowding meant more filth and heightened competition for scarce resources (space, water), especially in centers of high-density immigrant settlement.[26]

IMMIGRANT WOMEN

The conditions under which a female migrant left her home and sought to build a new life differed from those of men.[27] Like men, women traveled to Venice in search of work, political stability, and religious tolerance. But when they migrated alone, without husbands or fathers, women were likely to fill the ranks of the poorest immigrants. Few women were welcomed the way some men were. Male newcomers might be artisans, recruited in times of need; or they might be members of the city's steady stream of elite visitors—diplomats or wealthy travelers. The foreign women who arrived in Venice rarely received much of a welcome from the authorities, unless they came as the wives of artisans or privileged men.[28]

Immigrant men were often inveterate travelers. Although they settled in Venice, merchants, artisans, and sailors might easily up and move again, perhaps leaving the city for a time and returning later. Female immigrants, as we see in chapter 5, although part of a larger, mobile female population, were more stable, less likely to move as often or as far as men. Partly this was due to a paucity of resources: female migrants often lacked the means to travel easily. And women were more likely than men to be encumbered by children; for women, travel could be more difficult and costly.

Female migrants, then, as a group were more stable and poorer than male migrants. In spite of all this, many of the immigrants to Venice were women. They often moved to Venice in hopes of earning enough money, usually in domestic service, to accumulate a dowry.[29] In the parish of San Giovanni Novo, for example, foreign servants filled the homes in the Campo della Chiesa. To cite two cases on the same street, PierAntonio Orsin, an official with the courts, included on his household staff one male servant and two foreign maids: Maria from Asolo and Maria da Guda. Two houses down we find three foreign servants *(massere)*: Lucia from Zara and Agnese of Trent, plus a male servant from Portogruaro.[30] Some streets away, in the Corte da cha Molin, where the prosperous *(l'illustre)* Marco Fratina and his family employed five female domestics and six manservants, the women came from Milan, Brescia, Treviso, and Florence. The two Florentine women may have known two of the manservants from home, for they, too, were Florentine. Another manservant came from Verona, another from the Friuli. Foreigners also staffed another household in San Giovanni Novo, that of the highborn *(clarissimo)* Alvise Bragadin, a censor, his wife, and their six children. One of the family's two maids, Maria Pola, came from Cadore; the other, Isabetta, had traveled from Uderzo. Jacomina, the family's wet-nurse (the family's youngest child was 2 months old) hailed from Cividal de Belluno.[31]

Immigrants formed a substantial part of the servant population, perhaps even the majority at times. A study of one noble family from 1460 to 1582 shows that, at most, locals comprised less than 10 percent of the family's large staff.[32] Work conditions were not always the best: immigrant women were particularly powerless when it came to defending themselves against unfair treatment by employers. They sometimes drew lower wages than did their native counterparts, especially when they came as indentured servants, as many from Dalmatia and Albania did.[33] To be a servant, especially a female one, often meant to be vulnerable to financial and sexual exploitation, which is why those who could sought other forms of employment. Whether they worked as domestic servants or not, immigrant women were in a precarious position. When they came up against a powerful individual or the authorities, they could find themselves with little or no recourse, at least in the first months after arrival.

In 1576 one such case came before the Pien Collegio. A woman named Anzola explained to the court that soon after arriving in the city (she did not specify from where) she was plunged into a spiral of treachery and bad luck. She had found lodgings at an inn near the Piazza San Marco, and it was there that her troubles began. She claimed she was falsely accused of attacking a second-hand clothes dealer who lived near her inn, near San Marco. She was summarily arrested and spent four months in prison waiting for a trial. To gain the court's sympathy, Anzola emphasized her isolation and vulnerability, both as a foreigner and a woman.[34] In another case, Catterina, from Brescia, explained that her foreign status had made her particularly gullible when she purchased a love charm from a neighbor: "[She] taught me how I should go about [making a man fall in love with me], me, a poor unhappy foreigner, far from my homeland, I believed her words."[35]

WOMEN FROM THE COLONIES

Most of the women settling in Venice had traveled relatively short distances, from the Istrian coast, the Friuli, or Lombardy. A few, from further afield, came from the German-speaking lands and southern Italy. But in the sixteenth century Venice also offered shelter to a particular sort of immigrant, many of them women, who had traveled to the city under particularly brutal circumstances. This was the century in which Venice fought a losing battle against the encroachments of its empire by the Ottomans. As Venetian strongholds along the Adriatic coast and the Peloponnese islands fell to the Turks one by one, a steady stream of refugees made their way to the capital of the diminished empire.[36] The Venetian government did what it could for these subjects when they settled in the city.

The Pien Collegio heard many harrowing tales from immigrants who hoped to receive more aid. Many of the stories were recounted by women, but one of them—told by a son—told of a woman who herself did not make it to Venice. The son, Luca Mosua, told the tale to support his plea for financial assistance for himself and his sister. His mother, Todara, having been left a widow with a young daughter in the Peloponnesian city of Nauplia, was taken prisoner along with her daughter by an Ottoman after the Venetian colony fell to Suleiman's forces. Mother and child remained in captivity for seven years. "That Turk [made] dishonest use of my mother, [thus] he impregnated her with me, poor Luca," the son told the court. Todara's desire to escape had remained strong throughout the years, he explained, because she burned "with the desire to return among Christians." Eventually she managed to flee with her two children during an Ottoman ceremony. The family walked for eight days and nights before reaching the port city of Zante, under Venetian control, "and then we came to Zaffa where I was baptized, and a short while later our poor mother was killed under some houses in an earthquake." [37]

Another refugee, Margarita Mugie, was more fortunate than Todara, though she too endured considerable hardship as a resident of the Venetian colony of Cyprus. Her story emphasized the economic ties her family had enjoyed with Venice—ties that ultimately had saved her. Now a Venetian resident, her story came out when she filed a supplica with the Pien Collegio in 1585 regarding property her father had purchased in Venice years before. She told the court that her father Gieronimo, a Cypriot, had first visited Venice more than twenty years earlier in the service of the Cypriot ambassador. While in Venice, Gieronimo purchased a lease from a local man named Anzolo di Zorzi. Later he returned to his homeland. Years afterward, the adult Margarita saw her life destroyed as the Ottomans conquered Cyprus, taking her and her children as slaves. Margarita was able to use the income from her father's Venetian lease to buy her freedom from the Turks and pay for her daughter's dowry. Eventually she made her way to Venice and settled there.[38]

Another tale from Cyprus was that of Helena Bertucci, the widow of Giovanbattista Bertucci, who also filed a request for aid with the Pien

Collegio. Helena explained that her husband, a doctor, had worked at the University of Nicosia until he was called to the fortress town of Famagusta to care for its elite. As the long siege by the Turks continued, Bertucci continued to treat the sick. In 1573, Venice formally renounced Cyprus to the Ottoman sultan, a death knell for island residents who had enjoyed Venetian protection for decades. Like many others, the members of Helena's family were enslaved. Somehow they made their way into Christian territory, eventually reaching Marseilles and from there moving on to Venice, where they settled. There, "deprived of all of his worldly goods," Giovanbattista died, leaving Helena impoverished and with five children. Her expectation, in return for her husband's long service to Cypriot Venetian elites, was a pension from the state.[39]

Such expectations were common. Another female fugitive, Elena Apostolli, did not mention the travails of slavery to the Pien Collegio, but she did refer to the substantial loss of property her family had suffered when Nauplia fell to the Turks.[40] Elena filed her request on behalf of herself and her brother: it was not uncommon for a family member to speak for others, as we have already seen in the case of Luca Mosua. Many women arrived in Venice with relatives, especially children, to support. Another refugee from Nauplia, the widow Marieta, had four children (three girls) and a mother who was 100 years old to support.[41]

Sometimes the government was able to meet expectations of support. Caterina Chatario, also from Nauplia, enjoyed Venetian hospitality for a decade: the government put her up in a home for ten years, although not at the most stylish address: Caterina lived in the ghetto, an unusual and not very prestigious choice for a Christian.[42] Even when a pension was granted, it was not necessarily enough to live on. Marina Petrucena, a refugee from Napoli di Romania, requested an increase in her current pension; in the meantime, she supported herself by working as a servant.[43]

Financial interest continued to link some immigrant women to their old homes. Women coming to Venice could stay close to their homelands by maintaining financial investments there. Madonna Chiaretta, who had family in the Tyrol, filed papers concerning her inheritance from an uncle in the mountains. She filed the application on her own, but asserted that in doing so she had the approval of her Venetian husband (*consenso del marito*).[44] Another woman with affairs in a distant place was a Greek named

Sofia. Having filed a supplica on another matter, Sofia needed to acquire documentation from her native Corfu. The only way to do this was to go there herself and deal with the bureaucracy directly. For this trip, she asked for financial assistance from the court since she was going on a court-related matter (it appears that the Pien Collegio granted her request). Sofia did not mention travel companions—either a retinue or family members; she gave every indication of making the voyage alone.[45] Another traveler was Zuanna, an immigrant from the city of Mel, who explained that she had been back home on family matters when a charge was made against her in Venice, charges she learned of only upon her return.[46]

Most immigrant women, of course, emigrated without leaving behind patrimonies. Immigrants typically had few assets and made up one of the poorest and most vulnerable groups in the city. Their experiences with the Inquisition reveal one dimension of their treatment by both the authorities and their neighbors.

IMMIGRANT WOMEN AND THE INQUISITION

The index of the S. Uffizio, which lists everyone tried by that office by name, accusation, and place of origin, includes women from as far away as Hungary, Flanders, and Portugal. Almost two-thirds of the women and one-third of the men brought before the S. Uffizio were identified as native Venetians (see table 4.1). Most of the others represented Venice's largest immigrant groups: Greeks, German speakers, Slavs, and Italians from elsewhere on the peninsula. Many more foreign men than foreign women appear in the S. Uffizio records because the office was above all concerned with rooting out heresy.[47] To that end it focused mainly on the German-speaking European traders and artisans who migrated to Venice and sometimes brought Lutheran ideas with them.[48]

The number of women brought before the Inquisition, 766, is relatively small when set against Venice's total female population.[49] The ratio of foreign to local women is not representative of the city's wider population. More than 40 percent of the women accused were described as foreign by the authorities and witnesses in their cases, which suggests that an immigrant woman was more likely to find herself before the Holy Office than a native-born Venetian.[50]

TABLE 4.1

*People Brought before the Sant'Uffizio in Venice, by Place of Origin,
1541–1794*

Place of Origin	Men (%)	Women (%)	Total (%)
Venice	948 (36)	456 (59)	1,404 (41)
Other parts of Italy	1,214 (47)	257 (34)	1,471 (44)
Other countries	448 (17)	53 (7)	501 (15)
Total	2,610 (100)	766 (100)	3,376* (100)

Source: ASV, Indice del S. Uffizio, indice 303.

*This figure does not include the thirty-two cases listed in the index for which the accused's city of origin could not be identified.

Most of these women came from places near to Venice (between 1548 and 1732, women accounted for nearly two-thirds of people from the Friuli who appeared before the Inquisition—28 out of 43). But a considerable number of women came from Greece, a greater distance away—for example, the refugees from the Turks (here women made up nearly two-thirds of the accused immigrants: 63 percent, or 19 out of 30, of the Greeks). Other defendants came from beyond the Venetian empire—from Lyon, Languedoc, and Poland, for example.

The presence of foreign women in the S. Uffizio trials suggests two points. First, immigrant women often found themselves targets of their neighbors' anger: as newcomers with few long-standing allies, sometimes displaying exotic customs, they were particularly visible, vulnerable, and easy to accuse.[51] Second, and paradoxically, their accused status shows that they managed to insert themselves into the neighborhood community enough to challenge the status quo. That is, even as immigrant women threatened neighborhood solidarities, they became a part of them.

The majority of women brought before the Holy Office faced charges of witchcraft and magic (*stregoneria* and *magia*), whereas most of the men who appeared before the inquisitor were charged with heresy.[52] Immigrant women were easy targets for accusations of malefecia: in addition to being in a particularly vulnerable group, some women actually claimed to be practitioners of stregoneria, often drawing on folkloric traditions that had a rural component. Women who came to Venice from the country-side were thus closer to those traditions and more deeply committed to them than were the urban women who would become their neighbors. When Orseta Garzolo was confronted with a lengthy list of her activities as a healer and herbalist, she readily admitted using special potions, herbs, and incantations, explaining that "in Portogruaro, where I used to live, there were women who did such things and that was how I learned about them."[53] Immigrant women also shared their knowlege with other immigrants. Maria, a Greek servant accused of witchery by her former employees, was said to have learned her craft from a Jewish woman.[54] And foreign women themselves could sometimes contribute to the suspicion that surrounded them. By playing up their foreignness, those who marketed their magical skills could enhance their exotic qualities, and hence their legitimacy, as experts of the mysterious. The trial of Andriana Schiavona, a Slav, is an example. Throwing into relief the ways in which immigrant women might use their secret knowledge to gain some power or control over their environment, it reveals this dynamic at work in at least one Venetian neighborhood in the parish of S. Martino.

ANDRIANA SCHIAVONA

Over the course of her trial, Andriana Schiavona and other immigrant witnesses simultaneously asserted their place within local society and reinforced the view that foreign women were dangerous elements in its midst.[55] The *denuntio,* or accusation, that began the trial was supported by a list of witnesses ready to testify on its behalf. According to the accusation, Andriana had left Venice some time before but subsequently returned, bringing nothing but trouble with her. Andriana's general problem seemed to be a lack of respect for authority, especially church authority: she was "without fear of God" and frequently disrupted mass with her "dishonest words."[56]

She also allegedly dabbled in witchcraft. Her most serious offense, according to the denuntio, was her recruitment of three young girls to look into an enchanted jug of water and divine secret knowledge for her. The knowledge Andriana reportedly wanted to acquire was rather banal: she had lost a ring and wanted to know where to find it. By using a magical spell and three virgins, she hoped to learn its location.

The witness list that follows the denuntio tells us that the witnesses against Andriana were a mix of locals and immigrants. Another Andriana, this one a local, and her sister gave testimony, as did two mother and daughter teams from the Greek city of Candia (the *candiote* Agatina and Orsa, Madalena and Caterina). Another mother and daughter, the herb seller *(herbardina)* Vicenza and Zanetta, also appeared. Orsa, Caterina, and Zanetta were the three girls whom Andriana had persuaded to help her retrieve the missing ring. Their indignant mothers accompanied them to court.

In her testimony, Andriana admitted to trying to find her lost ring by using a magic jug. She explained that "a Greek woman taught me that to find the lost ring I should do the following: she brought me a jug filled with well water and then she told me to find three small candles, so that I gave her some money and sent her to buy some, she brought me a young girl, 16 or 18 years old, and then she told me that she would find two others, that the young girls should look in the jug, putting the candles in their hands." Andriana added: "The Greek is named Oliva . . . I don't know if she's married."[57]

Testimony from witnesses, along with Andriana's own story, made several implicit points. Until her accusation, Andriana, although an immigrant who continued to travel, had inserted herself into her neighborhood world. The girls who had entered her home did so trustingly, giggling, curious and eager to help. None testified to thinking that Andriana was a bad woman to be avoided. Nor did the girls' mothers insist that they had repeatedly warned their daughters to stay away from their Slavic neighbor. Yet her dabbling in magic was well known—part of her foreign identity. This was acknowledged even in the denuntio. The foreign component of magical arts was reinforced by Andriana herself when she implicated another foreigner, the Greek Oliva.

If Andriana's dabbling in magic was common knowledge, why was she denounced? The Inquisition operated with two primary goals: to root out and prosecute heretics; and, in the process of doing that, to define heresy and, more generally, inappropriate, unorthodox behavior. For reasons that do not appear in the trial record, someone in Andriana's neighborhood had decided that her activities were dangerous and merited investigation. In the defensive, uncertain climate of the Counter Reformation, the witnesses against her found themselves agreeing with that condemnation.

The Immigrant Identity

Andriana's difference, her foreignness, contributed to the collective belief that she was a witch. But what exactly was a foreigner in early modern Venice? What did it mean when Andriana was called a Slav? Had she arrived in Venice a week before or a decade before? Immigrants appear throughout Venetian documents, both secular and ecclesiastical. As we have seen, the census takers noted scores of immigrant women and men living in their parishes. The Inquisition records regularly described defendants and witnesses by their origins. Not only witnesses called to testify about their neighbors, but the officials who labeled the subjects of trials were careful to note the geographic provenance of defendants if they were not Venetian.

But what made an immigrant an immigrant? And how long did a person remain one? We do not know when the immigrants listed in the parish registers arrived in Venice. Some were clearly recent immigrants while others had been in Venice for years, even brought by their parents as children. The refugees from the Peloponnese islands who sought help from the Pien Collegio are easily identifiable as recent arrivals. Many of the protagonists of the Inquisition trials, by contrast, recounted a past that included many years of residence in Venice. A woman called Felicità Greca (the Greek, as she was described both by the inquisitor and the witnesses in her trial) was typical.[58] Felicità was accused of being a witch. She had lived on the Venetian island of Murano, in Corte da Cha Badoer, since she was a young woman. Many of the witnesses in her trial were nearby neighbors, some of whom had known her for more than a decade. One neighbor, Camillus Serena, said he had known "the Greek woman" for nearly twelve years, as did another witness.[59] Yet she was still considered distinctive, foreign, and was described by all as Greek.

Labels such as *Greek* or *Slav* tell us relatively little about an individual migrant: they can refer to one who arrived in Venice a week earlier or several decades before. The labels may tell us more about those who used them. What is significant here is that as far as Felicità's neighbors were concerned, she was not Venetian, but Greek; she was still distinctive after all those years. Her level of integration into local society (evident by the number of people who knew her and associated with her) did not remove her foreignness from her identity, even if that distinction was ultimately a superficial one. That is, long-term residents might have been identified by their birthplace simply as a way of distinguishing among several people with the same name or profession. A neighborhood might have two Margaritas, for example, so that neighbors would refer to one of them simply as Margarita and the other as Margarita from Trieste.

Whether immigrants were largely closed off from the wider society, dwelling in self-contained areas of the city where they could communicate primarily in their own language or dialect with others of their kind, often depended on their place of origin. Clearly, Jews were largely (though not always successfully) confined to the ghetto. The Greek and German populations often lived in informal immigrant neighborhoods — the Greeks in Castello, the Germans around Rialto. The Turkish merchants were housed in the Fondaco dei Turchi. But although such patterns existed, Inquisition trials paint a portrait of integration, mixed with occasional discord, between native and immigrant. It is clear that immigrants and locals socialized and worked together; did they also share lodgings? The censuses offer an additional perspective.

IMMIGRANT STREETS

Venetian neighborhoods were dotted with streets filled with immigrants. Sometimes the streets were filled with foreigners from around Europe, with neighbors linked not by a common point of origin but rather by their shared identity as immigrants. In the parish of San Giovanni Novo, Nicolò, a merchant from Ragusa, lived with his servant (*massera*) Lugrezia, who had immigrated from Cyprus. Elsewhere in the same parish, around the Corte Nova and the Ruga Giuffa, was an area particularly dense with Lombardian immigrant families, most of them from Brescia. Bortholo, a cloth merchant, hailed from Brescia. He, his wife, and their three children shared their home with two boarders: the Rev. Zuandomenego Romagnuol, a priest at the church of S. Severo, and Battista, another Brescian. Next door lived an elderly widow, Simona, with her widowed daughter Julia and Julia's children; they, too, were from Brescia.[60] Following Simona in the census is Pietro, a carpenter from Bergamo, who lived with his assistant, a compatriot. Two houses later came Angelo, a bread maker from Brescia. One street over, in the Corte dell'Hospedaletto, Marita from Padua presided over a household that included the widowed Caterina from Zara and her 2-year-old child.

S. Ternità was dotted with women and men from the Friuli. In the

Corte da Ca' Baffo, Antonio from the Friuli lived two doors away from Lucia, a Friulian widow with her four children. Next door, another Friulian, Pietro, and his wife shared their home with an orphan named Iseppo. After Pietro's family came his compatriot Lundardo with his wife, children, and sister.[61] A few streets away lived a group of three Friulian women in the home of Menega de Squaldo. Next door was the widowed Valentina, another Friulian (she shared her home with two other widows). Two doors away, three more Friulian widows appear in the census, one after the other.

Even more common than such groupings were immigrant streets populated by foreigners from a mixture of lands. The Calle da Cha Zane in the parish of San Giovanni Novo, home to immigrants from different parts of the Istrian coast, is typical. The widow Christina headed a home that included Dorothia, from Spalato, and her young son. Next door, Anzola, from Zara, and her 4-year-old rented a room from Giacomo, an unmarried tailor. Giacomo's two male boarders also came from Zara. It seems that women, especially, found common ground in their immigrant experiences. In the parish of San Provolo, women from across the empire pooled resources by sharing a home. One household contained Bella Cipriota, from Cyprus; Catarina Bressana, from Brescia; Livia Castellana, probably from Castelfranco, although she could also be from the Venetian *sestiere* of Castello; Christina da Spurch, from the Tirol; and Fiordelise dalla Gambarare, from Gambarare on the Venetian mainland.[62] In the parish of S. Giovanni Novo, on the Calle da Cha Balbi, more immigrant women and men clustered together. Iseppa, a widow with two children, was from Udine. Next door lived Caterina, from Cavarzere, a town on the banks of the Adige river. Caterina shared her home with two other migrants: Stella, from Lubiana, and Margarita, from Camin, another mainland town. Laura Trevisana, in the Corte da Cha Emo, rented rooms to Anzola, from Padua, and Lucieta, from Capodistria. Another Paduan, Anzola, lived next door with her 10-month-old infant. The foreign mix continued in the Corte de Cha Trevisan: the widow Caterina housed two nubili boarders, Lugretia, from Belgrade, and Paula, from the Veneto town of Oriago, as well as a Bergamese couple, Jacomo and Vittoria.[63]

Records of the Inquisition trial of the Friulian Angela reveal a neighborhood packed with immigrants and working women. Many of them appear on the witness list. There was Venturo, a sailor from San Agnese; Ippolito from Ferrara; Faustina, a fruit vendor at S. Moisè; Maria, a Friulian living in S. Moisè with another woman who hailed from Chioggia; Giulia, another Paduan now in San Moisè; Catarina, another Friulian; the Friulian Portia; and Cecilia Castellana.[64] Immigrants on streets such as these, housing other recent arrivals and even compatriots who spoke the same language, must have found their adjustment to Venetian life eased by the immigrant presence. Such clusterings gave them neighbors who had confronted similar obstacles.

The immigrant experience was not the only one that foreign women shared with their neighbors. Women alone, whether native or foreign, often clustered together. In the parish of S. Ternità, in the Calle in Ca' Erizzo, Meneghina—a Slav who had separated from her husband *(non sta col marido)*—made ends meet with rent from three boarders: Tomasina, Antonia from the Friuli, and Lucrezia, a local separated from her husband. Nearby lived the *nubile* Marieta, with four other women—one, Franceschina, a widow with three children, was the only one of Marieta's boarders who was local; of the other three, two were sisters from Istria, Marieta and Antonia; and Chiara came from the Friuli. Women like Chiara, both foreign and native, had location and status in common: as women without men they must have depended particularly on their neighbors for comfort and aid in times of need.

IMMIGRANTS AS A SOURCE OF INCOME

The Venetian popolane profited from the presence of immigrants. Immigrants were ready consumers of Venetian products and skills, purchasing food and services from their neighbors. They were also renters. Foreigners, both female and male, made up a substantial part of the boarder population, thus providing their neighbors with an additional (for some local women perhaps the primary) source of income. Two examples will suffice: In the Calle de Corte Rotta, Ambroso, a porter, and his wife rented out rooms to three women and two men. Two of the women and one of the men, a baker, were immigrants; Leandra was a widow from Concordia; Madalena was German, as was Zuane, the baker. In the parish of San Giovanni Novo, in the Corte da cha Briani, Pietro, a maker of rosaries, and his wife rented rooms to two women and two men: Oliva, a widow, was from the nearby town of Martelago; Margarita was from Zara. Both of the men were rosary makers, like Pietro: one of them, 18-year-old Valentin, was from Friuli.

The authorities took an interest in the business of boarding houses. In a 1612 ordinance, the Esecutori contro la Bestemmia, a Venetian court concerned primarily with blasphemous activities but with a wide range of prosecutorial powers, made clear the substantial presence of women innkeepers in the city: "Both male and female innkeepers *[albergatori et albergatrici]* who keep rooms to let, and who want to lodge foreigners must, within eight days present their documents to their excellencies the Signori Setti Savi, along with their rental [agreements] for approval."[65] The ordinance took note of a way in which renters of rooms—women, in particular—had been circumventing the regulations. Apparently some women had let rooms but claimed that their lodgers were relatives. The esecutori, whose office monitored the entry and behavior of foreigners, emphasized that anyone, regardless of sex, who sheltered a foreigner would be punished if he or she neglected to register the lodger and follow proper procedure: "Women are not to lodge any foreigners in their homes under the pretext of a blood relationship *[parentela]* . . . nor may anyone, man or woman, rent rooms or apartments or sublet to any foreigners, unless they give notice according to the law. [Violators] of these laws will be mercilessly punished according to the laws."[66]

There was a difference between innkeeping and simply letting rooms. Legitimate hostelries registered with the authorities and offered several beds as well as food. These inns might host as many as six or seven guests at a time. More costly for the guest and more profitable for the host, inns were usually owned and patronized by men.[67] The other source of lodgings for immigrants or visitors was in private homes. It was an informal, unofficial system based on capacity and demand. Women with a room or two available could rent out rooms when they needed the income: Orsetta Piriotta, who came up before the Inquisition in 1618, when asked for her profession replied: "I spin, and I also run a boarding house, but I have never rented more than one room."[68]

Some women did comply with the requirement to register their lodgers. In 1608, a woman named Antonia registered her foreign boarder, Mercurio of Ancona. One of Chiara Medici's two tenants the same year was a weaver from Milan. Immigrant women themselves got in on the act: Fiorenza, an immigrant from Istria, registered two foreign men living under her roof.[69]

A number of different offices concerned themselves with boarders and inns, and women who neglected to follow the appropriate procedures faced severe sanctions. The Provveditori alla Sanità, for example, was concerned with preventing the spread of contagion. In 1555, the provveditori condemned Lucia, originally from Verona, for harboring foreigners "in violation of this office's rules" (the charge did not explain what this violation entailed). For her offense, Lucia was to be arrested and displayed in chains in front of the Sanità building from morning to mid-afternoon, with a placard explaining her crime.[70] Rosa, condemned by the provveditori two months later, was punished more seriously. She had taken in as a boarder one Piero di Benettodi, a man the authorities said should have been quarantined. For placing the city in danger, Rosa was to be whipped and banned from Venice for a year.[71]

Though the censuses show that women most often let rooms to other women, the esecutori and the Inquisition focused on the perils associated with women who hosted foreign men. Here the concern was obviously moral. Paolina Briani gives us one example. When she was called before the Inquisition in 1581 on charges of heresy, Paolina de Viscardi, called Briana, was living in the parish of San Giovanni Novo. She was accused by multiple witnesses of having engaged in all sorts of blasphemous activities. The root of her crimes was said to be her association with foreign men, notably Greeks and Turks.[72] One of the charges was that Paolina had been seen eating meat on Fridays, under the malevolent influence of her Orthodox and Muslim clients. Such "wrong" consumption of food was often cited in Inquisition trials as proof of a deeper heretical bent. Another case involved Cristina Collari, a Christian woman accused of sexual relations with a Jew. One of the charges against her stated that her alleged lover, Don Enfrin, had brought meat to her from the ghetto — meat "prepared in various ways" and to be eaten on Fridays.[73] In Paolina's case, when asked if she cooked meat for the men on holy days, she replied, "No sirs, they cook their own food, and they cook better than women."[74]

Paolina had to answer serious charges, foremost among them the accusation that she was engaged in carnal relations with her clients. Paolina understood that suspicion of foreigners lay at the heart of the case against her. First, she dismissed their origin by offering her own version of why she had come before the tribunal in the first place: "I don't know why I was called here to this holy office; only that I was told about three months ago that the captain Hieronimo Venier wanted to get me into trouble, because my sister Samaritana had beat up his girl friend Maddalena." [75] Paolina then went on to explain her profession as an innkeeper and demonstrate, reasonably, that her moral health was not in jeopardy: "I work by renting rooms to Christians, Greeks, Turks, and in this way I earn a living by keeping a small inn. . . . These Turks and Greeks that stay in my house for a while, the Greeks do according to the Greek custom and the Turks according to the Turkish custom, so that the Turks eat meat on Friday and the Greeks on Saturday—but that I have ever had carnal relations with any of them, or that any of them impregnated me, certainly not, sirs." [76] The other woman mentioned above, Cristina, had to contend with similar charges; though the evidence against her pointed to an intense sexual relationship with only one man, she was accused, to damage her character further, of having multiple sexual partners, in her case foreign Jews. [77]

IMMIGRANTS AND INTERMARRIAGE

Venetian authorities feared that illicit sexual unions between Venetians and foreigners would ensue from contact between the two groups. Even legitimate marriages were sometimes discouraged, especially in cases where a wealthy local woman planned to marry a foreign man. [78] Nevertheless, successful marriages between immigrants and native Venetians did occur. We can speculate about the dynamics of such marriages. When a local woman married an immigrant man, she may have found power in the relationship because the husband, lacking his own family base, depended on his mate and on her family. In the other configuration, an immigrant woman married to a local man, while lacking a local family support group, might have learned to be independent by necessity, having traveled to Venice and survived there alone for a time. Such women may also, of course, have been more vulnerable, especially those who arrived in the city as young girls, alone. Information about age at marriage for women of the popular class, let alone those who were immigrants, is practically nonexistent for Venice; sources from other early modern communities suggests a pattern of more independent behavior on the part of some immigrant wives. [79] Then there were couples who immigrated to Venice together. They may well have created de facto partnerships to make their way in a new city, based on mutual dependence as they created their new lives.

Many notarial records concern couples in which at least one of the spouses was an immigrant to Venice. In these transactions about money or property, husband and wife often participated together.[80] Immigrant couples (i.e., couples in which at least one partner was foreign) met on a relatively equal footing, both with each other and their immediate environs. Young local couples whose match had been brokered by family members would remain tied to those families, a situation that could promise control as well as support. Immigrant couples could make a fresher start.

There are numerous mentions of immigrant couples in the notarial records. Caterina, a Piedmontese woman, was married to a Venetian milliner when she employed a notary's services in 1575.[81] Margarita, originally from Verona, was married to a local man when in 1615 she and her sister Lucia filed some financial papers.[82] Angelica, who hailed from Bassano, identified herself as the wife of a wool weaver when she contacted the notary Girolamo Brinis that same year.[83]

Not only foreign women married to local men displayed independence: local women who married foreigners did so, too. Hortensia was a Venetian born and bred, but her husband came from the town of Aquileia. They drew up a contract together in 1575.[84] Chiara's husband came from Padua. She handled her own dowry contract in 1615.[85] And we also hear of foreigners who married other foreigners: Meneghina, originally from Verona, was married to a Brescian when she filed a complaint in 1605 against two men who had done shoddy work for her.[86]

❧

LIFE WAS not easy for immigrants. They usually began their new lives with few resources, either financial or familial. Immigrant women were often singled out by their neighbors as targets of witchcraft accusations. Long after they had settled in Venice, many still found themselves labeled Slav or Greek, unable to escape their earlier identities. Perhaps some did not wish to: those whose communities had been dispersed or destroyed (for example, the victims of Ottoman expansion) and those who built small new communities within Venetian neighborhoods may have drawn sustenance from their shared customs and shared past.

Most, though, settled in neighborhoods predominantly composed of Venetians. There, they gradually integrated into local society, sometimes by drawing on traditional skills such as healing (and sometimes exploiting myths about such skills). Most often they engaged in the same economic and social exchanges as native Venetians, building networks of clients and companions in the process. Marriage was sometimes the result. Marriage and extramarital relationships developed between local women and foreign men and foreign women and local men, though perhaps neither with the frequency that the authorities feared, nor with dire consequences.

Immigrant women were deeply embedded in Venetian society. Living with one another and with native-born Venetians, these women formed part of a female world in flux: even women who did not travel could not help knowing about a wider world with different ideas and customs. As the next chapter demonstrates, the mobility of immigrant women was woven into a larger tapestry of female spaces throughout the city.

CHAPTER FIVE

Beyond the Contrada
Women and Mobility

W HEN immigrant women settled in a Venetian parish, they did not enter a tightly closed world from which local women rarely ventured. Rather, the immigrants to Venice were part of a larger community of women who were free to move about the city.

Venetian women have usually been portrayed as relegated to the relatively private spaces of home and local square. Dennis Romano has described a Venice where sharp distinctions were drawn between female and male territory in the fifteenth century. Male space was public, the centers of political and economic life; female space was private, domestic, pious.[1] Robert Davis has suggested a similar state for the sixteenth century, pointing out that even female fashions, particularly the impossibly high clogs (zoccoli) that were in fashion at the time, restricted women's physical movement.[2] A Scottish visitor to Venice, Fynes Moryson, reported that Venetian women were "locked up at home, as if in prison."[3]

In fact, the "female" spaces of home and the neighboring square rarely fit our definition of private. Among the noble and wealthy, the home consisted at least in part of spaces used for hosting important visitors and business partners.[4] For the popular classes, too, the home was a locus of business and social exchange. The business of the home spilled into the neighborhood, and vice versa. If so much social and commercial traffic took place within the neighborhood and home, can the women who resided there have been as limited in their movements as historians have suggested?

Common sense tells us that women left their neighborhoods more rarely than did men. Certainly there were practical reasons why a woman was less likely than a man to range far from her residence in early modern Europe. Married woman spent a good portion of their lives pregnant, which limited their ability to walk quickly or traverse great distances. Rearing children also ensured that women spent the balance of their days close to home. Finally, whether married or not, women bore most of the burden of housekeeping. With so much of their daily activity located in and around the household, they had fewer incentives and less opportunity to roam far.[5]

But while it is clear that women's access to the wider city was more limited than men's, they nonetheless displayed surprising mobility, in several ways. They walked from one parish to another on daily business or to see friends and relatives. Some journeyed clear across the city in search of clients or to appear before a tribunal. They could pick up and move to another part of town for personal reasons. They even moved out of and back into the city itself. Finally, travel and mobility were part of women's world more generally, as they said goodbye to relatives who emigrated or who temporarily left the city, and encountered women and men who had changed residence.

GETTING AROUND

"There are two ways of getting about in Venice: by foot, on the dry land, and by boat," wrote the Venetian noble Marin Sanudo in the late fifteenth century. He then expanded on the watery means of transport, extolling the beauty of the boats and the opulence of their decoration. But traveling by water could be expensive. The purchase price of a standard private boat, he wrote, was 15 ducats (in 1499), close to a year's salary for an unskilled worker.[6] Furthermore "ornaments are always required, either dolphins or other things, so that it is a great expense, costing more than a horse. The servants, if they are not slaves, have to be paid a wage, usually 1 ducat with expenses, so that, adding it all up, the cost is very high." Sanudo went on to say that "there is no gentleman or citizen who does not have one or two or even more boats in the family, according to household, etc."[7]

If the wealthy could afford multiple boats to ferry their families around in style, humbler folk could not. Most Venetians moved around the city on foot. People sometimes paid to be transported across the Grand Canal to get from one part of town to another.[8] Otherwise, they walked to the Rialto bridge to cross on foot. A walk across Venice was not normally arduous; even today, much of the city can be reached from any point in about half an hour. Walking through this crowded, lively city ensured that women had contact with people both like and unlike themselves; walking exposed them to all of the activity, opulence, and squalor that characterized early modern urban centers.[9]

Walking could certainly be risky. Venice was as dangerous a city as any, with more than its share of bandits and more generally rowdy folk.[10] Even games played by young men could spell danger for passers-by. One popular game called Pandolo involved hurling a long, sharply pointed stick in the air and trying to catch it safely before it fell to earth. Because "boys and even men" played this game in open areas, the authorities worried about the danger that it and similar diversions posed to innocent people walking the streets.[11] It was despite such dangers that women ventured beyond their *contrade*, for a range of reasons.

DAILY TRAVELS

Although women lived and worked the balance of their lives in their own neighborhoods, the boundaries between the parish and the wider city were still remarkably porous. Women left their homes and *campi* on a regular basis for all sorts of business. Any woman who had contact with a tribunal—civil or criminal, as a defendant, plaintiff, or witness—had to travel to that office. Women who visited charitable institutions might travel to distant parts of the city, including the Giudecca island.[12] Those who filed suppliche with the Pien Collegio had to visit a notary's office and maybe the collegio itself. Making a will also sometimes required women to leave their homes. To draw up her will, for example, Claudia Stella met her notary in the home of a silk merchant, who lived in the parish of the SS. Apostoli (see map on page 2). Claudia lived in the adjacent parish of S. Cancian.[13]

Women who testified before the Inquisition often referred to their forays beyond their neighborhoods. Such references came in the form of casual asides, as witnesses and defendants described their networks of acquaintances and friends, both former and present. Only rarely did the women offer explanations for their trips beyond the borders of the parish. Evidently explanations were unnecessary because traveling among different neighborhoods was an entirely normal activity. Those who did offer a context for their movements painted a portrait of overlapping social, familial, and economic motives that drew women away from their homes.

Family ties were the cause of some trips to other neighborhoods. The sisters Andriana and Paola Lodovoci lived in S. Barnaba and S. Stefano, respectively, two parishes on opposite sides of the Grand Canal. Yet the two were often seen together and accused of leveling curses on innocent acquaintances as a team. Nor did they leave their parishes only to visit one another. One witness reported that Andriana had come to her home in the parish of S. Samuele—closer to her sister's parish than to her own—determined to make trouble.[14]

Other sisters living apart who appeared before the S. Uffizio included two witnesses in Orsetta Piriotta's trial: Orseta Gelana and Bella. Orseta lived near the *traghetto* (boat) stop of S. Tomà; Bella lived in the parish of S. Maria Formosa, a completely different section of the city.[15] Yet another pair of sisters linked together in a witchcraft and heresy trial, Samaritana and Paolina Briani, spent time together but lived some distance from one another: Paolina lived in the parish of S. Giovanni Novo; Samaritana lived in the Corte Nova of S. Maria Formosa.[16] Women apparently often maintained close connections with their sisters even if they moved to different parts of the city. This could be true for both unmarried and married women: Samaritana Briani was married (although at the time of the trial she was estranged from her husband).

Women also often maintained contact with parents after leaving home, especially their mothers. Prudentia, the unmarried daughter of a caulker, resided in the parish of S. Moisè, next to the Piazza S. Marco; her mother and sister lived across town in Canareggio, near the Jewish ghetto. But we can surmise that Prudentia probably visited her mother and sister fairly regularly since she provided for them in her will.[17] The family remained important for her into adulthood. But women like Prudentia presumably moved where their work or marriage took them. Why sisters and others spread across the city as adults is not clear from the sources, but it seems reasonable to assume that they easily traversed the distances between family members to meet.

Not only family bonds but also women's social networks thrived beyond their members' immediate neighborhoods. Orsetta Piriotta was 46 years old when she appeared before the Inquisition. She had lived in Venice for many years and the list of witnesses in her case was long. Most of these were from Orsetta's parish of S. Moisè, a large contrada close to the Piazza S. Marco. But some came from other parishes as well: Elena was a widow from Castello, the eastern part of the city; she went to the tribunal and spoke of her relationship with Orsetta, from whom she had purchased a love charm.[18] Whether the women met in Elena's neighborhood or Orsetta's, one of them had to cross several parishes to reach the other.

Another witness in Orsetta's trial was a young man named Ambrogio, currently residing in the parish of S. Matteo, several parishes away and across the Grand Canal from S. Moisè. Of Orsetta he said: "I have known her for several years, and had her friendship."[19] Ambrogio also named others who knew the accused woman and might have insight into her guilt: Bernardo, a carpenter at the Arsenale, due east of Orsetta's home, and a servant named Helena, who was now living in S. Barnaba, far to the west. When Bernardo appeared before the tribunal he testified that he had known the accused woman for eight or nine years. "I know her in the way that young people are friends," he explained, "and the friendship between us lasted for quite a while, around three years." Their friendship cooled, but Bernardo maintained that the two had parted amicably and remained cordial: "Since then I have always said hello to her."[20] Bernardo explained that he had earlier lived at S. Moisè, but he had resided in the Arsenale district for several years. How and where did he and Orsetta meet? Perhaps they continued to see each other occasionally after Bernardo moved away; perhaps Bernardo returned to his old neighborhood; or perhaps they encountered each other at the home of a mutual friend before or after Bernardo's move. This is what had happened to 18-year-old Margherita, another witness in the trial and a current neighbor of Orsetta's. She testified that she had seen Orsetta around Easter when she visited the home of a friend who lived across the Piazza S. Marco and at least one parish away from the young woman's home in S. Moisè.[21] On that occasion, both the older woman and the younger one had left their parish to visit a mutual acquaintance.

What does such testimony reveal? Orsetta's contacts across the city appear to have been primarily social. She was known to people as far away as S. Barnaba and the Arsenale, opposite points on the city map. She encountered a fellow parishioner, Margherita, in the home of a third party, outside the parish itself. Such contacts indicate that a woman's friendships were not limited to her immediate neighbors.

Women also left their parishes daily for economic reasons. Travel was sometimes necessary to seek out and meet clients. Women who cleaned homes, did laundry, or performed other sorts of domestic service moved across streets and parishes to the homes of their customers. Women who worked as healers, especially, had to traverse neighborhoods as they visited the ill and tried to cure them. This was true of the healer Camilla Garzolo, tried for witchcraft in 1590. She readily admitted traveling throughout Venice to meet her customers.[22] Another case was Marietta Greca (the Greek), who in 1620 found herself on trial for witchcraft. Her trial illustrates the ease with which both women and men moved through different parishes on a daily basis.

Marietta's trial began with the testimony of Laura, a teenager from the parish of S. Agostin. Three years earlier, Laura had fallen gravely ill. The girl told the court: "I had a terrible illness, which the doctors did not know how to cure. They said that they did not recognize my malady. . . . I felt a great pain in my stomach and in my heart."[23] Laura's father, Gabriele, a wool cloth shearer, was desperate. As he told it, after learning that the physicians could do no more, he found his way to the church of the Frari, in the parish of S. Tomà. There he wept and told everyone who would listen of his daughter's plight and his fears for her. Some women in the church took pity on him and offered him advice, telling him of a healer who might help his daughter: "[They] told me of a Greek named Marietta who lived in Castello by the church of S. Francesco di Paolo, a woman with a few years on her, and fat."[24]

Gabriele went to Castello to find Marietta. When he found her, he explained his predicament and asked her to come to his home and examine Laura. Marietta agreed and accompanied the distraught father. (To reach Gabriele's home they crossed a minimum of nine parishes and the Grand Canal.)[25] As soon as Marietta saw Laura, Gabriele told the inquisitor, she declared that the girl had been bewitched. Eventually, she managed to cure Laura with a mixture of potions, signing, and prayers and chants.

It was Marietta's use of chants and potions that interested the inquisitor. But though Marietta readily acknowledged practicing the art of healing, she admitted no wrongdoing. As she described her profession, she made clear the degree to which she had to travel across Venice for her work. For the client Gabriele, she had walked from Castello to the sestiere of S. Polo, where the man's family lived and where the women who knew her work attended church. But she also ventured even further on a regular basis: Marietta explained to the court that she made use of various tools, including potions and lotions, to help the sick. She bought the powder to mix one particular potion, the one that "brings up the phlegm, from a spice dealer in San Pantalon." This parish is located in the sestiere of Dorsoduro, at the other end of the city from Marietta's residence.[26]

Marietta claimed that she was not a witch but, rather, a healer; and in fact she was never accused of trying to foretell the future or of selling curses and love charms. Other women, however, did market themselves as wise women with special powers. Like healers, such women relied on word of mouth to drum up business. The case of Orsolina is illustrative. When a baker named Pietro testified before the Holy Office in a witchcraft trial, he described his family's encounter with the accused witch. Pietro and his family were residents of Malamocco, a remote area on the Lido island, distant from the main island cluster of Venice. Pietro needed access to a boat to reach Venice proper. If he did not own one, he needed to borrow or hire one. At a minimum, the journey would take at least three hours, maybe more, depending on the weather. Yet it appears that he and his wife moved easily between the Lido and Venice proper.

The seeds were planted for Pietro's encounter with Orsolina a year before they actually met. Back then, he had lost a certain sum of money. Some time later, his wife Helena traveled from their Malamocco home to the Venetian parish of S. Margherita. Pietro did not explain why Helena found herself in Venice that day, only that she went to a building called Ca' Bolani, where she met Orsolina. Orsolina was called "da Mestre" because she had originally moved to Venice from that mainland town. We do not know whether Helena had sought Orsolina out or whether the two women met by chance. Whatever the case, Orsolina lost no time in telling Helena that she enjoyed a certain fame on the Terraferma, as one who possessed special powers. Pietro reported that "after talking with her Helena understood that in Mestre this woman was known as one who could divine unknown things." Little happened after that first meeting, but after Helena ran into Orsolina again—on another trip to Venice—

she returned to Malamocco and told Pietro of this *Mestrina* who might be able to help them. Hopeful, the couple traveled from Malamocco to Orsolina's home in the parish of S. Margherita, where she told them that their neighbor Rizzo was the thief.[27]

Pietro and Helena had visited Orsolina on business, in search of a service. We do not know Helena's reasons for visiting Venice earlier; they could have been familial, social, or economic; Helena may have been visiting friends or relatives, or she may have gone to sell or purchase something. Friendship, work, and family all drew women from their neighborhoods to other parishes and parts of the city. In Helena's case, something drew her to another island altogether, more than once. Whatever her motives, Helena's travels were not unusual. Her husband's testimony offered no explanation for her presence in Venice because there was no need. Naturally anxious to portray himself and his wife as innocents in the affair, Pietro made no attempt to hide or excuse his wife's trips because he knew that by themselves they would not excite comment or suspicion.

CHANGING HOMES AND NEIGHBORHOODS

The mobility that women displayed in their daily activities was mirrored by their readiness to relocate when circumstances demanded. Why did women change their residence? Work was one reason. Prudentia, mentioned earlier, had moved from her family's home near the Jewish ghetto clear across town near the Piazza S. Marco. She pointed this out in her will, when she left legacies to her family and gave their address. She had moved for economic reasons, she explained, to live in the home of her employer, Alvise Zorzi, in the parish of S. Moisè.[28] Prudentia was not unusual: many women moved permanently from one home to another for work. This was especially true for domestic servants, the majority of whom lived in their place of work.[29]

It has long been thought that in the early modern period a woman's major transition was marriage, when a woman left her parents' home for that of her husband. The Inquisition trials indicate that marriage was in fact only one of a number of factors that might compel a woman to change homes. Caterina de Freddis, a S. Uffizio witness, was a 25-year-old bride who had recently moved to the parish of S. Silvestro. She explained to the court that she had previously lived in the adjacent parish of S. Aponal. Apparently she had set up house alone in that earlier dwelling since she used the first person to describe her decision to move and rent out a room in S. Aponal. She told the court she had not been there long before packing up again to move to S. Silvestro. It was while living in S. Aponal that she knew the accused couple in the case, a carpenter named Raffaele and his wife Margherita.

Caterina knew Margherita well, even though the young woman had been only a short-term resident of her parish; in fact, Margherita was Caterina's godmother, which suggests that Margherita knew the young woman's parents. One possible explanation is that Margherita and Caterina's mother were neighbors in another parish before Margherita moved to S. Aponal. If Caterina did not grow up in S. Aponal, as she maintained, she had probably lived nearby. In any event, by the time she was 25, this young woman lived alone, earned money as a landlady, and moved again, probably because of her marriage. Another resident of S. Aponal who relocated was Agnese, the wife of a *fachin,* or porter. Agnese, according to another witness in the same trial, "used to live on the same street [as me] but then moved, though she is still close by." [30]

Caterina was vague about her reasons for changing homes so often; marriage seems to have played only a minor role in her changes of address. Sometimes the reasons for women's moves were clear, the circumstances pressing. For example, the end of a marriage led some of them to change homes. And relocation was an unpleasant necessity for a woman who could no longer afford to stay in the same home when her husband died. Such was the case of Zanetta, who after the death of her husband was forced to move with her children into a neighbor's home, where she then worked as a servant.[31] Another woman, Claudia Stella, hinted in her 1629 will that she might have moved in with another man after the death of her husband, changing households in the process.[32]

Some women found new mates and relocated without waiting for their husbands to die. Samaritana Briana did just that, according to her jilted husband. He explained in a trial against his sister-in-law that he was married to Samaritana, recalling that they had been married by the priest Pasqualigo of S. Maria Formosa. He also remembered buying the wedding ring from a certain Giovanni, who had a fruit stand at S. Aponal. But after ten years of marriage, Samaritana "ran away, leaving me with the house, and she gave me a little money." Samaritana had not left alone, but with the fishmonger. Now, according to Samaritana's aggrieved former husband, the couple "live together in the Corte Nova."[33]

Women who moved in and out of a parish were a regular feature of neighborhood life. One of the first witnesses in the trial of Vincenza and Dianora de Gilioli (originally from Ferrara) was Paolina, a married woman. She had lived in the same parish for many years, she explained, but had been living next to the Gilioli sisters for only three years. Either she or the two sisters had changed dwellings at that time. Cecilia, another witness in the same trial, told the court that she, too, had moved to the Gilioli sisters' parish only three years before.[34] One witness in Camila Garzolo's trial was a Cremonese widow, another Camila. She seems to have been positively peripatetic, having moved at least four times in the last decade. She testified: "I have lived in the street *[ruga]* with two wells at Santa Sofia since fifteen days before the *feste*.[35] And before that I lived in San Rocco in the *campiello*, where I lived for two years and six months. I have lived in Venice for six years."[36]

Usually women stayed in one place long enough to be remembered years later by their former neighbors. Angela Friuli changed neighborhoods at least once as an adult.[37] In her 1591 trial, both former and current neighbors gave testimony.[38] Angela was living in the parish of S. Moisè when she was denounced as a witch by her neighbor Ancilla, originally from Padua. Ancilla accused Angela of a range of crimes, most of which consisted of moral laxity: not going to confession or communion, and seducing men left and right, a charge made even more scandalous because Angela was a married woman. She also allegedly tormented her "poor" husband and, worst of all, "she is the most serious witch of herbs that one can imagine."[39]

Giulia from Padua was one of the first to testify in the case against Angela. A recent arrival to the accused woman's parish, she told the court: "I know this Friulian Angela, who is my neighbor in S. Moisè, in the court of Ca' Barci, and I have known her in this way, by sight, for two months, which is how long I have lived in that courtyard."[40] Another neighbor, Cecilia Castellana, had known Angela longer, and even lived with her briefly: "I have known this Angela for five or six years, and I lived in her house for three months, but it's been eight or nine months since I left there."

Sometimes, as in the case of Angela, women remained in contact with their former neighbors after moving; but other times, they simply vanished as far as those former neighbors were concerned. In the trial of Camila Garzolo, the witness Leona, a widow, suggested that the tribunal contact another neighbor, named Pasqua. But there was a problem: "This Pasqua, I don't know where she is now, because it's been two years since she moved away from here."[41] Caterina da Maggia, accused of witchcraft in 1591, was another woman who had cut ties with her former neighbors after moving. At the time of her allegedly evil deeds, Caterina resided in the parish of S. Marcuola. She later moved, according to her main accuser, who did not know her current whereabouts.[42]

In a different case, a 43-year-old matron named Paola explained that she had known the accused woman Cristina when they lived near one another for a few years: "Yes, I know her because four years ago more or less she lived in Rio Terrà, where I lived, too, and it has been about two years since we are no longer neighbors."[43] Both had moved away since then. When women moved across town, it was obviously more difficult for them to stay in touch than if they stayed within one district, especially women who moved among the border islands of Venice. For there were women who never lived in the central city itself but remained at its edges. Libera di Rossi resided on the island of Burano when she was accused of witchcraft by her neighbors. Earlier, she had lived on the Giudecca island. Her former neighbors there still remembered her, though she had moved away more than eight years before.[44]

The frequency with which Venetian women changed addresses meant that they had to form friendships quickly, sometimes again and again. Knowing their neighbors was essential, since neighbors could step in and help when families were unwilling or unable to do so. Many economic transactions took place within the neighborhood—another good reason to cultivate good local relations. Sabina, a 25-year-old witness in Orsetta Piriotta's trial, understood this. She explained that she had known the older woman by sight for some time, but that it was only when Orsetta moved near Sabina's home, five or six months earlier, that they began to run into each other and socialize. Sabina had been in Orsetta's home more than once by the time the trial was in session.[45]

Another witness in Orsetta's trial was the 30-year-old Catarina. She was the wife of a manservant who worked for the Council of Forty. The couple currently lived in the parish of S. Niccolò, a fisherman's district at the southwestern tip of the city. She professed nervous ignorance about why she had been called to the Inquisition: "I almost died when I was summoned." But when asked she readily admitted that she knew the accused: "I know her because she lives in the Calle Balaressa, where, four years ago, I lived for six months." In this case, proximity did not breed friendship, at least not in Catarina's account to the inquisitor: "But we never spent much time together."[46]

Certain factors predisposed some women to move. One was place of origin. Lacking a traditional support network, foreign women were more likely than women born and raised in the city to change their residences more than once. Indeed, immigrant women exemplify the double-edged sword of mobility better than any other group: certain freedoms (for example, the freedom to leave one occupation or neighborhood or town for another) often resulted in desperation or danger. Mobility often went hand-in-hand with risk. Another factor was wealth, or the lack of it. Financial well-being made women less likely to move, for several reasons. Prosperous women had fewer motives to relocate, especially for employment. And wealthy family members had a greater stake in their women's honor—an honor that risked compromise by too much independence. In addition, fathers, husbands, and brothers could control large portions of a woman's wealth, making her economically as well as legally dependent on them. It was, of course, also more physically difficult for a propertied woman to move, her possessions being more numerous and heavier than those of a woman in more humble circumstances.

A look at twenty-nine wills spanning the period 1555 to 1635 suggests that the amount, value, and weight of a popolana's belongings could vary widely. Anzola Zanotta took great pride in itemizing her feather bed *(letto di piuma)* and its sheets and many cushions.[47] But among the women whose wills are collected at the archive of the Istituzioni di Ricovero e di Educazione (IRE), we also find a high proportion of light, portable possessions, like clothing and scarves. One woman's goods (in addition to her cash) consisted merely of the following: one black undergarment, a small carpet, several shirts *(camise da donna diverse)*, aprons, head scarves, shawls, napkins, two tablecloths, a woman's hat, a handkerchief, and a pair of scarlet sleeves.[48] Another's most precious possession was a fur cloak.[49] Moving across the city would not have been physically prohibitive for such women. They could even leave Venice itself, and easily.

BEYOND VENICE: WOMEN TRAVELERS

In addition to the women who moved around Venice, women made up part of a less definable group of people who traveled out of town and back again, engaging in the sort of temporary travel normally associated with merchants or journeymen.[50] Women may not have traveled as far or as often as men, but they did move back and forth between Venice and its surrounding territory, and sometimes they roamed beyond. Wealthy women left to visit family and friends or to check on their business interests. Humbler women left town for periods stretching into months or years. Their descriptions of trips away from and back to Venice show that female travelers were a regular part of the landscape.

Some women moved in and out of Venice on social visits with family and friends. When a woman named Perina made her last will and testament, she remembered among other relatives her niece Maria who lived on the mainland, leaving her two dresses, a shirt, and two aprons. She left additional clothing to her sister Philippa, Maria's mother, with the request that "these things should be lovingly shared between mother and daughter." Maria was clearly dear to her aunt, who was unmarried; aunt and niece almost certainly visited one another on occasion.[51] Financial interest, too, could draw women from Venice. Women who had business interests on the mainland visited their properties occasionally. The sisters Giulia, Anna, Isabetta, and Veniera listed property holdings in the Vicentine territory of Lonigo. Their holdings included a villa, tracts of land that spanned several parishes, and leases.[52] Justina Zane was another woman with business interests outside of the city. She was living in the parish of S. Stin when she declared her holdings to the Dieci Savi and acknowledged ownership of several mainland properties. These included one undeveloped property *(terreno vacuo)* that boasted a few modest houses. Justina rented them out. She also had property near Padua.[53] Such properties, central to the financial security of women like Justina and Giulia and her sisters, linked them to a world of investment and travel beyond the city.

But most women who left their homes in Venice were visiting kin or friends, or left under duress, even exile.[54] In 1555, Franceschina Buranella, the wife of a Paduan called Marchio, had to appear before the board of health, the Provveditori alla Sanità, on the charge of giving false testimony in a case of broken quarantine. Along with her husband and two

other men, Franceschina was exiled from Venice for two full years. Flout-
ing this ban was strongly discouraged by the provveditori: "If at any time
one or more of them breaks this rule and is caught, they shall be locked
in prison for six months, and then must return to exile serving out the
full sentence from the beginning [*et poi debbin ritornar a principiar il bando*],
and pay a fine of 200 lire di piccoli." [55]

A fourth exile in this case was Violante, whose previous trip out of the
city had landed her in trouble. The wife of a printer named Domenego,
Violante had been away from Venice for an unspecified period of time.
She apparently had been traveling without Domenego; he was not mentioned in the court's discussion of her travels. Upon her return, she flouted
regulations by not spending the appropriate amount of time in quarantine, on the island of S. Lazzaretto. This reckless action had "risked infec-
tion of the city." Her punishment matched those of the others: Violante
was banished from Venice for two years. [56]

The board of health regularly delivered such swift, cold justice to
women who put the city at risk of disease. A woman named Rosa, already
mentioned in chapter 4, was sanctioned severely by the Provveditori alla
Sanità when she violated their regulations by taking in a boarder without
following the proper registration procedures. For her crime, Rosa was first
sentenced to be whipped and then banned from Venice and its environs
for one year. The provveditori also warned her sternly against ignoring
the punishment: "If she violates this ban and is caught, the person who
catches her will receive 50 lire di piccoli from her goods . . . and she
shall be locked up in prison for six months and then will be banned once
more." [57]

Exile was a relatively common punishment handed out by the Inquisition as well as the Provveditori alla Sanità. When Emilia Catena was
found guilty of witchcraft in 1586, the Inquisition sentenced her to five
years of exile. Thirty months into her punishment, in 1588, Emilia asked
for permission to return to Venice before her sentence was served in full.
Her plea described both her longing for Venice and the dire circumstances
into which the exile had plunged her. According to the notary who presented her request, "she throws herself at the feet of this illustrious court,
begging them with humility and with tears in her eyes, that they may
be moved by compassion by the great misery and unhappiness in which
this poor woman finds herself, far from her homeland, and lacking any
resources." [58]

Franceschina dal Dedo also pleaded with the authorities—in her case with the Pien Collegio—to lift a ban. She had been exiled from Venice and its dominion in perpetuo for bearing false witness in a trial before the Signori di Notte al Criminal, a powerful and secretive branch of the government concerned with crime. Ironically, Franceschina was out of the city when the charge was brought before the court. Her traveling was her downfall: unable to defend herself because she was away, she was found guilty. Three years later, she begged for a chance to state her case. Echoing Emilia's words, Franceschina said that she was living in torment and had been ruined by her exile: "I stay far from my *patria,* and I find myself in great need, always weeping. . . . So that I no longer must live in this misery and pain for what remains of my life, I beg your serene court to let me defend myself before you."[59]

Sometimes exile was self-imposed. In 1565 a woman named Magdalena petitioned the Great Council of Venice for mercy upon her return to the city. She had fled the city two years earlier because, she said, she had been accused of using a pestle "to hit a certain Bernardina . . . on the basis of which accusation a case was built against me." Once accused, Magdalena received a summons to the prisons office of the dreaded Signori di Notte. Magdalena was terrified, although as she explained in her petition it was not guilt that fed her terror, but rather "natural female imbecility and foolish fear." She had panicked. "I fled in haste, abandoning my homeland." Magdalena had fled alone, leaving her children behind. But she was "by now tired of these long travels and this pernicious exile, [and wish] to make known my innocence."[60]

Magdalena was not anomalous: other women fled the city under a cloud of crime or scandal. Camilla, the wife of a miller, was accused of adultery and forced to flee the anger of her husband Piero. She sought refuge with her father, Nicola, but he, too, threw her out and so she was absent from the city (she did not specify where) when the Council of Forty convicted her of the offense.[61] It was a different sort of scandal that drew another woman away from Venice. She asked the Pien Collegio for assistance to travel to the city of Ragusa, across the Adriatic, where she intended to confront her husband. She explained that he had abandoned her and was currently living in the coastal city in the company of her sister.[62]

Many women who left the city had every intention of returning, even after considerable time had passed. Anzelica told the Pien Collegio in 1565 that she had been away from Venice "in foreign lands" for a time when, unbeknown to her, two merchants named Angelo de Zorzi and Zuan-pietro accused her of stealing some silk from them. Found guilty, Anzelica was banned in absentia from the city for a whopping twenty years. When she innocently returned to town, she was discovered and arrested in short order.[63] A year later, Lucietta, a Venetian widow, found herself in a similar predicament. She claimed to have been in Treviso in the service of a wellborn woman (Lucieta was vague about her employer's identity, describing her only as "a magnifica gentlewoman") when an accusation and then a condemnation were lodged against her. Like Anzelica, Lucieta had returned to Venice to find herself banned.[64]

Lucieta had been away for innocent reasons, in the service of an employer—at least, that was her excuse. Anzelica also implied that her activities abroad had been blameless. Both women had been traveling outside of Venice on apparently normal business. Others left simply to maintain contact with their home towns. In 1575 a woman named Zuana filed a supplica regarding a charge brought against her some time earlier. She had been away at the time, she said, visiting her native city of Mel. She explained that when the accusation was filed, "I was given eight days to appear at the prison and defend myself against the blows [accusations] dealt me, but I could not do this during the period of the proclamation because I was in my homeland Mel then, and I had no news of what was happening."[65]

It was so easy for women to move in and out of Venice that in at least two Inquisition trials, the female defendants tried to persuade female witnesses to leave the city temporarily in order to avoid testifying. In the 1588 trial of Cristina discussed in chapter 3, one witness reported that the accused woman had attempted to pay her to leave Venice for the duration of the trial. The woman virtuously claimed: "I told [the accused] that I would not leave [even] if she gave me all of her worldly goods, and I did not go away from here."[66]

When women left the city, they had to first reach the mainland by boat, taking what they could with them. The wealthier traveled accompanied by servants and guards, but the poor had to fend for themselves. Most did so without help. When the women discussed above described their journeys, they implied that they were traveling alone. Servants may not have counted as company in some accounts, of course, and women pleading their case before a court may have exaggerated their plight to win sympathy. But even women speaking casually of earlier journeys rarely mention traveling companions. One exception was a woman on her way to Ragusa, who assured the authorities that she was traveling with an elderly male companion.[67] It therefore cannot have been an unusual sight to see women travelers on city streets and country roads, stopping at inns just as men did, asking for directions, lodging, or a meal.

Though some cases show women leaving the city in moments of crisis, others show women traveling out of and returning to Venice for prosaic reasons. Most Venetians probably did not leave the city regularly or at all; yet even if the experiences of most of the women described above were not typical, they do indicate the potential women had for travel beyond Venice's confines. Women must have been a presence on the roads of northern Italy. Whether they wanted to or not, Venetian women left their homes, parishes, and city, and often with every intention of returning.

A MOBILE WORLD

Even women who might never leave the city had a relationship to a wider world. When Lucieta, a 36-year-old in the parish of S. Vidal, referred the Inquisition to one of her neighbors as a witness, she was quick to add that he could be hard to track down, explaining that the neighbor, Leonardo Gardin, "right now might be in Corfu or Zara."[68] Lucieta may never have journeyed to these exotic lands, but she knew about them, and knew at least one person who had visited them. The connection to the wider world could also hit closer to home. Because Venice was a town built on travel and trade, many women had male relatives who served as sailors on private or military ships. Husbands, brothers, and sons went abroad to seek their fortune in the Venetian empire or beyond. Less fortunate women had male relatives consigned to the galleys as punishment for a crime.

In a supplica dated 1585, a widow named Cattarina asked the Pien Collegio for financial assistance. Like some of the women discussed in chapter 2, she expected help because of the service her male kin had given to the state. Cattarina had lost her father-in-law, her husband, and three sons in battle. All had served the republic at sea on Venetian galleys.[69] Andriana da Cerigo, another widow whose husband had worked on a galley ship, also asked for aid. In her petition she described how her husband had traveled all over the Middle East.[70] Anzola Barbarigo's husband had fought with the Venetian navy against the Turks and the Uskok pirates who were terrorizing the Adriatic. He had died in this service, and Anzola now expected government aid to support herself and her children.[71] Not only wives, but also children of men abroad were connected to the wider world. The siblings Laura and Zuane asked for assistance in reclaiming the property of their father, who having served the republic on a Venetian ship died in 1569 after becoming a slave to the Ottomans.[72] Livia Mafei's husband had left Venice for no less dramatic, but more scandalous, reasons. According to Livia's supplica, he moved to France after the Inquisition banished him for heresy. Livia recounted to the Pien Collegio that when he was unable to persuade her to accompany him, "he cruelly stripped me of all my goods and left me without any sustenance." She asked the court to help her with the taxes she was expected to pay in his absence.[73]

❧

ONE REASON that historians have pointed to a general female exclusion from the wider city is that the richest sources of women's activities concern members of the elite. Such sources do suggest that women's activities and movements were largely restricted to their residence and immediate vicinity.[74] However, in the area of urban mobility, we find a clear difference of opportunity between privileged and humble women.

Robert Davis and Dennis Romano make compelling cases for the seclusion of elite women. Their honor needed protecting, and their clothing, especially their unwieldy, high-heeled shoes, hampered easy movement across a street, let alone a bridge. By contrast, popolane wore less restrictive clothing and worried less about their honor, or at least conceived of it in a different way. Popolana honor could be jeopardized by suffering verbal and physical attacks, but not simply by being seen in public or in the company of a man.[75] Such freedom of movement gave them the liberty to range beyond their streets and *campi*.

Certainly women's lives were primarily built around their family and local networks of neighbors. But women's networks—familial, social, and occupational, all of which often overlapped—could extend across the city and even beyond. They created networks of relationships both near and distant. Even those women who remained largely within their neighborhoods regularly encountered women who had traveled. And people who had traveled—be they Venetians or immigrants—all contributed to a horizon for early modern women that was broad, even expansive.

CHAPTER SIX

City of Women

Institutions and Communities

INDIVIDUAL women in Venice moved beyond their homes and neigh-borhoods for a wide variety of reasons, both professional and personal. But sometimes a collective interest or project drew women from their homes as well. A group of charitable institutions founded in the second half of the sixteenth century offered many women the opportunity to par-ticipate in a citywide network that was almost entirely female. Women affiliated with these institutions in some way hailed from across Venice, and from across class boundaries: nobles and popolane found satisfaction, and sometimes salvation, through these *case di carità* (charitable homes).

In 1660, the noblewoman Elisabetta Polani found herself the target of a complaint by the governors of the Casa dei Catecumeni. This institu-tion's mandate was to convert people (often those captured in Venice's battles with the Ottoman Turks) to Christianity. A number of the Catecu-meni's charges were children; after conversion and education, some were adopted by Venetian families, others were sent into service. This was the case with a young girl named Marta, "also known as Zicale, originally Turkish and then made Christian." Marta had served Elisabetta Polani's household for five years. According to the Catecumeni's complaint, the girl had endured harsh, even brutal treatment under Elisabetta and had yet to receive payment for her service. "This [behavior on the part of Elisa-betta Polani] goes against the ethic of Christian piety, and we governors, having established that [Marta] was badly treated, have had her return to this charitable house." On Marta's behalf, the governors demanded that Polani now pay the girl five years' worth of salary. Further, they noted that "when said daughter [Marta] was sent to said noblewoman Polani, we gave her a few items of furniture to take with her." At some point during her service to Polani, Marta fell ill and spent time in hospital; upon her return to Polani's house, she found that those items had disappeared without explanation.[1]

Elisabetta Polani defended herself vigorously. She had always treated Marta with Christian love, she asserted in her rebuttal to the accusation, even taking care of her when she was ill. "For more than two years Marta suffered from the *tegna* [ulcerating head sores], and to help heal her I put her in the hospital of SS. Giovanni and Paolo and for six months, to help her health improve, I arranged for her to go out of Venice."[2] Elisabetta denied the charges of stealing the girl's furniture, refusing to pay her, and mistreating her. Such accusations, Elisabetta said, were just Marta's "fantasies," and she could explain their origin in damning terms: Marta's "false and mendacious assertions" were pathetic attempts "to cover up her bad deeds."[3] The truth, according to Elisabetta, was that Marta had betrayed her at the Polani home on the mainland. "Around three years ago I trusted her with the keys to my granary in Portogruaro," Elisabetta stated, angrily accusing her former servant of betraying her trust. She claimed that Marta "robbed me there" and "robbed me of many other things as well."[4] The flurry of accusations ceased when, according to the final document in the case, Elisabetta agreed to return Marta's possessions to her and make good on her promise to provide the girl with 25 ducats upon her marriage.[5]

The conflict between Elisabetta Polani on the one hand, and Marta and the Catecumeni, on the other, reveals how complicated women's relationships could be in early modern Venice. At the heart of this narrative lie two competing stories, with different interpretations of the power dynamic that existed between the older woman and the young girl. According to Marta (and the Catecumeni as her representative) she was the innocent victim of an exploitative employer. But Elisabetta told a different story, one of a woman who had reached out to her young servant, even tended to her while she was ill, only to have her thoughtfulness returned with venality and false accusations. This tale also demonstrates the vulnerability of servants in this period, especially women.[6] Yet we also see that even an orphan like Marta could find protection from a charitable institution.

Perhaps most interesting here is the role of the Catecumeni and its relationship to the two women. The charitable house provided Elisabetta with a servant and Marta with a livelihood by brokering the arrangement between the two. Its investment in or at least concern for Marta continued after the contract was drawn up and the young woman settled in her new home. The Catecumeni had raised Marta and converted her to Christianity and they continued to protect her after she left their care. When her relationship with Elisabetta fell apart, they took her back. But this Casa dei Catecumeni was important to Elisabetta Polani as well, and her business relationship with the institution was a typical one. It was one of several institutions that placed the young people in its care as domestic servants, while attempting to protect them by insisting on a fair wage and just treatment. Elisabetta was one of many Venetians who made such arrangements with them.

Marta's and Elisabetta Polani's relationships with the Catecumeni were only two types of exchange between women and Venice's charitable institutions in the sixteenth and seventeenth centuries. Women were the main actors in these *case:* they figured prominently among their patrons and governors and almost exclusively as their staff and charges. Charitable houses, even when designed to isolate their wards from the wider world, were embedded in a civic network of institutional, occupational, and individual relationships. Women shared, expressed, and promoted these interests. In this way, they participated in a series of relationships and institutions that connected them to the larger civic society in which they lived. Taken together, these institutions formed a community that extended across the city, connecting employers and employees, families and neighbors. By focusing on a few such institutions, the Zitelle, Soccorso, Derelitti, and Catecumeni, we can explore patterns of exchange between these *case,* women, and wider Venetian society.

CHARITY, ZEAL, AND COMMUNITY

In an earlier period, religious orders had founded small hospitals in Venice to serve the needs of small, specific groups of deserving unfortunates, such as war veterans or elderly religious laywomen. But from the 1540s on, a new movement advocating the creation of institutions that provided both salvation and shelter swept through Italy.[7] Such *case* and *ospedali* reflected a growing public focus on the shelter and upbringing of poor girls and young women.[8] Private individuals formed societies or linked up with charismatic religious leaders like Guillaume Postel to form charitable houses, or *case di carità,* which would extend civic charity more deeply and more broadly by sheltering and reforming the morally weak and materially poor and then returning them to society as productive members.

In the period between the 1540s and the 1580s, a group of Venetian nobles, many of them women, founded several institutions that ministered primarily or exclusively to women. These included the Casa delle Zitelle for young girls and the Casa del Soccorso for retired prostitutes and women seeking temporary shelter from difficult family situations. The Catecumeni and the Derelitti were not founded to help women and girls exclusively, but these homes prominently included popolane in their mission of salvation and protection.[9]

Over the course of the sixteenth and seventeenth centuries, the specific focus of some institutions blurred, as in the case of the Derelitti. Known also by its formal name, the Ospedaletto di SS. Giovanni e Paolo, the Derelitti was originally founded to shelter orphans, but came to accept wayward girls and women as well.[10] Venetians were not always sure of the differences among such institutions. A contemporary document grouping the houses together described the Derelitti, the Soccorso, and other *case* as homes for virtually anyone in need: "Places charged with the help and maintenance of various poor citizens and artisans, men, women, children, *convertite* [reformed prostitutes]."[11]

The records of these institutions reveal another dimension of Venetian life that drew women beyond their familial or neighborhood boundaries. First, women of all classes were involved in the *case,* as administrators, workers, and charges. Second, women moved beyond their neighborhoods to work, visit, or seek shelter at these houses. Finally, women participated in multiple exchanges between the institutions and the city outside its walls. By studying such exchanges, we find elements of Venetian society in which women of all classes participated in communities that challenged the boundaries of both their families and neighborhoods.

The idea behind all of these institutions was enclosure, to remove women and girls, at least for a while, from a world that had been cruel to them and offered dangerous temptations. Their charters emphasized the teaching component of their mission, and the importance of instructing the women and children in their care in religious devotion. To accomplish this, it was essential that their charges be temporarily isolated from the outside world. For example, the builders of the Casa delle Zitelle included a high wall that barred even visual access to the city beyond.[12] All of the houses worked to limit entry onto their grounds. A Derelitti document of 1572 was typical when it emphasized the necessity of keeping men who happened to be on the premises, like day laborers, away from the female wards to prevent "the scandals and dangers that could otherwise develop."[13]

Thus isolated, the casa's wards were instructed to devote themselves to pious contemplation mixed with industriousness. The Zitelle charter is illustrative of the spirit with which such institutions were founded and structured.[14] Set up by elite women, this house's mission was to shelter and train its charges in pious comportment. The young women also learned a skill, like sewing, that would make them useful employees or wives when they left. The fortunate few who gained admission to the Zitelle eventually emerged with three options: they could marry, enter the religious life, or stay on as employees of the home, overseeing the care and education of their successors.

Admission policies were stringent. The Derelitti, Zitelle, and Soccorso were particularly attractive resources for poor girls and their parents. The Catecumeni, founded to convert children and adults to Christianity, drew its wards from a different pool. All of them most basically provided their charges with shelter, clothing, and food. They could also offer them a degree of insurance for the future, since they all provided some type of dowry to enable girls to marry. It may be the high demand for entry that led the Zitelle, Derelitti, and Soccorso to establish strict guidelines for admission, sometimes repeatedly.[15]

Women who found shelter at the Soccorso were generally chosen by the noblemen and noblewomen who acted as its benefactors and administrators.[16] Once a woman came to the attention of this group, two of the governors visited her. They inspected her and her home to ensure that she was deserving. If she was found to be "without sin, . . . old, ugly, ill, pregnant, or living with her husband . . . she may not be accepted."[17] A woman, then, had clearly to have sinned (through prostitution or adultery) and be relatively healthy, young, and attractive (hence presumably in danger of sinning again) in order to hope for a place at the Soccorso. Youth and beauty were also prime prerequisites for admission to the Zitelle, where the governors focused on young girls who had been pushed by family members into a life of sin. To ensure that applicants hailed from such difficult circumstances, a member of the governing board was supposed to visit each applicant in her home to ensure that she was as lovely, and her situation as dire, as she or her relatives had described.[18]

Applicants and governors sometimes tried to bend the rules of admission for individual cases. The Zitelle and Soccorso both passed resolutions admonishing governors who tried to sponsor particular candidates without going through the proper channels. The Derelitti passed several measures reiterating the importance of following procedure. In 1566, the board reminded its members that a quorum was necessary to vote on girls before they could be accepted into the casa.[19] Twenty years later, the board complained that too many girls were gaining entry by claiming illness and checking into the infirmary, afterwards simply staying on.[20]

However they managed to enter a casa, women and girls did so from across the city. In 1597, a Zitelle administrator recorded the origins of the shelter's current charges, listing them by charitable fraternity, or *scuola*. That year, all six of the Scuole Grandi were represented: seven girls came from the Scuola della Carità, eight from the Misericordia, four from San Teodoro, five from San Rocco, nine from San Marco, and four from San Giovanni.[21]

Once a girl or woman gained entry to one of these institutions, she found herself in a female environment. At the head of the Zitelle and Soccorso was the *madonna*, a wellborn woman who was either widowed or unmarried and at least 40 years old.[22] She was selected by the female governors, or *governatrici*, and the women who would serve her in the house, the *coadjutrici*.[23] Once established in the casa, the madonna relied on the coadjutrici (usually two in the case of the Soccorso, one in the house of the Zitelle) and the *maestre*, or housekeepers. The former were from noble families, often selected at a young age to be trained for a job that was seen as a vocation.[24]

The case of the Zitelle provides the clearest example of an intensely female environment. At the Zitelle, the coadjutrici dealt with the girls on a daily basis, oversaw the physical maintenance of both the girls and their quarters, and reported regularly to the madonna. Their duties were carefully spelled out in the constitution.[25] The coadjutrice was elected by the governatrici and the presiding madonna. A candidate had to be at least 30 years of age and to have spent at least "five or six" years at the house, presumably in some sort of apprenticeship. In addition, she was to "know how to write and figure" and be "an alert woman, yet humble and devout."[26]

At the lowest rung in the staff hierarchy of the Zitelle were the maestre. These women acted both as housekeepers and big sisters to the young girls. The madonna and the coadjutrici were instructed never to reprimand the maestre in front of the young girls, "so that the respect for and the authority of [the maestre] shall be maintained."[27] For their part, the women administering the house were reminded that without the maestre "this house could not be governed effectively, for they are like great columns which support the place."[28] The maestre enjoyed the closest daily contact with the girls and were exhorted not to engage in either excessive violence or affection toward them.

The maestre, elected from among the zitelle themselves, began their tenure as young women.[29] Their duties included teaching the girls to read, training them in a skill, supervising their prayers, and making sure they dressed properly.[30] The charter instructed the maestre to live according to the creed that "the hours spent in the governance, care, and administration of these virgins are hours well spent, and the distractions and difficulties [distrazzioni e le fatiche] of these duties . . . will pass."[31] In addition to their function as role models to the girls in their care, each maestra had a particular duty. One woman guarded the chapel; another acted as porter to protect the house from unwanted visitors. The latter was also in charge of buying bread for the house and accompanying (male) manual laborers to their work site, presumably to prevent contact between them and the virgin wards.[32]

At the Soccorso, Derelitti, and Zitelle, women dominated the staff. The girls and women who entered these houses found themselves enclosed in a world defined by female authority, discipline, and support. These communities drew on two traditions: that of the convent; and that of neighborhood networks, where wealthier or older women could exercise some authority by virtue of their status and role as potential benefactresses.[33] In the *case,* a web of relationships built on those models and fused them by linking an enclosed, primarily female community to the wider world. As we shall see, these sheltered environments were in fact the site of regular and varied exchanges with the city beyond their walls.

INSIDE THE INSTITUTION

Despite the desire of these institutions' founders to isolate their charges from the world, people moved into and out of the *case* with relative ease. Those entering the homes brought news, experiences, and reminders of the outside world, eroding the barriers between them and the women and girls confined to the grounds. While new wards and employees settled permanently into the home, renouncing wider society for the moment, they nonetheless brought descriptions of that society with them as they told their own stories.

There was less permanent traffic into the *case* as well. Day laborers came to work on the grounds and make repairs. These were the men that the maestre were advised to keep apart from the *zitelle* and *soccorse,* as the wards of the Zitelle and Soccorso were known. There were other, higher-class visitors to the *case:* the governatrici, of course—the women on the board of governors—and noblewomen called *protettrici,* the financial patrons of the casa. Governatrici had to be of mature age and to have lived an exemplary life of deep spirituality and good works. They also had to demonstrate sincere devotion to the project at hand; the Soccorso charter mandated that a governatrice's work with a house not simply be one of many charitable activities: "They are not to be greatly occupied with other pious works, so that with the maximum diligence they can attend to this place without harming another."[34] Their power was considerable: governatrici of the Soccorso had the final say when it came to selecting new wards. The Soccorso's madonna was cautioned not to attempt to bring wards of her choice into the hospital but to leave the selection to these wealthy, illustrious women.[35] Given their assumption of such responsibilities, it was expected that governatrici would visit their favorite charity regularly. The Soccorso charter offered its esteemed guests one gentle suggestion: when governatrici visited the casa, they should treat all of the women they encountered there equally, without favoring any one ward in particular.[36]

As patrons, prottetrici were also invited and expected to visit their charities frequently. They were given a personal tour by a governatrice, a woman of the same social standing. The madonna and the coadjutrici gave these special visitors free rein: they were allowed to view the grounds and speak with the wards. Other elite women, too, especially potential benefactresses, were able to visit. The casa hoped thereby to gain their approval and secure their largesse: visits by women of privilege were a crucial way of cultivating sponsorship. So important were such guests that the Zitelle charter included a chapter entitled "On the Manner in which the Governatrici, with the Madonna, Should Show the House to Those Gentlewomen and Ladies Who Wish to See It."[37] The charter also noted that these women might wish to offer advice and that the staff would be wise to heed any and all suggestions. In the case of board members and patronesses, words could be backed by action: if a protettrice noted a serious problem, she had the power, along with the governatrici, to replace the woman responsible.[38]

In addition to these highly prized visitors, other Venetians came to the *case* to leave donations, large and small. By 1590 the Derelitti governors had to create a new position to deal with these informal contributions. From the maestre, they appointed a *portiniera,* a woman whose duty it was to stay by the door and receive casual donations. She was to keep a careful written account of all income and to deliver it promptly to the governatrici or madonna.[39]

The wards of the Soccorso, Zitelle, and Derelitti had some contact with their patrons, but the staff took pains to guard them from the male laborers who worked on the grounds. It is also unlikely that they saw much of the passers-by who left contributions for their sustenance. Nor were they supposed to have much contact with their family and friends. The Casa del Soccorso was particularly strict about such encounters. Visits to women or girls by men were generally forbidden, and even visits by women were strictly controlled.[40] The Soccorso charter viewed female relatives as presenting a particular danger: "The relatives of the soccorse, like mothers, sisters and other scandalous women of corrupt ways [*mala vita*], shall never be permitted to speak with them." Encounters between soccorse and outside visitors were permitted only when the prospective visitor met the staff's standards: "If they have female acquaintances who are virtuous, they may be permitted to visit occasionally, but very rarely and then only in the presence of a governatrice."[41] Rules about visits were less strict at the Derelitti, but—as the case of Paolina and Madona Faustina with which this book opens demonstrates—such visits could have disastrous results.[42]

Wards of the Zitelle, too, were supposed to remain secluded for the duration of their stay. Yet they must have had contact with relatives because when they married and left the casa, they sometimes did so with familial assistance. Although the casa was the architect of the marriages and provided the bulk of the ward's dowry, extant dowry contracts drawn up for zitelle in the early seventeenth century show a high level of involvement on the part of uncles and fathers, who supplemented dowries and gave formal consent to the match. Some of the brides had maintained close enough relations with their families to marry into their father's profession. Of the twenty-nine documents that give the occupations of both the zitella's father and her husband, twelve name men with the same occupation as the bride's father. In four of these cases, the trade was weaving; the list also includes masons, boatmen, servants, tailors, and spice vendors.[43] In these cases, the families of the bride were likely involved in arranging the match.[44]

LEAVING THE INSTITUTION

There was as much traffic out of the houses as into them, which deepened their connection to civic society. As they married or entered employment, wards exited, sometimes for weeks or months at a time and sometimes forever. Employees, of course, regularly ventured out to the city on errands. At the Soccorso and Zitelle, one of the maestre's primary duties was to visit the residences of wealthy Venetians to ask for financial help for the house. Particular maestre were selected for the job. They had to be articulate and presentable enough to describe their institution's mission in terms that would elicit sympathy and respect. Such maestre, according to the charter, had to be of impeccable reputation and at least 40 years old (presumably past the age of temptation). "And upon their return to the house, they will inform the madonna or the coadjutrice of the balance of their day's activities, and they will turn in the charity, be it bread or money or whatever has been given to the house."[45]

The Casa dei Derelitti appears to have been the only house that permitted its female wards to enjoy a change of scenery before leaving the place permanently.[46] According to its charter, girls could leave the home under certain conditions (these were not explicitly described). They had to request permission and explain the circumstances. If the request was approved, the girl had to travel by boat, not on foot (presumably to minimize casual or planned encounters of which the board would not approve). Of course, she could not travel alone; a female guardian had to accompany her.[47]

Wards also left the Derelitti for lengthier periods of time to work, usually in domestic service. Leaving the institution in this way did not mean the wards broke off all their ties with it, even if they left permanently. Because the Derelitti sponsored their charges and drew up the contracts with employers, they remained responsible for the young servants after they had left the premises. The Derelitti charter even included a chapter entitled "The Defense of Orphans Put Out to Service."[48] The girls (and boys) were placed with employers for a trial period of fifteen days, at which point a more binding contract was agreed upon. When conflicts between master and servant arose, the Derelitti urged an objective hearing to ensure that the servant was not exploited because of her vulnerable position. In cases of runaway servants, for example, the Derelitti acknowledged that employers deserved reimbursement, but also recommended that a hearing determine whether or not the girl had been treated unjustly.[49]

When the Catecumeni defended Marta against Elisabetta Polani, therefore, the charitable house was behaving in an appropriate, normal way; it was not being unusually or surprisingly altruistic. When the Derelitti charter was drafted, its framers recognized the potential for exploitation that existed when orphans entered the world of domestic service. The staff were urged to bear in mind "the piety and charity that one must exercise in this holy place, placing above all else the care of the poor orphaned boys and girls for the Lord our God." The charter enjoined the staff to "always be vigilant for the health of the souls [of these children] and the use of their bodies, and not permit that those who for a day are given [a child in service], after having reached a written agreement, think themselves free, with little fear of God, to keep these girls and boys [in service]." The charter went on to lament that some unscrupulous employers also held on to the children's few possessions and disregarded the contracts they had signed with the institution.[50]

Some wards left the Derelitti and the Catecumeni to enter domestic service; many others eventually left these institutions and the Zitelle permanently by entering Venetian society as wives; and sometimes they left as daughters. The Catecumeni offered Venetian families the possibility of adopting its charges, thus permitting them to enter a family on the most intimate level. Seven-year-old Cattarina, a Turkish girl, was adopted by Bortholo, a sandal maker, and his wife Madalena, in 1576.[51] In their formal request to adopt her, Bortholo and Madalena explained that they were "married but without children, and at an age when they can no longer have any." Were they merely looking for a servant? The language used suggests otherwise. They wrote that they had decided "to adopt a little daughter for comfort, comfort in their old age." Even if Bortholo and Madalena were cynically using adoption to acquire cheap labor, it is significant that they felt the need to create the image of their shared loneliness and need for a child. To reassure the Catecumeni that their motives were sincere, they promised that they "would accept her as an adoptive daughter, treating her, raising her, and teaching her good habits, and persevering in the teachings of the holy faith just as if she were born of them."[52]

Such assurances were not unusual. The Catecumeni insisted that people wishing to adopt affirm their good intentions regarding their prospective sons and daughters. When possible, they were expected to back up their words with contractual actions. In 1577, a tailor named Zordan and his wife Margarita, from the parish of S. Felice, adopted an 11-year old girl. Like Bortolo and Madalena, Zordan and Margarita promised to raise and educate the girl as they would a biological daughter and to provide her with a dowry at the time of marriage.[53]

Sometimes women adopted girls on their own. The noble widow Leonarda Tron, originally from Ferrara, petitioned to "accept as a daughter of the soul the young and honest Nicolosa, daughter of Teodor from Lepanto, made a Christian and raised in the house of the Catecumeni." Leonarda vowed to care for Nicolosa "with the appropriate charity and love, supplying, feeding and dressing her with the proper decency [*con quella carittà, et amorevolezza che si conviene, spesandola, alimentandola et vestendola condecentemente*]." As proof of her commitment, Leonarda promised to will Nicolosa some substantial properties, including real estate in the town of Este.[54]

Marriage, however, was perhaps the most common circumstance under which a Zitella or a Derelitti ward left a charitable house. And even if a girl had already left to start work, when she married the institution was still involved. Marietta, the daughter of a spice vendor, had once lived at the Derelitti. In 1574, after she had moved out to work as a washerwoman for the noble Giulia Pisani, she left her place of employment to marry. The Derelitti governors agreed to give her 15 ducats as a dowry, "along with the things that were promised to her in the event of her marriage."[55] We have already seen that the Zitelle regularly dowered its charges, and brides from the Catecumeni, too, also received help. Maria, a "daughter of the venerable Catecumeni," received a dowry from that institution to marry a tailor named Francesco.[56]

Contact did not cease once the marriage was sealed. Former zitelle, for example, were sure to meet with governatrici after they married. The Zitelle charter required that governatrici visit their newlyweds regularly, for three reasons. First, governatrici were reminded that the young women still had emotional ties to their former homes and institutional family: "The governatrici must remember that these daughters do not have mothers other than themselves." Second, such visits were good for the girls' souls: "Visiting them frequently will keep the fear of God in them." Third, the visits of powerful women to the bride's home could have a salutary effect on the new marriage itself: "It is also good that with these visits the husband will not treat [their wives] badly, since they will see that they are under the protection of many matrons." Thus, the former zitelle would know that they always had someone to whom they could turn in a crisis: "When these daughters are in need, they must notify the congregation of governatrici, who will have [already] visited them, to ask advice regarding what they should do to resolve the issue."[57]

Leaving such an institution for good, then, did not mean breaking off all contact. As women moved into the city, they kept ties to their former homes, and probably received news of their former companions. Whether a ward turned servant, adoptee, or bride, she could rely on protection in times of trouble. At least, this was the institutions' intention.

Fleeting Encounters

Was former residence at the institutions described above something to be hidden or denied? Living at such a place may or may not have been a source of shame. The successful matches between former wards and respectable men suggest it was not. The charitable institutions were woven into a larger civic tapestry—an aspect of Venetian life that people knew on different levels. If most Venetians did not work or lodge at the Derelitti, Zitelle, Soccorso, or Catecumeni, they may well have known someone who did, and when graduates of these institutions entered or reentered Venetian neighborhoods as wives, servants, or adopted daughters, they brought with them information about life in the *case*.

Even Venetians who had not lived in, sent a relative to, or married someone from a charitable house could engage in an exchange with one. The Derelitti and Catecumeni were sources of labor, so men and women might journey to them to contract for a servant. Venetians had a visual familiarity with the *case* simply by walking past them. They were scattered across the city: the Zitelle on the Giudecca, the Catecumeni at SS. Apostoli, the Soccorso at Santa Maria del Carmine, and the Derelitti by the hospital of San Giovanni and Paolo (see map on page 2).

Those who neither traveled to the *case* on business, passed by them while walking elsewhere, nor knew someone connected to one of them might still hear about them when drawing up a will. Notaries were required to suggest charitable donations to testators, and some included these institutions in their list of options.[58] The results were mixed: people often left bequests to the institutions only on the condition that a long list of heirs predeceased the testator. Nevertheless, testamentary bequests made up an important source of funds for such houses.

Two sisters, Lodovica and Borthola di Marinoni, drafted a joint will in 1584. Apparently neither woman was married. With no husbands or children to provide for, they left the bulk of their wealth to three pious institutions: the Incurabili (a hospital for those with incurable diseases); SS. Giovanni and Paolo, and the Casa delle Zitelle. Each institution received 300 ducats. The sisters left explicit instructions on how their legacies should be used: "with these conditions, that the governors of the two hospitals and the above-named house invest these monies in the name of the sisters and benefactresses, but invest the money well, so that there will be something each year for the governors to use to help the daughters of these three institutions to marry or become nuns."[59] For the Marinoni sisters, the primary function of these institutions was to shelter girls in anticipation of marriage or entering a convent. The association, for them, between charitable houses and the plight of young women was indelible.

Lodovica and Borthola were typical in their instructions. Testaments that left money to these institutions almost always contained specific directions for its distribution.[60] The instructions reflected the benefactors' investment in and knowledge of these institutions and their role in Venetian society. The noble Andrea Marcello left a bequest of 200 ducats to the Derelitti to dower ten girls.[61] Domenico Bonaro did the same.[62] In 1611, Vicenzo di Garzoni's bequest of money to the Casa di Catecumeni included details on how the legacy should be distributed—"to Jews, or Turks, or Moors, male and female, over the age of twelve."[63] Prudentia Calafado was less specific; in her will of 1557, she made a simple bequest to the "little children of SS. Giovanni e Paolo" (i.e., the Derelitti).[64]

℃

AT LEAST since Michel Foucault's *Discipline and Punish* and *Madness and Civilization,* scholars have interpreted institutions such as the Derelitti and the Zitelle as tools of repression and control.[65] Here I have suggested ways in which they could also function as part of an expansive female society. The *case* described above certainly restricted the movements of women who lived within them. But they also offered those women new ways of interacting with one another and with the larger urban environment. Once they left the institution, girls and women reentered Venetian society equipped with skills and the protection of an institution behind them; if they married, they also received a partial dowry. The very existence of these institutions signaled a new level of social consciousness about the plight of poor women. That such institutions, designed to rehabilitate and protect women and girls, should exist, should enjoy the protection of Venice's elite, and should merit mention by notaries as they counseled their clients, placed women on the map of civic concerns and responsibilities.

As Counter Reformation institutions, the *case* were founded with the pious mission of salvation. They brought rich and poor women together, united to improve the lives of unfortunate members of their sex and to improve society in the process. The Catecumeni saw conversion to Christianity as consistent with that aim. But the founders defined salvation in a new way: salvation of the body as well as the soul. Women and girls, especially, had to be taken from the streets, from poverty, from sin (as prostitutes or heathens) and sheltered and nourished in body and spirit to prepare them for reentry into the world. To do this, a community of women cared for and taught the women and girls who entered the *case*, though inevitably they had to turn away some who wanted to stay.

Two levels of community emerge from the histories of these institutions. The first was local, within the houses themselves. It was a predominantly if not exclusively female environment, grounded in the belief that society as much as internal weakness can contribute to sin. The mission of the *case* was twofold: to remove the charges to a safe place, away from the squalor of their lives outside, and at the same time to prepare them to return to that society when their education was complete.

The charitable houses offered women access to a new kind of community, albeit one with a great many restrictions. Life in a charitable institution was one option for women across the city of Venice away from traditional networks; choosing it allowed (or forced) them to participate in communities largely independent of their neighborhoods or families. The success and usefulness of the *case* for many women is evident from the institutions' longevity; they continued to minister to the needs of Venetian women until the end of the eighteenth century. Of course, the majority of sixteenth-century Venetians were neither charges nor employees of any of the *case*. But that many of them were certainly aware of the existence and mission of such institutions is shown by the many bequests Venetians made to them.

The institutions were not perfect. Nor is our information about them definitive. Their spotty records cannot tell us the consistency with which the *case* placed their charges in successful situations after they left their walls. We know little about the reality of daily life within the houses themselves. But we do know that girls and women left the *case* to enter families as adopted daughters and to build their own families as wives. We know that when one servant, Marta, accused her employer of exploitation, her parent institution was quick to support her. In some cases, at least, the institutions made good on their intentions to protect their charges during and after their stay.

The second level of community was citywide. Venetians knew about the *case* because they had friends or relatives who worked or lived there, because they had hired servants from them, or because they had neighbors who had a connection to them. They knew about the Zitelle and Derelitti enough to want to send more children there than the places could handle. They also knew about them because notaries asked testators to consider bequeathing money to them in their wills.

Through these institutions, Venetian women participated in a citywide network of charity, adoption, marriage, and employment. The *case* offered a multitude of roles, and in these roles women moved definitively beyond the boundaries of their neighborhoods, families, and households. For the women who entered the institutions, and their families, it was a radical move. For others, whose contact with a charitable house was fleeting or temporary, the casa was simply one thread in the tapestry of their world. My point is not that these institutions were of crucial importance to many Venetian women (though they were for some), but that women's connections to the *case* reveal the broad and complex pattern of citywide relationships women enjoyed in early modern Venice—relationships that took them, mentally and physically, out of their homes and neighborhoods into the city at large.

Conclusion

THE women of early modern Venice, whether popolana or privileged, lived multidimensional lives. They participated one way or another in a variety of civic bodies—some of them poor women in need of help; some of them privileged women seeking to live socially engaged lives. It was not only institutions such as the Zitelle and the Soccorso that gave women an opportunity to assert their place in Venetian life beyond the neighborhood: they also came before the Inquisition or secular courts as plaintiffs and witnesses; they traveled to the office of the Pien Collegio to plead for or demand assistance.

Venetian women's lives were layered with different levels of experience, challenge, and possibility. Within their homes, women shared their lodgings with men and women, parents and children, relatives, friends, boarders, and landlords. A woman's position within the home was not fixed: it was nuanced by—and sometimes even defined by—her economic situation. Income, occupation, ownership of property, and inheritances all played a part in creating living patterns through which women reinforced or broke the ties that linked them to people near and far—kin, friends, and neighbors. For both economic and personal reasons, women and men moved freely between street and household. Neighbors helped one another and could at times provide support, economic and emotional, if it was lacking in the home.

In the living patterns and property disbursements revealed by the civic records, we see that women's lives were intimately bound up with family members, especially immediate family. But female networks of work and sociability complemented familial support systems. Those networks could begin in the home, where women sometimes lived and worked together. Such networks extended out into a neighborhood of women and men who exchanged goods, services, and gossip; and sometimes the networks moved beyond the neighborhood and even beyond Venice itself. The city was one into which immigrants poured and from which the populace, including women, traveled, not only between parishes but to the mainland and beyond in search of work, companionship, or freedom.

Venice was not an isolated case. Early modern Europe was fluid and urban women moved easily between their communities of family, neighborhood, and the wider world. They had overlapping networks of familial, social, and business relationships. Whether in London, Florence, or the cities of the Low Countries, women forged connections to other women and men, expanding their options and their world in the process.[1]

Being a popolana in early modern Venice was certainly not easy. The lives of working women were difficult, plagued by poverty, disease, overcrowding, and crime. Recognizing female agency and mobility does not mean ignoring the difficult circumstances under which most poor people labored in early modern Venice. But female spaces, and with them the range of women's options, were greater than have been imagined. Women's roles within the home, the neighborhood, and the city at large bespeak agency, strength, and confidence. This was manifested in the petitions women brought to the city's appeals court and their requests for marital separation to the patriarchal court. It was displayed in the relative ease with which women might hold property or earn money. It was displayed in the choices women made about where they lived, what sort of labor they performed, whom they associated with, and whom they loved. Daily, Venetian women worked, traveled, and contested obstacles in ways that made the city their own.

Appendix

A Note about the

Status Animarum

The *status animarum,* or soul counts, are housed at the Patriarchal Archive of Venice.[1] Forty-seven censuses are in the collection—almost exactly two-thirds of the seventy-one Venetian parishes of the period.[2] Most of them appear to have been recorded in the 1590s, although one is dated 1607. Taken together, the censuses cover a total of 94,862 persons and 19,444 households.[3] Individual members of households are listed in the following way: the head of the household is named first, followed by other inhabitants who are identified by name and relation to the first person listed. The order is consistent: after the head of household comes that person's spouse, followed by any children of the couple. Then come parents, then brothers and sisters, then servants, and finally other people, most of whom appear to be boarders. A typical entry for a household with a couple at its head appears as:

Jacopo, baker
Simonetta, his wife
Zuanne, his son
Lucieta, his daughter
Margarita, his mother-in-law
Susanna and Chiara, his maids
Tommaso, his apprentice
Carlo, builder, who rents
Maria, Carlo's wife

A household with a widow at the head typically appears as:

Giustina, widow
Francesco, her son, worker
Catarina, her daughter, widow
Filippo, her grandson, 1 year old
Orsetta, widow, who rents

Notes

INTRODUCTION

1. ASV, Ospedali e Luoghi Pii, B. 921, filza 5, doc. 97, sixteenth century, un-dated. This document has been transcribed by Giuseppe Ellero in *Un'Ospedale della riforma cattolica*, pp. 161–62.

2. On noblewomen, see Stanley Chojnacki's work, including "Marriage Legis-lation" and "Nobility, Women, and the State"; on women writers in early mod-ern Venice, see Patricia Labalme, "Venetian Women on Women"; on the writer Moderata Fonte specifically, see Ginevra Conti Odorisio, *Donna e società*; and on the courtesan Veronica Franco, see Margaret Rosenthal, *The Honest Courtesan*.

3. Some examples: Marilyn Boxer and Jean H. Quataert, eds., *Connecting Spheres*; Isabelle Chabot, "La Reconnaissance du travail des femmes"; Sherrill Cohen, *The Evolution of Women's Asylums since 1500*; Natalie Zemon Davis, "Women in the Crafts"; R. B. Outhwaite, ed., *Marriage and Society*, pp. 81–100; Renate Bri-denthal and Claudia Koonz, eds., *Becoming Visible*; Barbara A. Hanawalt, ed., *Women and Work*; Julie Hardwick, "Widowhood and Patriarchy"; Martha C. Howell, *Women, Production, and Patriarchy*; Margaret Leah King, *Women of the Re-naissance*; Christiane Klapisch-Zuber, *Women, Family, and Ritual*; Odorisio, *Donna e società*; Mary Prior, ed., *Women in English Society*; Joan W. Scott and Louise A. Tilly, *Women, Work, and Family*; Merry E. Wiesner, *Working Women in Renaissance Germany*.

4. See, for example, King, *Women of the Renaissance*; Klapisch-Zuber, *Women, Family, and Ritual*; and Robert C. Davis, "The Geography of Gender." Not all histo-rians focus primarily on women's activities within the home. See Samuel Cohn Jr., "Donne in piazza e donne in tribunale."

5. For example, Chojnacki's work, including "Patrician Women," "La Posi-zione della Donna," and "The Power of Love." See also James Grubb, *Provincial Families of the Renaissance*, and Anna Bellavitis, " 'Per cittadini.' " Bellavitis also has a book on citizen women forthcoming.

6. Edward Muir, in *Civic Ritual*, has described how women were increasingly pushed out of public rituals after the fifteenth century. Davis asserts that male fes-tivals and general rowdiness sometimes resulted in violence to ensure that sections of town would remain resolutely male. Davis, "Geography of Gender."

7. King, chap. 1 of *Women of the Renaissance*, Grubb, *Provincial Families;* David Herlihy and Christiane Klapisch-Zuber, *Tuscans and Their Families;* for Northern Europe, see Martha C. Howell, *The Marriage Exchange.* Grubb and Herlihy and Klapisch-Zuber examine the lives of both women and men by organizing their studies along stages of life. On single women specifically, see Chojnacka in the recently published collection *Singlewomen in the European Past,* ed. Judith Bennett and Amy Froide. On widowhood, see Barbara J. Todd, "The Remarrying Widow"; Christiane Klapisch-Zuber, *Women, Family, and Ritual;* and Ida Blom, "The History of Widowhood." On the differences, including the different risks, between wealthy and poor widowhood, see Maura Palazzi, "Abitare da sole," esp. p. 46.

8. For work in the same vein, see Samuel Cohn Jr., *Women in the Streets.*

9. Chojnacki, "Patrician Women" and "Power of Love"; and Maria Pia Pedani, "L'osservanza imposta." There is also a smaller body of work on upper-class, non-patrician women. See, for example, Labalme, "Venetian Women"; Odorisio, *Donna e società;* and Bellavitis, " 'Per cittadini.' "

10. Romano discusses female servants in his *Housecraft and Statecraft.* Guido Ruggiero has studied cases of magic involving popular-class women in *Binding Passions.* Florence has been the richest source for work on Italian women of the popular classes. See Christiane Klapisch-Zuber's work in *Women, Family, and Ritual;* Chabot, "La Reconnaissance"; Cohn, "Donne in piazza"; and Judith C. Brown, "A Woman's Place Was in the Home." For Rome, see Elisabeth Cohen, "Honor and Gender."

11. Class is hard to define in early modern Venice. Technically, there were three distinct secular classes: the patriciate, the citizen class, and the popolani. On the patriciate, see Stanley Chojnacki, "Political Adulthood" and "In Search of the Venetian Patriciate"; also Alexander Cowan, *The Urban Patriciate.* On the citizen class, see Bellavitis, " 'Per cittadini,' " and Andrea Zannini, "Un ceto di funzionari." The popolani were the largest class, comprising a wide range of wealth and status since the category stretched from merchants to beggars. Most popolani were humble people, but some were prosperous folk who employed servants and married up. On different branches of the popolani, see Richard Mackenney, *Tradesmen and Traders,* and esp. Dennis Romano, *Patricians and Popolani.*

12. On the uses and definitions of experience and identity for investigations into the lives of women or other marginalized groups in history, see Joan W. Scott, "Experience."

13. On Venice's shift to manufacturing in the sixteenth century, see Domenico Sella, "The Rise and Fall," and Frederic Lane, *Venice: A Maritime Republic,* pp. 309–21.

14. John J. Martin has shown in several works how the religious turmoil of the sixteenth century fostered a new atmosphere of debate in which men and women of the popular classes were active participants. Martin, "Out of the Shadow," "Salvation and Society," and *Venice's Hidden Enemies.*

15. Because they are so rich, these trial records, or *processi,* have been explored by many historians asking different questions about Venetian society. See, for example, Pier Cesare Ioly Zorattini, *Processi del S. Uffizio;* Ruggiero, *Binding Passions;* Martin, *Venice's Hidden Enemies;* and Ruth Martin, *Witchcraft and the Inquisition.*

16. The importance of defining parish boundaries was discussed in the Council of Trent's twenty-fourth session. See *Canons and Decrees of the Council of Trent,* chap. 13, pp. 203–4.

17. For brief references to these censuses by other historians, see Paolo Ulvioni, *Il gran castigo di Dio,* intro.; and Giovanni Favero et al., "Le anime dei demografi."

18. See Dennis Romano, "Gender and the Urban Geography"; and Davis, "Geography of Gender."

ONE. RESIDENCE, SEX, AND MARRIAGE

1. Both parish registers can be found at the Archivio Storico della Curia Patriarcale in Venice (ASCP), status animarum, B. 3.

2. Although information on the marriage age of sixteenth-century commoners is scant for Venice, the general trend throughout Europe was that of a later marriage age among the general population than among the elites. See Anthony Molho, *Marriage Alliance,* pp. 138–39. Marzio Barbagli has suggested that age at marriage is related to the spouses' type of residence, with patrilocal settings encouraging marriage at an earlier age and neolocal settings favoring unions at a later age. See his "La famiglia nel mutamento." More recently, Barbagli's article "Three Household Formation Systems" offers an excellent synopsis of the relevant historiography on the subject. For other countries, see Lawrence Stone, *The Family, Sex, and Marriage,* pp. 42–45; Peter Laslett, *The World We Have Lost,* pp. 81–92; Jean-Louis Flandrin, *Families in Former Times,* pp. 185–86; and Dorothy McLaren, "Marital Fertility," pp. 38–39.

3. On the impatience of young nobles who had to to wait for economic independence and entry into political society, see Chojnacki, "Political Adulthood."

4. IRE, TEST, 834, Feb. 1579 and TEST, 598, Mar. 1610. For other examples, see ibid., TEST, 660, doc. 2, Mar. 1551.

5. On the culture of the shipyards and other trades in early modern Venice, as well as apprenticeships, see Richard Rapp, *Industry and Economic Decline,* and Robert C. Davis, *Shipbuilders of the Venetian Arsenal.*

6. On domestic service in Venice, see Romano, *Housecraft and Statecraft.* On female occupations in early modern Tuscany, see Brown, "A Woman's Place."

7. Paola Pavanini, "Abitazioni popolari."

8. Pavanini has calculated sixteenth-century rents in Venice by working backward from the data collected by Daniele Beltrami for 1661. Pavanini makes her calculations based on the assumption of 250 working days a year. Pavanini, "Abitazioni popolari." pp. 66–68, 89, 109.

9. Pavanini offers a tentative description of expenses for a typical family of four: "Around the middle of the sixteenth century we have, for a nuclear family of four people (two of whom are children): around twenty ducats a year for bread, 5–6 ducats for rent, two ducats approximately for meat (for three pounds weekly), four to six ducats for condiments, wine, and miscellaneous. We arrive at 30 to 35 ducats, to which we must add the cost of heat and light . . . on an annual salary of little more than forty ducats, there is not much room for anything else." Ibid., p. 72.

10. I have identified as widows those women in the "sibling" category who carry the title *vedova* (widow) after their names.

11. ASCP, Archivio Segreto, status animarum, B. 3, S. Ternità.

12. Herlihy and Klapisch-Zuber found a few cases of siblings sheltering siblings in their study of Florence's 1427 catasto, but their conclusions suggest that the vast majority of these were men who were living in the house of a married brother. *Tuscans and Their Families,* pp. 292–94.

13. Unlike that of women, men's marital status is almost never specified in the census. Thus, we have no way of knowing whether or not these men were widowed, unless they appear to have children. For more information on widowers, see Monica Chojnacka, "City of Women," pp. 234–35.

14. ASCP, Archivio Segreto, status animarum, SS. Apostoli.

15. Christiane Klapisch-Zuber has been one of the most compelling voices suggesting that women's roles with both their natal and marital family circles were generally limited. More recently, however, Thomas Kuehn has suggested that "we may be placing an excessive emphasis on the degree to which marriage severed a woman from her natal patriline." Klapisch-Zuber, *Women, Family, and Ritual;* and Kuehn, *Law, Family, and Women,* p. 240.

16. On the relation between a married woman's earning power and her authority within her family, see Brown, "A Woman's Place."

17. ASCP, Archivio Segreto, status animarum, B. 3, S. Giovanni Novo.

18. Ibid., B. A. 1., SS. Apostoli.

19. Ibid.

20. For an excellent survey of Venice's economic growth in the sixteenth century, see Domenico Sella, "L'Economia."

21. ASCP, Archivio Segreto, status animarum, B. 3, S. Giovanni Novo.

22. Ibid.

23. On servants living with their employers, see Romano, *Housecraft and Statecraft,* chap. 3.

24. ASCP, Archivio Segreto, status animarum, B. 3, S. Giovanni Novo. We have no way of knowing whether Vienna was the widowed sister of Jacomo's wife or the widow of Jacomo's brother.

25. Ibid., B. 2, S. Matteo.

26. Ibid., B. 3, S. Ternità.

27. Ibid., S. Giovanni Novo.

28. Archivio di Stato di Venezia (ASV), S. Uffizio, B. 70, #16.

29. That statement requires some qualification. The number of both unmarried men and women living with parents was almost certainly higher than the figure indicated by the parish registers. Since age was rarely recorded in the registers, the only means of identifying a son or daughter as an adult are the presence in the records of a spouse, children, occupation, or title of some kind, such as "*Donna Elisabetta, sua figlia*" instead of merely "Elisabetta, sua figlia." The single men listed as living in the homes of their parents were generally identified by occupation; adult daughters without husbands were most commonly described as widows. The result is that never-married adult women are those most likely to have been excluded from my census count.

30. See Klapisch-Zuber, " 'Cruel Mother.' "

31. This is not to suggest that elite brides maintained no contact whatever with their natal families. Recent studies of noblewomen's wills show that Venetian *patrizie* remembered siblings, nieces, nephews, and other relatives from their own families many years after leaving the natal home for marriage. See Chojnacki, "Patrician Women" and "The Power of Love."

32. Angela's household consisted of herself, her two daughters and their husbands, her mother, and two sisters. ASCP, Archivio Segreto, status animarum, B. 3, S. Matteo.

33. Patrician households are difficult to identify in these registers because of the fluidity of certain titles, specifically *Clarissimo* and *Magnifico*. Sometimes these refer to nobles and at other times to citizens in the merchant class. The merchants were below the hereditary patriciate but they enjoyed certain privileges that distinguished them from rank-and-file popolani. Thus, this sample is quite small and represents only those households that appeared to be unequivocally patrician, based on title and name. For more on identifying the patriciate and the citizen classes, see most recently Pavanini, "Abitazioni," esp. pp. 63–69; and Zannini, "Un ceto di funzionari."

34. ASCP, Archivio Segreto, status animarum, B. 3, S. Giovanni Novo.

35. This figure is imprecise since a young man who was widowed with no children, although likely to board, would be impossible to identify.

36. The number of widows comes directly from the registers. The number of widowers, as explained above, has been deduced.

37. Samuel Cohn Jr., "Le Ultime Volontà"; Hardwick, "Widowhood and Patriarchy"; Palazzi, "Abitare da sole"; Todd, "Remarrying Widow"; Klapisch-Zuber, " 'Cruel Mother' "; Olwen Hufton, "Women without Men"; Boxer and Quataert, eds., *Connecting Spheres*.

38. ASV, Dieci Savi Sopra le Decime, Condizioni, B. 166, #400.

39. ASCP, Archivio Segreto, status animarum, B. 3, S. Giovanni Novo.

40. Romano, *Housecraft and Statecraft*, pp. 155–60, 178–82.

41. ASV, S. Uffizio, Processi, B. 73, #8 (trial of Raffaele Marangon), doc. 8, 1620.

42. "Fiola adotiva di anni 7." ASCP, Archivio Segreto, status animarum, B. 3, S. Giovanni Novo.

43. Ibid., S. Ternità.

44. "Antonia, moglie di francesco . . . veronese, qual è fuori già 10 anni." Ibid., S. Giovanni Novo.

45. On propertied widows as desirable wives, see Todd, "Remarrying Widow."

46. ASCP, Archivio Segreto, status animarum, B. 3, S. Ternità.

47. "Tutte tre maritate non stano col marito." Ibid.

48. Ibid., B. A. 1, SS. Apostoli.

49. On children in domestic service in Venice, see Romano, *Housecraft and State-craft,* pp. 152–55.

50. Few ages are listed in the parish censuses, making it impossible to assess how many children actually worked as servants (the larger number of boys in table 1.14 reflects the number of apprentices whose ages were given). The children identified above ranged in age from 7 to 16 years. Undoubtedly there were many more. See ibid.

51. Romano points out that the *serve,* because they spent so much time in the environs of the neighborhood doing the laundry and running errands, could form friendships with other popolane outside of their home and workplace. Ibid., p. 171.

52. ASCP, Archivio Segreto, status animarum, B. A. 1, S. Hieremia.

53. One of the most influential historians in this field is J. Hajnal. See esp. his article "Two Kinds of Pre-industrial Household Formation System," esp. p. 66. See also Edward Crenshaw, "The Demographic Regime of Western Europe," p. 182. A recent summary of the literature on this subject can be found in Marzio Barbagli's "Three Household Formation Systems."

54. See Barbagli, "Three Household Formation Systems," and Kertzer and Brettell, "Advances."

Two. Women of Means

1. Archivio IRE, CAT, F. 4/6, doc. 12, Atti Giudiziari, 1660.

2. ASV, Dieci Savi, B. 166, #446. A ducat in the sixteenth century was a currency of account, meaning that it did not exist as real money. It was equivalent to 6 lire di piccoli and 4 soldi, which equals 124 soldi or 24 grossi. See David Chambers and Brian Pullan, with Jennifer Fletcher, eds., *Venice: A Documentary History,* p. 461. For an authoritative discussion of Venetian currencies, see Frederic C. Lane and Reinhold Mueller, *Venetian Coins and Monies of Account.*

3. ASV, Condizioni di Decima Straordinaria, B. 658, 1617.

4. See Gigi Corazzol, *Fitti e livelli a grano* and *Livelli stipulati a Venezia;* and more recently, Grubb, *Provincial Families.*

5. Chojnacki has written extensively on the power that noble widows could wield in renaissance Venice. See, for example, "Patrician Women" and "Measuring Adulthood."

6. Marco Ferro, *Dizionario del diritto comune e veneto* 2: 202–3. See Brian Pullan's discussion of livelli in "The Occupations and Investments of the Venetian Nobility," *Crisis and Change,* pp. 388–93.

7. Corazzol, *Livelli stipulati,* p. 69.

8. ASV, Dieci Savi Sopra le Decime, Condizioni, B. 166, #405.

9. "Uno livello su Certi Molini et Case in Vicenza de ducati centovinti a anno fatto con m. Franc.co dalagio fu de Ser Lorenzo e fratello, il qual m. Franc.o non avendo pagatto lo acquisto de detti beni me son sta contraditto alle stride del venditor qual sono m. Paulo q. Franc.o Inzenier abitante In bic.a et pero non ho mai Cavato cossa alchuna et come sara spedito che possa aver la Intrada darò in notta alla mac.cie." Ibid., #331.

10. ASV, Condizioni di Decime Straordinaria, B. 658, Anzola Beltrame, 1617.

11. IRE, CAT, C. 1, 73b–74, Nov. 17, 1602.

12. ASV, Condizioni di Decime Straordinaria, B. 658, Giustina Panizzosa, 1617.

13. ASV, Dieci Savi Sopra le Decime, Condizioni, B. 162, B. 464.

14. Ibid., B. 166, #323.

15. Ibid., B. 161, #1120.

16. IRE, TEST, 658, 1590.

17. Ibid., 672, doc. 1, 1600.

18. Marina was not alone in drawing on her widowed status to elicit sympathy. Orsa and Borthola di Zanchi reminded the court that it traditionally showed clemency to the young and the widowed *(pupille e vedove).*

19. ASV, Pien Collegio, Suppliche di Dentro, filza 1, #76.

20. IRE, TEST, 598, 1610: "Lasso alli Hospedali dell'Incurabeli, Pietra, Mendicante, et San Zanepolo la botegha, et inviamento della spiciana delli doi ochiali, qual ho tolto in pagamento de mia dote . . . et me puo aspetar . . . dui livelli de duc. 100/ de cavedal per cadauno."

21. The index was compiled by the archivists Claudia Salmini and Euregio Tonetti of the Archivio di Stato di Venezia. I particularly thank Dottoressa Salmini for making possible a search of the women who appear in the index.

22. Grubb points out that women's dowries enjoyed protection from certain types of confiscation due to debt. Grubb, *Provincial Families,* p. 148.

23. ASV, Dieci Savi Sopra le Decime, Condizioni, B. 166, #346. See also #331.

24. Ibid., Livelli, B. 464. See also ibid., Condizioni, B. 158, #858.

25. ASV, Pien Collegio, Suppliche, filza 1, #222, 1565.

26. It is possible that such collective holdings were ultimately consolidated in

the dowry of one sister, with the others never marrying, especially in the case of the patriciate. See James C. Davis's study of the Donà family in *A Venetian Family and Its Fortune.*

27. "Non fu mai intention de V. Ser.ta ne di quest'Ill.mo dominio, che alcun di suoi Cittadini sia astretto supportar maggior gravezza di quello puo portar la condition sua et massimamente le povere donne." ASV, Pien Collegio, Suppliche di Dentro, filza 1, #203, 1565. For another example of women drawing on the vulnerability of their sex, see ibid., filza 2, #110, 1566.

28. Ibid., filza 2, #60, Aug. 1564.

29. Ibid., #5, 1566. See also ibid., B. 8, #393, 1588, the sisters Caterina and Chiara.

30. Ibid., #68, 1585.

31. Ibid., #92, 1585.

32. Ibid., filza 7, #100, 1581.

33. Ibid., #298, 1584.

34. Ibid., filza 3, #100, Nov. 1568.

35. ASV, TEST, B. 57, #510.

36. Ibid.

37. IRE, TEST, 691, 1573.

38. ASV, Pien Collegio, Suppliche di Dentro, B. 8, #67, 1585.

39. ASV, Dieci Savi Sopra le Decime, Condizioni, B. 158, #902.

40. IRE, TEST, 476, Dec. 1576.

41. ASV, Pien Collegio, Suppliche di Dentro, B. 8, #206, 1587.

42. ASV, Dieci Savi Sopra le Decime, Condizioni, B. 162, #157, and B. 461, #461.

43. Ibid., B. 170, #450, and B. 168, #495.

44. IRE, CAT, C. 1, Catastico di Catecumeni, p. 70b, Oct. 10, 1598.

45. ASV, Dieci Savi Sopra le Decime, Condizioni, B. 172, #1493.

46. IRE, CAT, C. 1, 1562, pp. 22–24.

47. ASV, Dieci Savi Sopra le Decime, Condizioni, B. 158, #890.

48. ASV, Pien Collegio, Suppliche di Dentro, B. 8, #165, 1586.

49. Ibid., #52, 1585.

50. ASV, Dieci Savi Sopra le Decime a Rialto, B. 160, #607, and #421.

51. Ibid., B. 157/b, #595.

52. IRE, TEST, 38, doc. 1, Oct. 1574.

53. ASV, Pien Collegio, Suppliche di Dentro, filza 1, #69, 1564.

54. Ibid., filza 5, #190, 1573. Paulina asked that she be absolved of a tax that she insisted she could not and should not have to pay.

55. Ibid., filza 2, #17, 1566. For similar examples, see #92, 1566, and filza 6, #330, 1580, and filza 6, #370, 1580.

56. Ibid., filza 5, #65, 1577.

57. Ibid., filza 1, #155, 1565.

58. Ibid., filza 6, #331, 1580.

59. Ibid., filza 6, #338, 1580.

60. Archivio IRE, CAT, C. 1, 110/b, TEST, 21 Apr., 1626.

61. IRE, ZIT, E. 46, #2, pp. 18–19, 1597.

62. Ibid., E. 45, #2, p. 11, 1602.

63. Cohn has found a variety of occupations practiced by women for fifteenth-century Florence and its surrounding countryside, including bakers, vintners, oil merchants, and cheese dealers. Samuel Cohn Jr., "Women and Work," p. 115.

64. See ibid., and Brown, "A Woman's Place," pp. 223–24.

65. ASV, Pien Collegio, Suppliche di Dentro, filza 3, #172, 1569.

66. Ibid., filza 6, #314, 1579.

67. ASV, S. Uffizio, Processi, B. 72, #3, doc. 25.

68. IRE, TEST, 660, 1557.

69. Ibid., doc. 2, 1551.

70. IRE, TEST, 38, docs. 2 and 3, 1574.

71. Ibid., doc. 1.

72. Ibid., 37, doc. 1, 1574.

73. *Pagiarizzo*, defined in Boerio as the bedsack stuffed with straw. Giuseppe Boerio, *Dizionario del dialetto veneziano*, p. 462.

74. IRE, TEST, 37, doc. 1, 1574.

75. On women and moveables, see Howell, *Marriage Exchange*. Cohn has pointed out that what a widow might do with her inherited wealth varied from city to city. In the fifteenth century, for example, Florentine widows were much more restricted contractually in how they could manage and distribute their property than were their Pisan counterparts. Cohn, "Women and Work," p. 124.

76. It is also possible that husbands sometimes represented their wives without including them as plaintiffs.

77. Brown has argued for early modern Florence that married women who contributed a wage to their household may have enjoyed greater status within that household. See Brown, "A Woman's Place."

THREE. AROUND THE NEIGHBORHOOD

1. "Anticamente, rione, quartiere." Nicola Zingarelli, *Lo Zingarelli, 1998: Vocabolario della lingua italiana*, p. 428.

2. The meaning of Venetian neighborhoods has been explored elsewhere. See Elisabeth Crouzet-Pavan, "La maturazione dello spazio urbano"; and Donatella Calabi, "Il rinnovamento urbano del primo Cinquecento."

3. On women's mobility beyond their local parishes, see chap. 5.

4. On the evolution of the parish in Venice, see Romano, *Patricians and Popolani*, pp. 17–20.

5. Muir, *Civic Ritual*, pp. 154–55. Alan Macfarlane defines the word *commu-*

nity by assigning it a group' of characteristics. These include a role as an area of economic exchange, an arena for marriage, an area for recruitment to rituals, an administrative area, a field for informal social control, and a range of gossip and scandal. Alan Macfarlane, *Reconstructing Historical Communities,* pp. 1–27. Macfarlane's work focuses on rural Essex, rather than London, so it is not surprising that the parishes he has studied were more self-contained than either urban Venice or London could have been. The Venetian neighborhoods fulfill four out of five of these requirements since marriage may not have been confined to or even predominantly located within parish boundaries. For examples of scandal and conflict among neighbors in early modern Rome, see Cohen, "Honor and Gender." The importance of the neighborhood to daily life was still being felt well into the modern period. David Garrioch writes,

> For many of the inhabitants of eighteenth-century Paris . . . the neighbourhood was the hub of daily life. They relied on neighbours for material and psychological support; among them they found human contact and companionship; and their vision, shaped by day-to-day sociability, was parochial. But more than that, they were aware of belonging to a community, geographically circumscribed although without fixed boundaries. Garrioch, *Neighbourhood and Community in Paris,* p. 29

See also William Sewell, *Structure and Mobility,* pp. 109–26.

6. Frederic Lane points out that, while the doge chose the chief of each parish (called the *capo di contrada*), he had to choose from among the parish residents themselves. *Venice,* pp. 98–99.

7. Davis, *Shipbuilders,* pp. 84–85.

8. Ibid., pp. 86–87.

9. Roberto Zago, *I Nicolotti.*

10. ASCP, Archivio Segreto, status animarum, B. 1, S. Maddalena.

11. ASCP, Archivio Segreto, status animarum, B. 3, S. Giovanni Novo.

12. ASCP, Archivio Segreto, status animarum, B. 3, S. Ternità.

13. This was also true in early modern Rome. See Elizabeth Cohen, " 'Courtesans' and 'Whores,' " 201–8, esp. pp. 204–5.

14. ASCP, Archivio Segreto, status animarum, B. A. 1, SS. Apostoli.

15. Prostitution itself was also underrepresented in the censuses. See chap. 1.

16. "La mia profession é de lavorar, de cuser, de filar." ASV, S. Uffizio, Processi, B. 67, #14, 1590, doc. 6.

17. Recent work on the Inquisition trials includes John J. Martin, *Venice's Hidden Enemies;* Ruth Martin, *Witchcraft;* Ruggiero, *Binding Passions;* and Pier Cesare Ioly Zorattini, *Processi del S. Uffizio.*

18. "Et all'hora vi erano delle donne de corte alla mia porta ma non mi ricordo che erano, di piu in corte." ASV, S. Uffizio, Processi, B. 72, doc. 1.

19. Ibid., B. 37, #5, doc. 2, 1574.

20. Ibid., B. 72, #3, 1618–26.

21. The late date of the majority of these cases—most from the early seventeenth century—signal the shift in the Inquisition's focus from heresy to witchcraft. See Martin, *Witchcraft*.

22. ASV, S. Uffizio, Processi, B. 80, #3, doc. 5, 1625.

23. Ibid.

24. For another example, see the trial of Orsolina Mestre, where the female witnesses included Aneta, eyeglass seller *(ochialina)*. Ibid., B. 67, #19, Orsolina Mestre, doc. 1, May 1591.

25. Ibid., B. 67, #14, Orsola Garzolo (aka Orseta Frolade), doc. 6, Dec. 1590.

26. Ibid., B. 67, #5, Caterina da Maggia, 1591.

27. Ibid., doc. 1.

28. Ibid., B. 72, #2, doc. 6, 1618.

29. Ibid., doc. 12.

30. Ibid., #5, doc. 6, 1620.

31. Ibid., B. 80, #3, doc. 10, 1625.

32. Ibid., doc. 4.

33. "Io non so perche lei sia striga, ma sento dir che sia striga, perche ho sentito la s.ra Livia de Andrea fachiazzo a lamentarse che detta marina havesse strigato detto Andrea suo marito." Ibid., doc. 5.

34. Ibid., B. 58, #8, doc. 1, 1583–85.

35. Ibid., B. 75, #7, doc. 3, 1620.

36. Ibid., doc. 9.

37. Ibid., docs. 7 and 9.

38. See, for example, the case against the Gilioli sisters, where one witness deferred to the older women in her parish, most of whom were convinced that the sisters were diabolically inclined. Ibid., B. 70, #16, doc. 7, 1608.

39. Ibid., B. 80, #3, doc. 10, 1625.

40. Ibid., B. 67, #4, doc. 2, 1591.

41. Ibid., B. 29, #9, doc. 1, Jan. 1571.

42. Ibid., doc. 3.

43. For other cases similar to Marina's, see ibid., B. 72, #3, 1620; B. 59, #1, 1587; and B. 70, #16, 1608.

44. Ibid., B. 80, #2, doc. 9, 1625.

45. Ibid., B. 72, #3, doc. 8, 1618.

46. Ibid., B. 62, #6, doc. 1, 1588.

47. Ibid., doc. 2.

48. Ibid., B. 72, #5, doc. 1, 1620.

49. Ibid., doc. 8.

50. Ibid.

51. Ibid., doc. 13.

52. Ibid., B. 62, #6, doc. 3, 1588.

53. Ibid., doc. 4.

54. "Sta vicina a me, et é vecchia che affitta camere." Ibid., B. 72, #3, Orsetta Piriotta, doc. 36, 1618–26.

55. Ibid., B. 73, #8, Raffaele Marangon e sua moglie, doc. 8, 1620.

56. Ibid., B. 70, #15, Felicità Greca, doc. 8, 1610–17.

57. Ibid., B. 75, #7, doc. 3, 1620.

58. Ibid.

59. Ibid., doc. 4.

60. Several witnesses offered their own accounts of Libera's bad will, if not her magical powers. Rocco, a 60-year-old fisherman, testified to an altercation between the mother of Libera and Lazaro's wife on the street:

> I was walking on the *riva,* and passed by Anzoletta, Libera's mother. Lazaro's wife showed up, too; her name is Alessandrina. Anzoletta said to her: "Alessandrina, are you bewitched?" Alessandrina answered, "Don't you all know?" At this point Libera came out and said to Alessandrina, "Aren't you ashamed to be walking by here?" And she said back, "So now you also want to keep the street from me, after everything else that you've done to me?" And Libera answered, "Those things are roses and flowers compared to what we want to do to you now." And then Alessandrina went off about her own business. . . . This happened on the riva of the Zuecca next to my house, because Libera is my neighbor, and the others aren't far away either. This happened two months ago. Ibid., B. 75, #7, doc. 6, 1620.

61. For other cases that involve witnesses visiting the accused witch in her own home, see ibid., B. 59, #1, doc. 1, 1587; B. 67, #14, docs. 1–2, 1590; B. 246, #2, 1585.

62. Ibid., B. 58, #2, doc. 1, 1585.

63. Ibid., B. 67, #10, 1591.

64. Ibid., B. 29, #9, doc. 2, Jan. 1571.

65. Ibid.

66. Another example of male/female friendships can be found in a 1585 appeal *(supplica)* that was filed at the Venetian court of appeals by three men and a woman, unrelated, who banded together to complain of being taxed too highly in their old age. ASV, Pien Collegio, Suppliche di Dentro, B. 8, #67, Sept. 9, 1585.

67. ASV, S. Uffizio, Processi, B. 83, #3, doc. 2, 1625.

68. Ibid., B. 73, #8, 1620.

69. Ibid., doc. 9.

70. Ibid., B. 58, #16, 1583–85.

71. Presumably the stairs were greased to make them dangerously slippery.

72. ASV, S. Uffizio, Processi, B. 58, #16, doc. 1, affidavit of Fiametta, 1583.

73. "La conosco da 24 o 25 anni in qua, per vista, e perchè mi porto dei lavorieri, et Cattarina meretrice in Terrao perche erano vicen in terrao, dove anco habitava mia fia Fabia che l'andai visitare." Ibid., B. 83, #3, doc. 3, 1625. For another example, see B. 67, Caterina da Maggia, doc. 6, 1591.

74. Ibid., B. 70, #15, doc. 3, 1608.

75. For eighteenth-century Paris, David Garrioch has noted that

> it was gossip . . . based on familiarity and on a degree of vigilance requiring a considerable local commitment of interest and energy, which more than anything else defined the boundaries of the community. People gossiped primarily with and about people they knew. What they said could have little impact on outsiders, but for those who belonged to the community the way neighbours spoke of them and behaved towards them was a constant preoccupation. Because the neighbourhood, socially and materially, was central to people's existence, the place they occupied in it was vitally important to them. Garrioch, *Neighbourhood,* p. 33

76. "Io sto in casa mia, et non attendo a fatti d'altri et non so cosa alcuno di questo." ASV, S. Uffizio, Processi, B. 70, #15, doc. 7, 1612.

77. Ibid.

78. Ibid., B. 72, #3, doc. 3, 1618.

79. Ibid., doc. 4.

80. Ibid., doc. 5.

81. Ibid.

82. Ibid., doc. 19.

83. Ibid. Terms like *santolo* and *compare* are somewhat ambiguous. Boerio offers the traditional definition of godfather (for a baptism or confirmation). But here they seem to be used more loosely, even between peers, to connote strong bonds that go beyond normal friendship.

84. ASV, S. Uffizio, Processi, B. 72, #3, doc. 20, 1619. See also doc. 21, which is the testimony of another sister.

85. See chap. 5.

86. *Lucia occhialera,* is probably the wife of the eyeglass dealer. IRE, TEST, 38, Oct. 1574.

87. Ibid.

88. Ibid., 598, 1610.

89. Ibid., 574, Oct. 1596.

90. "Lasso a Donna Santina Vedoa che mi pratica per casa quatro delle mie camise da Dona, et una Vestura . . . sicome al deto mio commiss.o parera che sia nuova." Elisabeta also left a dress to Marcolina, her servant. Ibid., 672.

91. "Lasso ducati quattro a Serena furlana stà qui in casa." Ibid., 821, doc. 2, Dec. 1580. See also 598, Mar. 1610.

92. Ibid., 598, Mar. 1610.

93. Ibid. For more examples of male/female friendships, see also TEST, 574, Oct. 1596 and 476; and ASV, S. Uffizio, Processi, B. 72, #5, 1620; ibid., B. 73, #8, doc. 9, 1620; B. 67, #4, 1591; B. 59, #1, 1587; and B. 67, #14, doc. 1, 1590.

94. IRE, ZIT, E. 45, #2, p. 11, 1602.

95. Ibid.

96. IRE, TEST, 843, Aug. 1581. Chiara's will shows that a patrician woman's thoughtfulness toward her servants was not always benign: she also left money to, among other servants, one Nicolo: "Two hundred ducats once so that with this he can never ask anything more of [my heirs]." See also ibid., 740, Feb. 1635; IRE, ZIT, E. 45, #2, pp. 8–10, 1597; and IRE, ZIT, E. 45, #2, p. 11, 1602. On the role of noblewomen in Venetian neighborhoods of an earlier period, see Romano, *Patricians and Popolani,* pp. 131–38.

97. On sisters and inheritance, see chap. 2.

98. IRE, TEST, 476, Dec. 1576.

FOUR. IMMIGRANT WOMEN

1. ASV, S. Uffizio, Processi, B. 67, #9, 1561.

2. The phenomenon of women migrating in large numbers to cities in nineteenth-century Europe has been described by, among others, Olwen Hufton and Joan Scott. See Hufton, "Women and the Family Economy"; Scott, "L'ouvrière!"

3. See the work of both Hufton and Scott.

4. On migrant women in early modern London, see Vivien Brodsky Elliot, "Single Women in the London Marriage Market." On migrant women in fifteenth-century Florence, see Herlihy and Klapisch-Zuber, *Tuscans and Their Families.*

5. ASCP, Archivio Segreto, status animarum, B. 2, #8.

6. On the migration of people from the countryside to the city throughout early modern Europe, see Herman A. Diederiks, "The Measurement of the Immigration into Towns," pp. 11–13. See also Fernand Braudel, *The Mediterranean* 1: 334 and 433. Herlihy and Klapisch-Zuber describe a "Florence [that attracted] predominantly poverty-stricken rustics, humble folk adrift in the world, seeking the city's public or private charity, or young workers hoping to gain, even without fortune, a better lot." Herlihy and Klapisch-Zuber, *Tuscans and Their Families,* p. 114.

7. Pullan has written that "it is quite probable that in the Venetian Republic population may have gently increased in the middle and late fifteenth century, though the constant recurrence of epidemics of pestilence kept it under control. . . . But convincing evidence of population pressure, provoking economic action, generally appears only in the second and third quarters of the sixteenth century." Brian Pullan, *Rich and Poor in Renaissance Venice,* p. 217.

8. Pullan notes that after a loss of three-tenths of the population,

> Venice did not suffer from any lack of willing newcomers—its popula-
> tion, which the plague may have reduced to 120,000 by the summer of
> 1577, had reached 135,000 by 1581 and 150,000 by 1586. . . . The pull of
> Venice was such that even where the country's sufferings from plague
> were definitely severer than those of the [neighboring] towns . . . Venice
> could quickly repair many of its losses. . . . Immigration lowered the
> dearth of workers in the lower grades of the building industry so rapidly
> that in 1577–80 the money wage paid to *lavoranti* was slightly lower than
> in the early 1570s and, over the next ten years, became higher by only an
> eighth. Brian Pullan, "Wage-Earners," pp. 159–60.

9. Daniele Beltrami, *Storia della popolazione,* p. 43.

10. See Sella's lucid analysis of population growth in sixteenth-century Venice.
He offers the following analysis of the immigration rates:

> In 1509, the city counted 115,000 souls. In 1563, a census registered
> 168,627: within fifty years, therefore, there was an increase of almost
> 50 percent, at an average annual rate of 1 percent. . . . The 50 percent
> increase that we find in the period 1509–1563 can be attributed only to
> natural increase—that is, to a higher rate of births than deaths—with
> great difficulty; immigration contributed as well. . . . From the birth
> and death rates calculated by Beltrami for 1581 and 1586 we can deduce
> a natural population increase of 0.2 and 0.4 percent, respectively. . . . In
> early modern populations, the birth rate under normal circumstances
> was only slightly higher than the death rate: this implies that average
> annual increases of 1 percent or more were possible only because of
> immigration. [My translation]

It follows from Sella's analysis that if population increased at an average rate of
1 percent and that the natural rates of increase were at most 0.4 percent, the remainder, that is, more than one-half of the increase in population, can be attrib-
uted to immigration. Sella, "L'Economia," p. 652.

11. Beltrami, *Storia della popolazione,* chap. 2.

12. ASV, S. Uffizio, Processi, B. 80, #2, doc. 1.

13. ASV, Collegio Cinque Savi, Mariegola, Casaroli 34, Sept. 27, 1543.

14. Pullan, "Wage-Earners." Frederic Lane has written: "So many of these shop-
keepers were recent immigrants that Philippe de Commynes, the French ambassador who wrote a laudatory analysis of Venetian institutions at the beginning of the
sixteenth century, after declaring that 'the people' had no part in the government,
added: 'Most of the people are foreigners.'" Lane, *Venice,* p. 273. On the impact of
immigrant artisans on early modern Venetian society, see Martin, *In God's Image,*
pp. 168–81.

15. On the Bravi, see Jonathan Walker, "Bravi and Venetian Nobles, c. 1550–1650."

16. ASV, Consiglio di Dieci, 1578, die 25 Julii (Comp. Leggi, B. 210).

17. Biblioteca Marciana, 131.d.163, *Parti prese nell'Ecces. Consiglio di Dieci,* pp. 1–18.

18. John Martin, "Per un analisi quantitativa," and *Venice's Hidden Enemies.*

19. On the Bravi as rapists, see Walker, "Bravi and Venetian Nobles." Many of the Bravi were from the Terraferma.

20. "Men who left Bergamese lands and Alpine valleys relocated to Venice without families, perhaps leaving a wife and children at the old home. Once settled in the new city, they built new lives, found a new home, as well as another wife and new children to maintain." Angelo Rigo, "Giudici del Procurator e Donne 'Malmaritate'" [my translation], p. 243. See also pp. 244–46.

21. Pullan, *Rich and Poor,* p. 380.

22. ASV, Comp. Leggi, B. 210, p. 794, Ordini delli Eccel.mi Sig.ri Essecutori Contra la Biastema, 1612.

23. Ibid.

24. On the growth of cities across Europe in the sixteenth century, see Paul Bairoch, Jean Batou, and Pierre Chevre, *La Population des villes européennes,* pp. 46–49.

25. Beltrami, *Storia della popolazione,* chap. 2.

26. On the problems of space and water common to early modern urban dwellers, see Calabi, "Il rinnovamento urbano," and Paul M. Hohenberg and Lynn Hollen Lees, *The Making of Urban Europe,* p. 132.

27. On the immigration of women alone to cities, see Scott and Tilly, *Women, Work, and Family* and Elliot, "Single Women." Christopher R. Friedrichs has suggested that 60 percent of the seventeenth-century immigrants to one Swabian town were women. Friedrichs, "Immigration and Urban Society," p. 72. Regarding immigration in general in this period, Hohenberg and Lees point out that, although labor opportunities in rural areas were increasing in the early modern period, the lure of the city was still a powerful force. Hohenberg and Lees, *The Making of Urban Europe,* pp. 128–29. On the plight of female immigrants in early modern Europe, see Hufton, "Women and the Family Economy"; and Natalie Zemon Davis, "City Women," in *Society and Culture,* p. 69.

28. By comparing young, never-married women with older widows and abandoned wives, Klapisch-Zuber has found that

> percentages in both categories demonstrate the greater mobility of older women. Close to 15 percent of women of this age group were born outside of the territory of Florence, and more than one-half (52.5 percent) were born in the "subject" territories—that is, those more recently acquired by Florence (41.5 percent and 11 percent respectively). This re-

cruitment over a widespread area is not found among the servants we presume to have been unmarried, 56.4 percent of which, as we have seen, were probably Florentine in origin. Klapisch-Zuber, "Female Celibacy and Service," p. 172.

See also Herlihy and Klapisch-Zuber, *Les toscans,* p. 322, #43, which shows that women were more likely to head a migrant household than a Florentine one.

29. On migrant women and the earning of a dowry elsewhere, see Elliot, "Single Women," and Hufton, "Women, Work, and Marriage." Women who arrived in Venice and had to make their own way were usually, by definition, poor: women with any kind of patrimony would not have needed to risk such a perilous existence to accumulate a dowry. It may be that many of them succeeded in marrying up, as Elliot has shown was the case in London. But research in this field remains to be done for Venice. Friedrichs has distinguished between two types of immigrants in early modern Europe: temporary; and permanent, or definitive immigrant. The latter often married into the urban community. Friedrichs also notes that, for the northern European city of Nordlingen, 60 percent of the permanent immigrants were women. Friedrichs, "Immigration," pp. 67 and 72. In Lyons, "male immigrants contributed to every level of the vocational hierarchy — from notaries, judges, and merchants to craftsmen and unskilled day laborers . . . some were also drawn from faraway cities. . . . The female immigrants, on the other hand, clustered near the bottom of the social ladder and came mostly from villages and hamlets in surrounding provinces to seek domestic service in the city." Davis, "City Women," p. 69. This contrast between male and female immigrants seems to have been true well into the nineteenth century. See William Sewell, *Structure and Mobility,* pp. 190–91. For examples of foreign women alone in Venice, see ASV, Pien Collegio, Suppliche di Dentro, B. 8, #393, 1588, and #109, 1585.

30. ASCP, Archivio Segreto, status animarum, B. 1.

31. Ibid., B. 1, S. Giovanni Novo.

32. Romano, *Housecraft and Statecraft,* pp. 125–26, tables 4.2 and 4.3.

33. Ibid., p. 158.

34. ASV, Pien Collegio, Suppliche di Dentro, filza 6, #93, Anzola (m.v.), Jan. 20, 1576.

35. "Avermi venduto una Carta del ben voler . . . dicendomi che quel mi servia per far che li uomeni mi vora bene isegniandomi come dovevo fare me povera infelice et forestiera fora di mia patria credandoli alle sue parole." ASV, S. Uffizio, Processi, B. 72, #3, Orsetta Piriotta, doc. 31, 1618–26.

36. See Maria Pia Pedani-Fabris, "Venezia a Costantinopoli."

37. ASV, Pien Collegio, Suppliche di Dentro, filza 1, #73, Sept. 1564. For other examples, see ibid., B. 8, #1, 1587; ibid., filza 6, #278, 1579; filza 7, #260, 1584; and filza 1, #87, 1566.

38. Ibid., B. 8, filza 8, #109 (m.v.), Jan. 23, 1585.

39. Ibid., filza 7, #125, 1582.

40. Ibid., filza 6, #278, 1579.

41. Ibid., filza 12, #82, Apr. 24, 1607.

42. Ibid., filza 6, #342, July 14, 1580.

43. Ibid., filza 7, #260, 1584.

44. ASV, Notarile Atti, B. 775, p. 353v, Sept. 10, Brinis, 1615.

45. ASV, Pien Collegio, Suppliche di Dentro, filza 5, #252, 1574.

46. Ibid., filza 6, #36, 1575.

47. ASV, S. Uffizio, indice 303. Martin has studied the Inquisition cases regarding heresy that were heard between 1547 and 1583. Of these predominantly male defendants (5 percent were women), only 20 percent were born and bred in Venice. Martin, "Per un analisi quantitativa," p. 148. Only two defendants apparently came from France, and both were women: Maria Rozagli, tried in 1581, came from Lyon, and another woman, Maria Rompo, tried in 1610, came from Languedoc.

48. See Martin, *In God's Image.*

49. The number also pales in comparison with the number of men—2,610, or nearly three times as many.

50. This was even more true for men.

51. Immigrants, both male and female, were also easy targets for other types of accusations; they were disproportionately represented before the censors—a board that examined disputes between masters and servants. See Romano, *Housecraft and Statecraft,* p. 263, table N1.

52. See Martin, *Venice's Hidden Enemies.*

53. ASV, S. Uffizio, Processi, B. 67, #14, doc. 7, Dec. 1590. On the power of rural culture in popular magic, see Carlo Ginzburg, *Night Battles,* and Cecilia Gatto Trocchi, *Magia e medicina popolare in Italia,* esp. chap. 1.

54. ASV, S. Uffizio, Processi, B. 72, #1, doc. 5, 1617.

55. Ibid., #2, 1618.

56. Ibid., doc. 3.

57. Ibid., doc. 12.

58. Ibid., B. 70, #15, 1610–17.

59. Ibid., docs. 4 and 5.

60. ASCP, Archivio Segreto, status animarum, B. 3, S. Giovanni Novo.

61. Ibid., B. 3.

62. Ibid., B. 3, S. Provolo.

63. Ibid., B. 1, S. Giovanni Novo.

64. ASV, S. Uffizio, Processi, B. 67, #10, Angela Friuli, Feb. 23, 1591.

65. ASV, Comp. Leggi, B. 210, pp. 796/b–797, Esecutori contro la Biastema, 1612. On this court, see Gaetano Cozzi, "Religione, moralità, e giustizia"; and Renzo Derosas, "Moralità e giustizia."

66. ASV, Comp. Leggi, B. 210, pp. 796–796/b, Esecutori contro la Biastema, 1612.

67. Lina Urban, *Locande a Venezia.*

68. "Mi filo, et ho tenuto et ancora tengo camera locanda, et non ho affittato mai più di una camera sola." ASV, S. Uffizio, Processi, B. 72, #3, doc. 5, 1618–26.

69. ASV, Esecutori contro la Bestemmia, B. 75, filza 1, #2, "note per forestieri."

70. ASV, Provveditori alla Sanità, B. 730, #30, Oct. 2, 1555.

71. Ibid., #41, Dec. 10, 1555.

72. ASV, S. Uffizio, Processi, B. 47, #2, Paolina Briani, 1581.

73. Ibid., B. 80, #2, doc. 1.

74. Ibid., B. 47, #2, doc. 20, 1581.

75. Ibid.

76. Ibid.

77. Ibid., B. 80, #2, doc. 2.

78. Luciano Mopurgo, *Sulla condizione giuridica dei forestieri,* p. 23.

79. For example, a study of early modern English villages has shown that, for immigrant brides, "both the selection of partners and courtship behaviour were probably to a large degree outside the immediate control of parents and kin. The selection of partners was perhaps more likely to be governed by personal choice within a local pool of eligibles than by parental match-making." David Levine and Keith Wrightson, "The Social Context of Illegitimacy," p. 166. Elliot has found a higher age and greater independence among migrant brides in early modern London. Elliot, "Single Women."

80. For examples, see ASV, Notarile Atti, B. 3067, Cigrigni, 1557, pp. 108/b–109, and 129/b–130; ibid., B. 2627, Crivelli, 1575, pp. 19–20, 26/b, pt. 2, pp. 1–3, 26–26/b, 48–48/b, and pt. 3, p. 5/b; B. 559, Beazin, 1596, pp. 88/b–92, 99–100, and 159–60; and B. 2661, Crivelli, 1610, Dec. 14, 1610; Dec. 22, 1610; Feb. 4, 1610.

81. ASV, Notarile Atti, B. 2627, Crivelli, 1575, pt. 4, p. 47v., June 14.

82. Ibid., B. 775, Brinis, 1615, p. 171v., May 11.

83. Ibid., p. 456r., Dec. 16.

84. Ibid., B. 2627, Crivelli, 1575, p. 26v., July 9.

85. Ibid., B. 775, Brinis, 1615, p. 77r., Mar. 9.

86. Ibid., B. 765, Brinis, 1605, p. 109v., May 9.

FIVE. BEYOND THE *CONTRADA*

1. Romano, "Gender and the Urban Geography."

2. Davis, "Geography of Gender." For fourteenth- and fifteenth-century Florence, Cohn has suggested a gradual retreat of women from public life, as they appeared less often in courtrooms, both as plaintiffs and defendants. He sees the decreased participation of women in both formal (courtrooms) and informal (the

piazza) public venues as an important indicator of women's changing status in Renaissance Florence. Cohn, "Donne in piazza."

3. Fynes Moryson, *An Itinerary* 1: 70, quoted in Davis, "Geography of Gender," p. 21.

4. On the uses of private spaces for public display, see Richard A. Goldthwaite, *Wealth and the Demand for Art;* and Randolph Starn and Loren Partridge, *Arts of Power.*

5. For a good summary of women's experiences as mothers in early modern Europe, see King, *Women of the Renaissance,* and Merry E. Wiesner, *Women and Gender.*

6. See chap. 1 discussion of rents and incomes.

7. Marin Sanudo, *Laus urbis Venetae,* trans. David Chambers, in Chambers, Pullan, and Fletcher, *Venice,* p. 6.

8. See Guglielmo Zanelli, *Traghetti veneziani,* esp. pp. 46–79. See also the book's preface by Giovanni Caniato, where Caniato cites Marin Sanudo's fifteenth-century description of the numerous routes serviced by traghetti for the common people across the canal and from Venice to the mainland. Caniato, "Gondole e gondolieri," p. 13, #7.

9. Alexander Cowan, *The Early Modern City.*

10. On the lawless population of mercenary soldiers in Venice, see Walker, "Bravi and Venetian Nobles." See also Davis, "Geography of Gender," pp. 25–28.

11. ASV, Comp. Leggi, B. 215, pp. 201–3, Dec. 11, 1546.

12. For examples of women dealing with institutions, see the story of Paolina in the intro. and chap. 6.

13. IRE, TEST, 827, May 1629.

14. ASV, S. Uffizio, Processi, B. 58, doc. 1.

15. Ibid., B. 72, #3, Orsetta Piriotta, doc. 31, 1626.

16. Ibid., B. 47, #2, doc. 18, 1581.

17. IRE, TEST, 660, doc. 1, June 1557.

18. ASV, S. Uffizio, Processi, B. 72, #3, Orsetta Piriotta, doc. 2, 1618.

19. Ibid., doc. 15, 1620.

20. "La conosco, che possono esser circa 8 o 9 anni, con occasionale che ho tenuto sua amicitia com fanno li gioveni. Et l'amicitia fra noi duro' parecchio tempo, che duro' detta amicitia da 3 anni in circa." ASV, S. Uffizio, Processi, B. 72, #3, Orsetta Piriotta, doc. 17, 1620.

21. Ibid., doc. 36, 1620.

22. Ibid., B. 67, #14, esp. docs. 3 and 4, 1590. Camilla was also known as Orsola.

23. Ibid., B. 75, #3, Marietta Greca da Castello, doc. 1, 1620.

24. "Una donna de tempo et grassa." ASV, ibid., B. 75, #3, Marietta Greca da Castello, doc. 2, 1620.

25. The closest Castello parish to S. Agostin (and Gabriele's home) is S. Severo. From there, a direct path across the city to S. Agostin covers nine parishes.

26. ASV, S. Uffizio, Processi, B. 75, #3, Marietta Greca da Castello, doc. 4, 1620.

27. Ibid., B. 67, #19, doc. 6, 1591.

28. IRE, TEST, 660, doc. 1, June 1557.

29. See chap. 1 and Romano, *Housecraft and Statecraft.*

30. ASV, S. Uffizio, Processi, B. 73, #8, 1620.

31. Ibid. See also ibid., B. 58, #12, doc. 11, 1586.

32. IRE, TEST, 827, May 1629. Claudia describes herself as the widow of Piero Stella, a man who delivered flour at Rialto. At the present, she says, she lives in the nearby parish of S. Cancian, with (not in the home of, not in the employ of) one Rimondo Rimondi. See also the case of Angela Friuli, ASV, S. Uffizio, Processi, B. 67, #10, doc. 4, 1591.

33. ASV, S. Uffizio, Processi, B. 47, #2, doc. 17, 1581.

34. Ibid., B. 70, #16, doc. 3.

35. Her testimony was given in January. She had been living there for a couple of months, since shortly before Christmas.

36. ASV, S. Uffizio, Processi, B. 67, #14, doc. 5, Dec. 1590.

37. We do not have sources for her life before she moved to S. Moisè.

38. ASV, S. Uffizio, Processi, B. 67, #10, Angela Friuli, Feb. 23, 1591.

39. Ibid., doc. 1.

40. Ibid., doc. 3.

41. Ibid., #14, doc. 4, Dec. 1590.

42. "Che la stava in contra de S. Marcuola, ma adesso non la stata piu la, ma no so dove la staga." Ibid., B. 67, #5, Caterina da Maggia, doc. 1, 1591.

43. Ibid., B. 80, #2, Cristina Collarina, doc. 9, 1625.

44. Ibid., B. 75, #7, Libera di Rossi, doc. 6, 1620.

45. Ibid., B. 72, #3, Orsetta Piriotta, doc. 11, 1618.

46. Ibid., doc. 37, 1626.

47. IRE, TEST, 834, Feb. 1579.

48. Ibid., 835, doc. 2, Apr. 1632. See also TEST, 865, Aug. 1565.

49. Ibid., TEST, 574, doc. 2, Oct. 1596. In addition to her *pelizza*, Laura, the widow of Iseppo the linen dealer, had goods consisting of little more than some tin pots, pans, and utensils.

50. On the international community of merchants in Venice, both native and foreign, see Ugo Tucci, "The Psychology of the Venetian Merchant."

51. IRE, TEST, 865, Perina, Aug. 6, 1565.

52. ASV, Dieci Savi Sopra le Decime a Rialto, B. 166, #464.

53. Ibid., #360.

54. For examples of women traveling to and from Venice to check on families and investments, see chap. 4: Zuanna and Sofia both went home to check on families and investments.

55. ASV, Provveditori alla Sanità, B. 730, #39, 1555.

56. Ibid.

57. Ibid., B. 730, #30, Oct. 2, 1555. Concerns about convicted criminals (men as well as women) ignoring their exile and returning to the city occupied other courts as well. The Quarantia Criminal had addressed this problem in 1456. See Gaetano Cozzi, "Authority and Law," p. 293.

58. ASV, S. Uffizio, Processi, B. 58, #12, May 26–28, 1586, doc. 10, Dec. 1588.

59. ASV, Pien Collegio, Suppliche di Dentro, filza 6, #198, Nov. 13, 1577.

60. Ibid., filza 1, #142, 1565.

61. Ibid., filza 7, #213, Oct. 1, 1583.

62. Ibid., filza 5, #67, Aug. 12, 1572.

63. Ibid., filza 1, #146, 1565.

64. Ibid., filza 2, #110, 1566.

65. Ibid., filza 6, #36, 1575.

66. ASV, S. Uffizio, Processi, B. 62, #6, doc. 2, 1588.

67. ASV, Pien Collegio, Suppliche di Dentro, filza 5, #67, Aug. 12, 1572.

68. ASV, S. Uffizio, Processi, B. 80, #3, doc. 13, 1625.

69. ASV, Pien Collegio, Suppliche di Dentro, B. 8, #47, 1585.

70. Ibid., Suppliche di Dentro, filza 2, #89, and #114, 1566.

71. Ibid., filza 3, #72, 1568.

72. Ibid., Suppliche di Dentro, B. 8, Dec. 21, 1587.

73. Ibid., Suppliche di Dentro, filza 5, #103, Nov. 19, 1572.

74. Davis points this discrepancy out but goes on to conclude that popolane were also often banned from the "male spaces" that covered most public areas. Davis, "Geography of Gender," pp. 22–23.

75. On popolana honor, see Cohen, "Honor and Gender."

Six. City of Women

1. Archivio IRE, CAT, F. 4/6, doc. 1, Atti Giudiziari, 1660.

2. Ibid., doc. 5.

3. Ibid., docs. 2 and 5.

4. Ibid., doc. 5.

5. Ibid., doc. 11.

6. On this vulnerability, see Romano, *Housecraft and Statecraft*, esp. chap. 4.

7. See Sherrill Cohen, "Asylums for Women"; Luisa Ciammitti, "Quanto costa essere normali"; Lucia Ferrante, "L'onore ritrovato." Stone has noted a roughly similar development in early modern England. *Family, Sex, and Marriage*, pp. 106–7.

8. The authoritative work on the subject of these charitable institutions remains Pullan's *Rich and Poor in Renaissance Venice*. Before the sixteenth century, there were a number of hospices (shelters) set up for women in Venice. But, as Pullan explains, "in the era of the Reformation and of Catholic reform, clergy, laity, governments and city magistrates displayed a new sensitivity to the spiritual and

material needs of beggars, orphans and prostitutes. The new religious societies and religious Orders discharged a militant, evangelical function, directed ultimately at the salvation of souls imperilled by the ignorance and temptation which poverty brought in its train." Pullan, *Rich and Poor*, p. 216 and pp. 372–422.

9. Ibid., and Monica Chojnacka, "Women, Charity, and Community."

10. On the Derelitti and the other institutions, see Giuseppe Ellero, *L'Archivio IRE*. The information in this chapter was greatly supplemented by conversations with Dottor Ellero, who generously shared with me his knowledge of the history and contents of the IRE archive.

11. "Lochi deputati allo aiuto et conservation di vari poveri citadini et artesani, homeni, done, puti, convertite." ASV, Luoghi Pii, B. 910.

12. Silvia Lundardon, "Le Zitelle alla Giudecca."

13. "Proveder a quelli scandoli et pericole che altrimente potrebbero nassere." IRE, DER, B. 1, Libro di Parte, pp. 58–59, 1572. See also a 1566 resolution that access to the orphan girls be limited to female staff. Ibid., p. 37, 7 lug., 1566.

14. On the Zitelle, see Chojnacka, "Women, Charity, and Community."

15. The Catecumeni's applicant pool was markedly different, since its mission was to convert non-Christians to Roman Catholicism.

16. IRE, ZIT, A. 1, Capitoli per i Governatori.

17. "Et se in alcuna poliza fusse espressa alcuna conditione dela Donna, come che non sij cascata in peccato, che sij vecchia, brutta, inferma, gravida, in casa di suo marito, per le quali conditioni . . . non deve essere accettata." Ibid., p. 19.

18. Ibid.

19. IRE, DER, B. 1, Libro di Parte, p. 38, 1566.

20. Ibid., p. 101, Mar. 9, 1586. See also ibid., p. 57, Apr. 7, 1572.

21. It may be that the Scuole Grandi sponsored the girls in some way. See ZIT, G. 1, pp. 16–17.

22. Ibid., chap. 4.

23. "Questa elezzione appartiene alla Congregazione delle Governatrici, con la Coadjutrice." ZIT, A. 1, sec. 6, chap. 2. The constitution of the Zitelle goes on to warn these women not to allow their choice to be swayed by affection, but choose instead that woman best qualified to govern the house. Ibid., chaps. 1–4 and 6.

24. Chap. 31 speaks of "the care that the madonna and the coadjutrici must have to raise two noble daughters who may succeed them in governing the house." Ibid., sec. 5.

25. See, for example, ibid., chaps. 7–11.

26. "Che sappia scrivere, e tener conti, Donna svegliata, ma umile, devota." Ibid., sec. 6, chap. 21.

27. Ibid., sec. 5, chap. 21.

28. "La casa non si po governar bene senza l'ajuto delle Maestre, che sono come tante colonne, che la sostentano." Ibid., chap. 27.

29. Ibid., chap. 28. From among the maestre were chosen consultrici, who had special responsibilities and conferred regularly with the madonna and coadjutrici. Apparently to be chosen for consultrice was prestigious; the young woman so honored could easily become the object of jealousy. This suggests that even the popular-class women who served the Zitelle as maestre could attain a certain level of privilege and influence within the house. See ibid., sec. 6, chap. 21.

30. "O insegnadole leggere, o di lavorare, o ammaestrandole nelle divozioni, e buoni costumi Christiani, che tutto sanno per amore di Gesu Cristo." Ibid., sec. 7, chap. 2.

31. Ibid.

32. Ibid., chaps. 13 and 28.

33. See Chojnacka, "Women, Charity, and Community."

34. IRE, SOC, A. 1, Capitolari delle Governatrici, chap. 1. See also chaps. 2–5 of this charter.

35. "Non dover per se stessa accettare donna nissuna nel Soccorso, e promette di farla accettare, ma lasciar questo uffitio alli Governatori e Governatrici." Ibid., chap. 16, p. 46. See also ibid., chap. 11, p. 31.

36. Ibid., Capitolari della Casa del Soccorso, 1585, chap. 5, pp. 21–25.

37. "Del modo che hanno da osservare le Governatrici con Madonna per mostrare la casa ad alcune Gentildonne, e Signore che desiderassero vederla." Ibid., Constitutioni della Casa delle Zitelle, chap. 11, p. 32.

38. For the Zitelle, see ibid., sec. 5, chap. 43. For the Soccorso, see, ibid., Capitolari delle Governatrici, chap. 3.

39. IRE, DER, B. 1, Libro di Parte, p. 114.

40. "Et huomini non mai ammettino di qual si voglia sorte se non nelle necessita di confessori, e medici dati dalli Governatori colla presenza dela madre, et d'alcuna altra di quelle, che l'aiutano nel governo della casa, e colle circostanze convenienti alla maggiore custodia." IRE, SOC, A. 1, chap. 7, p. 26.

41. Ibid., chap. 8, p. 27. See also chaps. 9 and 10.

42. See the intro.

43. IRE, ZIT, G. 4.

44. The contact may have been maintained through correspondence. The Soccorso charter included a provision for the receipt of letters for its charges; letters were reviewed by the staff before delivery. IRE, SOC, A. 1, chap. 8, p. 27.

45. "Ritornate, che faranno a Casa, renderanno conto a Madonna, o alla Coadjutrice di quanto averanno fatto, e li consegnaranno la limosina, che averano raccolte si di pane, come di danari, o di qualsivoglia altra cosa che gli fosse data per la Casa." Ibid., chap. 29, esp. #7.

46. The Derelitti charter does not address the seclusion of the orphaned boys who lived there.

47. IRE, DER, B. 1, Libro di Parte, p. 36, Apr. 25, 1566. See also ibid., Apr. 20, 1579; and p. 90, Nov. 25, 1580.

48. "Defesa degli orfani collocati a servizio," ibid., p. 34, Dec. 18, 1565.

49. Ibid., p. 46, June 5, 1569.

50. Ibid., p. 34, Dec. 18, 1565.

51. For the adoption of a boy, see IRE, DER, 9.2, #2, fasc. 2, May 15, 1549.

52. IRE, CAT, C. 1, Catastico di Catecumeni, pp. 34–35, Jan. 26, 1576. For another adoption of a girl "about nine years old," see ibid., pp. 33–34, Oct. 16, 1572.

53. Ibid., pp. 34–35, Mar. 2, 1577.

54. Ibid., p. 69b, Nov. 16, 1591.

55. IRE, DER, B. 1, Libro di Parte, p. 64, Dec. 12, 1574.

56. IRE, CAT, C. 1, Catastico di Catecumeni, p. 68b, June 27, 1597.

57. IRE, ZIT, A. 1, parte 2, cap. 12.

58. In 1474, before the Counter Reformation institutions under discussion here were established, the Venetian senate, which was trying to raise funds for new hospitals to accommodate the flood of refugees fleeing the Turks, required all notaries to remind clients who were preparing wills of the existence of such institutions and to encourage testators to leave money to them. Pullan, *Rich and Poor,* pp. 212–13.

59. IRE, ZIT, E. 45, TEST, p. 6, July 13, 1584. See also ibid., #2, p. 11 (testament of Orsetta Moro); and pp. 18–19 (testament of Marieta).

60. For examples of women leaving money to the charitable institutions in the sixteenth and early seventeenth centuries, see the archive of IRE, Testamenti, e.g., TEST, 658, 660, 672, 693, 740, 798, and 821. One dying patient at the Derelitti gratefully singled out a nurse in her will. Ibid., 591, Feb. 1578.

61. IRE, DER, B. 1, Libro di Parte, July 12, 1560.

62. Ibid., p. 112, Mar. 14, 1593.

63. IRE, CAT, C. 1, Catastico di Catecumeni, pp. 107–9, Sept. 20, 1611. See also ibid., will of Tomaso Mocenigo, p. 110b., Apr. 21, 1626.

64. IRE, TEST, 660, Prudentia Calafado, June 21, 1557. See also the entire TEST archive at IRE, which contains copies of testaments that include bequests to charitable institutions.

65. Michel Foucault, *Discipline and Punish.* On the subject of social control by civic authorities in premodern Italy, see Cohen, *Evolution of Asylums;* and Carol Lansing, "Gender and Civic Authority."

CONCLUSION

1. Studies of active women in other cities include Chabot, "La Reconnaissance"; D'Amelia, "Scatole cinesi"; Davis, "Women in the Crafts"; Elliot, "Single Women"; Howell, *Women, Production, and Patriarchy;* Wiesner, *Working Women.* More generally, see Boxer and Quataert, eds., *Connecting Spheres;* Brown, "A Woman's Place"; and Wiesner, *Women and Gender.*

APPENDIX

1. An important contribution to Italian parish studies in the early modern period is Domenico Sella's "Coping with Famine." See also Giacomo Martina, "Rilievi su alcuni libri parrocchiali"; Louis Michard and Georges Couton, "Les registres de l'état des âmes"; Michael Zell, "Families and Households"; and Lyn Boothman, "On the Accuracy of a Late-Sixteenth-Century Parish Register."

2. Forty-six of the censuses are located at the Archivio Patriarcale in Venice. One census, that of the parish S. Nicolò di Mendicoli, remains in that church's archive. I would like to thank that parish's priest, Don Luigi Battagia, for making the census available to me.

3. Seven households did not provide information on their inhabitants; for each of those households, I listed one male inhabitant, although there were probably more.

Bibliography

PRIMARY SOURCES

ARCHIVAL SOURCES

Archivio di Stato di Venezia (ASV)

Atti Notarili
 Buste 452, 462, 559, 617, 765, 775, 2573, 2583, 2627, 2637, 2647, 2656, 2661,
  2667, 2696, 2697, 2703, 2713, 2723, 3067, 4992, 4993, 5004, 5821.
Avogadori di Comun
 Buste 246, 311
Dieci Savi alla Decima
 Indice
 B. 658, Condizioni, B. 157, B. 158, B. 160, B. 161, B. 162, B. 166, B. 170, B. 172
Collegio Cinque Savi, Mariegola, Casaroli 34.
Esecutori contro la Bestemmia
 Busta 75
Giudici del Proprio
 Pergamena 348
Ospedali e Luoghi Pii
 Buste 901, 921
Pien Collegio
 Suppliche di Dentro
 Busta 8, and filze 1, 2, 3, 5, 6, 7, 9, 11, 12
Provveditori alla Sanità
 Busta 730
S. Uffizio, Processi
 Buste 7, 8, 29, 37, 47, 58, 59, 62, 63, 67, 70, 72, 73, 75, 80, 81, 83
Testamenti
 Buste 33, 57

Archivio Storico della Curia Patriarcale (ASCP)

Archivio segreto, sezione antica
    Stati delle anime (parish censuses)
      Buste 1, 2, 3

Archivio delle Istituzioni di Ricovero e di Educazione (IRE)

CAT C. I, F. 2–F. 6

DER B. I, B. 2, G. I

SOC A. I

TESTAMENTI

ZIT Miscel., Costituzione, G. I, G. 4, E. 45, E. 46

Biblioteca Marciana

Parti prese nell'Ecces. Consiglio di Dieci. (Venezia, 1651)

PUBLISHED SOURCES

PRINTED PRIMARY SOURCES

Alberti, Leon Battista. *The Family in Renaissance Florence.* Trans. Renee Neu
    Watkins. Columbia, 1969.

Dolce, Lodovico. *Dialogo . . . della institution delle donne.* Venice, 1545.

Domenichi, Lodovico. *La nobiltà delle donne.* Venice, 1549.

Fonte, Moderata. *Il merito delle donne: Scritto da Moderata Fonte in due giornate . . .*
    Venezia, 1600.

Franco, Giacomo. *Abiti d'Uomini e Donne Veneziane ed altre cose principali.* Venice,
    1614.

Franco, Veronica. *Lettere dell'unica edizione del MDLXXX.* Ed. Benedetto Croce.
    Naples, 1949.

Marinella, Lucrezia. *La nobiltà et L'Eccellenza delle Donne, co' Diffetti e Mancamenti*
    de gli Huomini. Venice, 1621.

Sansovino, Francesco. *Venetia, città nobilissima e singolare . . .* Venice, 1603.

SECONDARY SOURCES

Aikema, B., and D. Meijers, eds. *Nel regno dei poveri.* Venice, 1989.

Arbel, Benjamin. "Colonie d'oltre mare." In *Storia di Venezia: Dalle origini alla*
    caduta della Serenissima, vol. 5, *Il rinascimento, società ed economia,* ed. Alberto
    Tenenti and Ugo Tucci. Rome, 1996.

Ariès, Philippe. *Centuries of Childhood: A Social History of Family Life.* Trans.
    Robert M. Baldick. New York, 1962.

———. "Thoughts on the History of Homosexuality." In *Western Sexuality:*

Practice and Precept in Past and Present Times, ed. Philippe Ariès and André Béjin, trans. Anthony Forster. Oxford, 1985.

Aymard, Maurice. "Friends and Neighbors" In *A History of Private Life,* vol. 3, *Passions of the Renaissance,* ed. Roger Chartier. Cambridge, Mass., 1989.

Baernstein, P. Renee. "In Widow's Habit: Women between Convent and Family in Sixteenth-Century Milan." *Sixteenth Century Journal* 25, no. 4 (1994): 787–807.

Bairoch, Paul, Jean Batou, and Pierre Chevre. *La population des villes européennes de 800 a 1850: Banque de données et analyse sommaire des résultats.* Paris, 1988.

Barbagli, Marzio. "La famiglia nel mutamento." *Passato e Presente* 7 (1985): 13–30.

———. "Three Household Formation Systems in Eighteenth- and Nineteenth-century Italy." In *The Family in Italy from Antiquity to the Present,* ed. David I. Kerzer and Richard P. Saller. New Haven, Conn., 1991.

Baulant, Micheline. "The Scattered Family: Another Aspect of Seventeenth-Century Demography." In *Family and Society: Selections from Annales: Economies, Sociétés, Civilisations,* ed. Robert Forster and Orest Ranum. Baltimore, 1976.

Bellavitis, Anna. " 'Per cittadini metterete . . .': La stratificazione della società veneziana cinquecentesca tra norma giuridica e riconoscimento sociale." *Quaderni Storici* 30, no. 2 (1995): 359–83.

Bellettini, Athos. "La demographie italienne au xvieme siècle: sources et possibilities de rechereche." *Annales de Demographie Historique* 36 (1980): 19–38.

Beloch, Karl Julius. "La popolazione di Venezia nei secoli xvi e xvii." *Nuovo Archivio Veneto* 3 (1902): 5–49.

Beltrami, Daniele. *Storia della popolazione di Venezia dalla fine del secolo XVI alla caduta della repubblica.* Padua, 1954.

Benigno, Francesco. "The Southern Italian Family in the Early Modern Period: A Discussion of Co-residential Patterns." *Continuity and Change* 4, no. 1 (1989): 165–94.

Bistort, Giulio. *Il Magistrato alla pompe nella republica di Venezia.* Bologna, 1912.

Blom, Ida. "The History of Widowhood: A Bibliographic Overview." *Journal of Family History* 16, no. 2 (1991): 191–210.

Boerio, Giuseppe. *Dizionario del dialetto veneziano.* Venezia, 1856.

Boothman, Lyn. "On the Accuracy of a Late-Sixteenth-Century Parish Register." *Local Population Studies* 49 (1992): 62–66.

Bossy, John. "The English Catholic Community, 1603–25." In *The Reign of James VI and I,* ed. A. G. R. Smith. London, 1973.

Boswell, John. *The Kindness of Strangers: The Abandonment of Children in Western Europe from Late Antiquity to the Renaissance.* New York, 1988.

Boxer, Marilyn, and Jean H. Quataert, eds. *Connecting Spheres: Women in the Western World, 1500 to the Present.* Oxford, 1987.

Braudel, Fernand. *The Mediterranean in the Age of Philip II.* Vol. 1. London, 1972.

Bravetti, Patrizia. "Giovanni Aider: L'ascesa sociale di un oste tedesco nella venezia di fine '500." *Annali Veneti: Società, Cultura, Istituzioni* 2, no. 2 (1985): 85–90.

Bridenthal, Renate, and Claudia Koonz, eds. *Becoming Visible: Women in European History.* Boston, 1977.

Brolio d'Ajano, Romolo. "L'industria della seta a Venezia." *Storia dell'Economia Italiana,* Carlo Cipolla, ed. Turin, 1959.

Brown, Judith C. *Immodest Acts: The Life of a Lesbian Nun in Renaissance Italy.* New York, 1986.

———. "A Woman's Place Was in the Home: Women's Work in Renaissance Tuscany." In *Rewriting the Renaissance: The Discourses of Sexual Difference in Early Modern Europe,* ed. Margaret W. Ferguson, Maureen Quilligan, and Nancy J. Vickers. Chicago, 1986.

Brucker, Gene. *Giovanni and Lusanna: Love and Marriage in Renaissance Florence.* Berkeley, 1986.

———. "Florentine Voices from the *Catasto,* 1427–1480." *I Tatti Studies: Essays in the Renaissance* 5 (1993): 11–32.

Bruni, Annalisa. "Mobiltà sociale e mobiltà geografica nella Venezia di fine '500: La parrocchia di San Salvador." *Annali Veneti: Società, Cultura, Istituzioni* 2, no. 2 (1985): 75–83.

Burguière, André. "The Formation of the Couple." In *Family History at the Crossroads: A Journal of Family History Reader,* eds. Tamara Hareven and Andrejs Plakans. Princeton, 1987.

Burke, Peter. "Classifying the People: The Census as Collective Representation." In *The Historical Anthropology of Early Modern Italy: Essays on Perception and Communication,* by Peter Burke. Cambridge, U.K., 1987, pp. 27–39.

Calabi, Donatella. "Il rinnovamento urbano del primo Cinquecento." In *Storia di Venezia: Dalle origini alla caduta della Serenissima,* vol. 5, *Il rinascimento, società ed economia,* ed. Alberto Tenenti and Ugo Tucci. Rome, 1996.

———. "Gli stranieri e la città." In *Storia di Venezia: Dalle origini alla caduta della Serenissima,* vol. 5, *Il rinascimento, società ed economia,* ed. Alberto Tenenti and Ugo Tucci. Rome, 1996.

Caniato, Giovanni. "Gondole e gondolieri: Ultimi testimoni della Serenissima." Foreword to Guglielmo Zanelli, *Traghetti veneziani: La gondola al servizio della città.* Venice, 1997.

Canons and Decrees of the Council of Trent. Trans. Rev. H. J. Schroeder, O.P. Rockford, Ill., 1978.

Canosa, Romano, and Isabella Colonnello. *Storia della prostituzione in Italia, dal quattrocento alla fine del settecento.* Rome, 1989.

Cantarella, Eva. "Homicides of Honor: The Development of Italian Adultery Law Over Two Millennia." In *The Family in Italy from Antiquity to the Present,* ed. David I. Kerzter and Richard P. Saller. New Haven, Conn., 1991.

Casey, James. *The History of the Family.* London, 1989.

Castan, Nicole. "The Public and the Private." In *A History of Private Life,* vol. 3, *Passions of the Renaissance,* ed. Roger Chartier. Cambridge, Mass., 1989.

Chabot, Isabelle. "La Reconnaissance du travail des femmes dans la Florence du bas Moyen Age: Contexte ideologique et realité." In *La Donna nell'Economia (XIII–XVIII).* Florence, 1990.

Chambers, David, and Brian Pullan, with Jennifer Fletcher, eds. *Venice: A Documentary History, 1450–1630.* Oxford, 1992.

Chartier, Roger, ed. *A History of Private Life,* vol. 3, *Passions of the Renaissance.* Cambridge, Mass., 1989.

Chojnacka, Monica. "City of Women: Gender, Family, and Community in Venice, 1540–1630." Ph.D. diss., Stanford University, 1994.

———. "Singlewomen in Early Modern Venice: Community and Opportunity." In *Singlewomen in the European Past,* ed. Judith Bennett and Amy Froide. Philadelphia, 1998.

———. "Women, Charity, and Community in Early Modern Venice: The Casa delle Zitelle." *Renaissance Quarterly* 51, no. 4 (1998): 68–91.

———. "Women, Men, and Residential Patterns in Early Modern Venice." *Journal of Family History* 25, no. 1 (2000): 1–25.

Chojnacki, Stanley. "In Search of the Venetian Patriciate: Families and Factions in the Fourteenth Century." In *Renaissance Venice,* ed. J. R. Hale. London, 1973.

———. "Marriage Legislation and Patrician Society in Fifteenth-Century Venice." In *Law, Custom, and the Social Fabric in Medieval Europe: Essays in Honor of Bryce Lyon,* ed. Barnard S. Bachrach and David Nicholas. Kalamazoo, Mich., 1990.

———. "Measuring Adulthood: Adolescence and Gender in Renaissance Venice." *Journal of Family History* 17, no. 4 (1992): 371–95.

———. "Nobility, Women, and the State: Marriage Regulation in Venice, 1420–1535." In *Marriage in Italy, 1300–1650,* ed. Trevor Dean and K. J. P. Lowe. Cambridge, U.K., 1998.

———. "Patrician Women in Early Renaissance Venice." *Studies in the Renaissance* 21 (1974): 176–203.

———. "Political Adulthood in Fifteenth-Century Venice." *American Historical Review* 91 (1986): 791–810.

———. "La Posizione della Donna a Venezia nel Cinquecento." In *Tiziano e Venezia: Convegno Internazionale di Studi.* Vicenza, 1980.

———. "The Power of Love: Wives and Husbands in Late Medieval Venice." In *Women and Power in the Middle Ages,* ed. Mary Erler and Maryanne Kowaleski. Athens, Ga., 1988.

Ciammitti, Luisa. "Una santa di meno: Storia di Angela Mellini, cucitrice bolognese." *Quaderni Storici* 41 (1979): 603–43.

———. "Quanto costa essere normali: La dote nel Conservatorio femminile di Santa Maria del Baraccano, 1630–1680." *Quaderni Storici* 53 (1983): 469–97.

Ciriacono, Salvatore. "Protoindustria, lavoro a domicilio e sviluppo economico nelle campagne venete in epoca moderna." *Quaderni Storici* 52, no. 1 (1983): 57–80.

Clark, Alice. *Working Life of Women in the Seventeenth Century.* London, 1919.

Clark, Peter. "The Reception of Migrants in English Towns in the Early Modern Period." In *Immigration et Société Urbaine en Europe Occidentale, XVIe–XXe Siècle,* ed. Etienne François. Paris, 1985.

Cohen, Elisabeth. " 'Courtesans' and 'Whores': Words and Behavior in Roman Streets." *Women's Studies* 19 (1991): 201–8.

———. "Honor and Gender in the Streets of Early Modern Rome." *Journal of Interdisciplinary History* 22, no. 4 (1992): 597–625.

Cohen, Elisabeth S., and Thomas V. Cohen. "Camilla the Go-between: The Politics of Gender in a Roman Household, 1559." *Continuity and Change* 4, no. 1 (1989): 53–77.

Cohen, Sherrill. "Asylums for Women in Counter-Reformation Italy." In *Women in Reformation and Counter-Reformation Europe: Private and Public Worlds,* ed. Sherrin Marshall. Bloomington, Ind., 1989.

———. "Convertite e Malmaritate: Donne 'irregolari' e ordini religiosi nella Firenze rinascimentale." *Memoria* 5 (1982): 23–65.

———. *The Evolution of Women's Asylums since 1500.* New York, 1992.

Cohn, Samuel, Jr. "Donne e controriforma a Siena: Autorità e proprietà nella famiglia." *Studi Storici* 30, no. 1 (1989): 203–24.

———. "Donne in piazza e donne in tribunale a Firenze nel rinascimento." *Studi Storici* 22, no. 3 (1981): 515–33.

———. "Le Ultime Volontà: Famiglia, Donne e Peste Nera nell'Italia Centrale." *Studi Storici* 32, no. 4 (1991): 859–75.

———. "Women and Work in Renaissance Italy." In *Gender and Society in Renaissance Italy,* ed. Judith C. Brown and Robert C. Davis. New York, 1998.

———. *Women in the Streets.* Baltimore, 1994.

Coleman, David. "Moral Formation and Social Control in the Catholic Reformation: The Case of San Juan de Avila." *Sixteenth Century Journal* 26, no.1 (1995): 17–30.

Concina, Ennio, Ugo Camerino, and Donatella Calabi. *La città degli ebrei: Il ghetto di Venezia: architettura e urbanistica.* Venice, 1991.

Corazzol, Gigi. *Fitti e livelli a grano: Un aspetto del credito rurale nel Veneto del '500.* Milan, 1979.

———. *Livelli stipulati a Venezia nel 1591.* Pisa, 1986.

Costantini, Massimo. "Le strutture dell'ospitalità." In *Storia di Venezia: Dalle origini alla caduta della Serenissima,* vol. 5, *Il rinascimento, società ed economia,* ed. Alberto Tenenti and Ugo Tucci. Rome, 1996.

Cowan, Alexander F. *The Early Modern City.* Oxford, 1998.

———. *The Urban Patriciate: Lubeck and Venice, 1580–1700.* Cologne, 1980.

Cox, Virginia. "The Single Self: Feminist Thought and the Marriage Market in Early Modern Venice." *Renaissance Quarterly* 48, no. 3 (1995): 513–81.

Cozzi, Gaetano. "Authority and Law in Renaissance Venice." In *Renaissance Venice,* ed. John Hale. London, 1973.

———. *Il dibattito sui matrimoni clandestini: Vicende giuridiche, sociali, religiose dell'istituzione matrimoniale tra medioevo ed età moderna.* Venice, 1985–86.

———. "Padri, figli, e matrimoni clandestini (metà sec. xvi–metà sec. xviii)." *La Cultura* 14, nos. 2–3 (1976): 169–213.

———. "Religione, moralità, e giustizia: Vicende degli Esecutori Contro la Bestemmia." In *Ateneo Veneto* 177 (1991).

Crenshaw, Edward. "The Demographic Regime of Western Europe in the Early Modern Period: A Review of Literature." *Journal of Family History* 14, no. 2 (1989): 177–89.

Crouzet-Pavan, Elisabeth. "La maturazione dello spazio urbano." In *Storia di Venezia: Dalle origini alla caduta della Serenissima,* vol. 5, *Il rinascimento, società ed economica,* ed. Alberto Tenenti and Ugo Tucci. Rome, 1996.

D'Amelia, Marina. "Scatole cinesi: Vedove e donne sole in una società d'*ancien régime.*" *Memoria* 18 (1986): 58–79.

Davidson, Nicholas. "Northern Italy in the 1590s." In *The European Crisis of the 1590s: Essays in Comparative History,* ed. Peter Clark. London, 1985.

Davis, James C. *A Venetian Family and Its Fortune, 1500–1900.* Philadelphia, 1975.

Davis, Natalie Zemon. *The Return of Martin Guerre.* Cambridge, Mass., 1983.

———. "The Shapes of Social History." *Storia della Storiografia* 17 (1990): 28–34.

———. *Society and Culture in Early Modern France.* Stanford, 1975.

———. "Women in the Crafts in Sixteenth-Century Lyon." In *Women and Work in Preindustrial Europe,* ed. Barbara A. Hanawalt. Bloomington, Ind., 1986.

Davis, Robert C. "The Geography of Gender in the Renaissance." In *Gender and Society in Renaissance Italy,* ed. Judith C. Brown and Robert C. Davis. New York, 1998.

———. *Shipbuilders of the Venetian Arsenal: Workers and Workplace in the Preindustrial City.* Baltimore, 1991.

DeRoover, Raymond. "Labour Conditions in Florence around 1400: Theory, Policy and Reality." In *Florentine Studies: Politics and Society in Renaissance Florence,* ed. Nicolai Rubenstein. London, 1968.

Derosas, Renzo. "Moralità e giustizia a Venezia nel '500–'600: Gli esecutori contro la bestemmia." In *Stato, società, e giustizia nella Repubblica Veneta* (secs. 15–18), ed. Gaetano Cozzi. Rome, 1980.

DeVries, Jan. *The Economy of Europe in an Age of Crisis, 1600–1750.* Cambridge, U.K., 1976.

Diederiks, Herman A. "The Measurement of the Immigration into Towns."

Immigration et Société Urbaine en Europe Occidentale, XVIe–XXe Siècle, ed. Etienne François. Paris, 1985.

Douglass, William A. "The South Italian Family: A Critique." *Journal of Family History* 5 (winter 1980): 338–59.

Dynes, Wayne, and Stephen Donaldson, eds. *The History of Homosexuality in Europe and America.* New York, 1992.

Ellero, Giuseppe. *Un'Ospedale della riforma cattolica a Venezia: I Derelitti di SS. Giovanni e Paolo.* Unpublished thesis, University of Venice at Ca' Foscari, 1981.

———, ed. *L'Archivio IRE: Inventari dei fondi antichi degli ospedali e luoghi pii di Venezia.* Venice, 1987.

Elliot, Vivien Brodsky. "Single Women in the London Marriage Market: Age, Status, and Mobility, 1598–1619." In *Marriage and Society: Studies in the Social History of Marriage,* ed. R. B. Outhwaite. London, 1981.

Fanfani, Amedeo. *La Storia del Lavoro in Italia dala Fine del Secolo XV agli inizi del XVIII.* Milan, 1943.

Favero, Giovanni, Maria Moro, Pierpaolo Spinelli, Francesca Trivellato, and Francesco Vianello. "Le anime dei demografi: Fonti per la rilevazione dello stato della popolazione di Venezia nei secoli XVI e XVII." *Bollettino di Demografia Storica* 5 (1991): 23–102.

Ferrante, Lucia. "L'onore ritrovato: Donne nella Casa del Soccorso di San Paolo a Bologna." *Quaderni Storici* 53 (1983): 499–527.

Ferraro, Joanne M. "The Power to Decide: Battered Wives in Early Modern Venice." *Renaissance Quarterly* 48, no. 3 (1995): 493–512.

Ferro, Marco. *Dizionario del diritto comune e veneto.* 5 vols. Venice, 1847.

Finley, Robert. *Politics in Renaissance Venice.* New Brunswick, N.J., 1980.

Flandrin, Jean-Louis. *Families in Former Times: Kinship, Household, and Sexuality.* Cambridge, U.K., 1976.

Foucault, Michel. *Discipline and Punish: The Birth of the Prison.* Trans. Alan Sheridan. New York, 1979.

Friedrichs, Christopher R. "Immigration and Urban Society: Seventeenth-century Nordlingen." In *Immigration et Société Urbaine en Europe Occidentale, XVIe–XXe Siècle,* ed. Etienne François. Paris, 1985.

Gadol, Joan Kelly. "Did Women Have a Renaissance?" In *Becoming Visible: Women in European History,* ed. Renate Bridenthal and Claudia Koonz. Boston, 1977.

———. *Women, History, and Theory.* Chicago, 1984.

Garrioch, David. *Neighbourhood and Community in Paris, 1740–1790.* Cambridge, U.K., 1982.

Gavitt, Philip. *Charity and Children in Renaissance Florence: The Ospedale degli Innocenti, 1410–1536.* Ann Arbor, 1990.

Gillis, John R. *Youth and History: Tradition and Change in European Age Relations, 1770–Present.* New York, 1974.

Ginzburg, Carlo. *The Cheese and the Worms: The Cosmos of a Sixteenth-Century Miller.* New York, 1982.

―――. *Night Battles: Witchcraft and Agrarian Cults in the Sixteenth and Seventeenth Centuries.* New York, 1983.

Goldthwaite, Richard. *Wealth and the Demand for Art.* Baltimore, 1993.

Goody, Jack. *The Development of the Family and Marriage in Europe.* Cambridge, U.K., 1983.

Grendler, Paul. *Schooling in Renaissance Italy: Literacy and Learning, 1300–1600.* Baltimore, 1989.

Grubb, James. *Provincial Families of the Renaissance: Private and Public Life in the Veneto.* Baltimore, 1996.

Hajnal, J. "Two Kinds of Pre-industrial Household Formation System." In *Family Forms in Historic Europe,* ed. Richard Wall, with Jean Robin and Peter Laslett. Cambridge, U.K., 1983.

Hale, John, ed. *Renaissance Venice.* London, 1973.

Hanawalt, Barbara A. *Growing Up in Medieval London: The Experience of Childhood in History.* New York, 1993.

―――. "Is There a Decline in Women's Economic Position in the Sixteenth Century?" Introduction to *Women and Work in Preindustrial Europe,* ed. Barbara A. Hanawalt. Bloomington, Ind., 1986.

―――. "Peasant Women's Contribution to the Home Economy." In *Women and Work in Preindustrial Europe,* ed. Barbara A. Hanawalt. Bloomington, Ind., 1986.

―――. *The Ties That Bound: Peasant Families in Medieval England.* New York, 1986.

―――, ed. *Women and Work in Preindustrial Europe.* Bloomington, Ind., 1986.

Hardwick, Julie. "Widowhood and Patriarchy in Seventeenth-Century France." *Journal of Social History* 26 (1992): 133–48.

Herlihy, David. *Medieval and Renaissance Pistoia.* New Haven, Conn., 1967.

―――. *Medieval Households.* Cambridge, Mass., 1985.

Herlihy, David, and Christiane Klapisch-Zuber. *Les toscans et leurs familles: Une etude du catasto florentin de 1427.* Paris, 1978. Published in English as *Tuscans and Their Families: A Study of the Florentine Catasto of 1427.* New Haven, Conn., 1983.

Hohenberg, Paul M., and Lynn Hollen Lees. *The Making of Urban Europe, 1000–1950.* Cambridge, Mass., 1985.

Howell, Martha C. *The Marriage Exchange: Property, Social Place, and Gender in Cities of the Low Countries, 1300–1550.* Chicago, 1998.

―――. *Women, Production, and Patriarchy in Late Medieval Cities.* Chicago, 1986.

Hufton, Olwen. "Women and the Family Economy in Eighteenth-Century France." *French Historical Studies* 9 (1975): 1–22.

————. "Women without Men: Widows and Spinsters in Britain and France in the Eighteenth Century." *Journal of Family History* 9, no. 4 (1984): 355–76.

————. "Women, Work, and Marriage in Eighteenth-Century France." In *Marriage and Society: Studies in the Social History of Marriage,* ed. R. B. Outhwaite. London, 1981.

Hughes, Diane Owen. "From Brideprice to Dowry in Mediterranean Europe." *Journal of Family History* 3 (1978): 262–96.

Imhaus, Brunehilde. *Le minoranze orientali a Venezia, 1300–1510.* Rome, 1997.

Kent, Dale V., and F. W. Kent. *Neighbours and Neighbourhood in Renaissance Florence: The District of the Red Lion in the Fifteenth Century.* Locust Valley, N.Y., 1982.

Kertzer, David I., and Caroline B. Brettell. "Advances in Italian and Iberian Family History." *Journal of Family History* 12 (1987): 87–120.

King, Margaret Leah. "Caldiera and the Barbaros on Marriage and the Family: Humanist Reflections of Venetian Realities." *Journal of Medieval and Renaissance Studies* 6, no. 1 (1976): 19–50.

————. *Women of the Renaissance.* Chicago, 1991.

Kirshner, Julius, and Anthony Molho. "The Dowry Fund and the Marriage Market in Early Quattrocento Florence." *Journal of Modern History* 50 (1978): 403–38.

Klapisch-Zuber, Christiane. *Women, Family, and Ritual in Renaissance Italy.* Chicago, 1987.

————. "Women Servants in Florence during the Fourteenth and Fifteenth Centuries." In *Women and Work in Preindustrial Europe,* ed. Barbara A. Hanawalt. Bloomington, Ind., 1986.

Kussmaul, A. S. *Servants in Husbandry in Early Modern England.* London, 1981.

Labalme, Patricia H. "Venetian Women on Women: Three Early Modern Feminists." *Archivio Veneto* 5, no. 177 (1981): 81–109.

Lachiver, Marcel. "La reconstitution des familles aux XVIe–XVIIe siècles (vers 1550–1670)." *Annales de Demographie Historique,* 1980, pp. 97–103.

Laiou, Angeliki E., ed. *Consent and Coercion to Sex and Marriage in Ancient and Medieval Societies.* Washington, D.C., 1993.

Lane, Frederic C. "Venetian Shipping during the Commercial Revolution." In *Crisis and Change in the Venetian Economy in the Sixteenth and Seventeenth Centuries,* ed. Brian Pullan. London, 1968.

————. *Venice: A Maritime Republic.* Baltimore, 1973.

Lane, Frederic C., and Reinhold C. Mueller. *Money and Banking in Renaissance Venice: Venetian Coins and Monies of Account.* Baltimore, 1985.

Lansing, Carol. "Gender and Civic Authority: Sexual Control in a Medieval Italian Town." *Journal of Social History* 31, no. 1 (1997): 33–59.

Laslett, Peter. *Household and Family in Past Time.* Cambridge, U.K., 1972.

————. *The World We Have Lost: England before the Industrial Age*. New York, 1965.

LeRoy Ladurie, Emmanuel. *Montaillou: The Promised Land of Error*. New York, 1979.

Levine, David, and Keith Wrightson. "The Social Context of Illegitimacy in Early Modern England." In *Bastardy and Its Comparative History: Studies in the History of Illegitimacy and Marital Nonconformism in Britain, France, Germany, Sweden, North America, Jamaica, and Japan*, ed. Peter Laslett, Karla Oosterveen, and Richard M. Smith. Cambridge, U.K., 1980.

Lindert, Peter H. "English Occupations, 1670–1811." *Journal of Economic History* 40, no. 4 (1980): 685–712.

Lundardon, Silvia. "Le Zitelle alla Giudecca: una storia lunga quattrocento anni." In *Le Zitelle: architettura, arte e storia di un'istituzione veneziana*, ed. Lionello Pupi. Venice, 1994.

Macfarlane, Alan. *Marriage and Love in England: Modes of Reproduction, 1300–1840*. New York, 1988.

————. *Reconstructing Historical Communities*. Cambridge, U.K., 1977.

————. *Witchcraft in Tudor and Stuart England*. London, 1970.

Mackenney, Richard, *Tradesmen and Traders: The World of the Guilds in Venice and Europe, c.1250–c.1650*. Totowa, N.J., 1987.

Malanima, P. *La decadenza di un economia cittadina: L'industria di Firenze nei secoli, xvi–xviii*. Bologna, 1982.

Marshall, Sherrin. "Childhood in Early Modern Europe." In *Children in Historical and Comparative Perspective: An International Handbook and Research Guide*, ed. Joseph M. Hawes and N. Ray Hiner. New York, 1991.

Martin, John J. "In God's Image: Artisans and Heretics in Counterreformation Venice." Ph.D. diss., Harvard University, 1982.

————. "Out of the Shadow: Heretical and Catholic Women in Renaissance Venice." *Journal of Family History* 10 (1985): 21–33.

————. "Per un analisi quantitativa dell'inquisizione veneziana." In *L'inquisizione romana in Italia nell'eta' moderna: . . . Seminario internationale Trieste, 18–20 maggio, 1988*. Rome, 1991.

————. "Salvation and Society in Sixteenth-Century Venice: Popular Evangelism in a Renaissance City." *Journal of Modern History* 60, no. 2 (1988): 205–33.

————. *Venice's Hidden Enemies: Italian Heretics in a Renaissance City*. Chicago, 1993.

Martin, Ruth. *Witchcraft and the Inquisition in Venice, 1550–1650*. Oxford, 1989.

Martina, Giacomo. "Rilievi su alcuni libri parrocchiali dell'Abruzzo." *Rivista di storia della Chiesa in Italia* 40, no. 2 (1986): 391–404.

Martini, Gabriele. "Rispetto dell'infanzia e violenza sui minori nella Venezia del seicento." *Società e Storia* 9, no. 34 (1986): 793–817.

McLaren, Dorothy. "Marital Fertility and Lactation, 1570–1720." In *Women in English Society, 1500–1800,* ed. Mary Prior. London, 1985.

Michard, Louis, and Georges Couton. "Les registres de l'état des âmes dans la diocese de Chambéry." *Cahiers d'Histoire* 26, no. 1 (1981): 65–76.

Midelfort, H. C. E. *Witchhunting in Southwestern Germany, 1562–1684.* Stanford, 1972.

Molho, Anthony. *Marriage Alliance in Late Medieval Florence.* Cambridge, Mass., 1994.

Molmenti, Pompeo. *La Storia di Venezia nella Vita Privata dalle Origini alla Caduta della Repubblica.* Turin, 1880.

Mopurgo, Luciano. *Sulla condizione giuridica dei forestieri in Italia nei secoli di mezzo.* Bologna, 1872.

Muir, Edward. *Civic Ritual in Renaissance Venice.* Princeton, 1981.

Murray, Jacqueline. "Agnolo Firenzuola on Female Sexuality and Women's Equality." *Sixteenth Century Journal* 22, no.2 (1991): 199–213.

Nani, Filippo. *Prattica civile delle corti del Palazzo Veneto.* Venice, 1663.

Newett, Mary Margaret. "The Sumptuary Laws of Venice in the Fourteenth and Fifteenth Centuries." In *Historical Essays of The Owens College, Manchester,* ed. T. F. Tout and James Tait. Manchester, 1902.

Odorisio, Ginevra Conti. *Donna e società nel seicento.* Rome, 1979.

O'Neil, Mary Rose. "Discerning Superstition: Popular Errors and Orthodox Response in Late-Sixteenth-Century Italy." Ph.D. diss., Stanford University, 1982.

Otis, Leah Lydia. *Prostitution in Medieval Society: The History of an Urban Institution in Languedoc.* Chicago, 1985.

Outhwaite, R. B., ed. *Marriage and Society: Studies in the Social History of Marriage.* London, 1981.

Ozment, Steven. *When Fathers Ruled: Family Life in Reformation Europe.* Cambridge, Mass., 1983.

Palazzi, Maura. "Abitare da sole: Donne capofamiglia alla fine del settecento." *Memoria* 18 (1986): 37–57.

Palli, Heldur. "Parish Registers and Revisions: Research Strategies in Estonian Historical Demography and Agrarian History." *Social Science History* 7, no. 3 (1983): 289–310.

Palumbo Fossati Casa, Isabella. "Gli interni della casa veneziana nel settecento: continuità e trasformazioni." In *L'uso dello spazio privato nell'età dell'Illuminismo,* ed. Giorgio Simoncini. Florence, 1995: 165–79.

———. "L'interno della casa dell'artigianato e dell'artista nella Venezia del Cinquecento." *Studi Veneziani* n.s. 8 (1984): 109–53.

Pastore, Alessandro. "Rapporti familiari e pratica testamentaria nella Bologna del Seicento." *Studi Storici* 25, no. 1 (1984): 153–68.

Pavanini, Paola. "Abitazioni popolari e borghesi nella Venezia cinquecentesca." *Studi Veneziani* 5 (1981): 63–126.

Pedani, Maria Pia. "L'osservanza imposta: I monasteri conventuali femminili a Venezia nei primi anni del Cinquecento." *Archivio Veneto* ser. 5, vol. 144, no. 179 (1995): 113–26.

Pedani-Fabris, Maria Pia. "Venezia a Costantinopoli alla fine del xvi secolo." *Quaderni di Studi Arabi* 15 (1997): suppl. 67–84.

Pinto, Giuliano. "Il personale, le balie, e i salariati dell'Ospedale di San Gallo di Firenze negli anni 1395–1406: Note per la storia del salariato nelle città medievali." *Ricerche Storiche* 4 (1974): 143–61.

Pollock, Linda. *Forgotten Children: Parent-Child Relations from 1500 to 1900.* Cambridge, U.K., 1983.

Poos, L. R. "The Historical Demography of Renaissance Europe: Recent Research and Current Issues." *Renaissance Quarterly* 42, no. 4 (1989): 794–811.

Prior, Mary. "Women and the Urban Economy: Oxford, 1500–1800." In *Women in English Society, 1500–1800,* ed. Mary Prior. London, 1985.

———, ed. *Women in English Society, 1500–1800.* London, 1985.

Pullan, Brian. "The Relief of Prisoners in Sixteenth-century Venice." *Studi Veneziani* 10 (1968): 221–30.

———. *Rich and Poor in Renaissance Venice: The Social Institutions of a Catholic State, 1580 to 1620.* Oxford, 1971.

———. "Wage-Earners and the Venetian Economy, 1550–1630." In *Crisis and Change in the Venetian Economy in the Sixteenth and Seventeenth Centuries,* ed. Brian Pullan. London, 1968.

———, ed. *Crisis and Change in the Venetian Economy in the Sixteenth and Seventeenth Centuries.* London, 1968.

Rapp, Richard. *Industry and Economic Decline in Seventeenth-century Venice.* Cambridge, Mass., 1976.

Rasi, Piero. "La conclusione del matrimonio nella dottrina prima del Concilio di Trento." *Annali della Facoltà Giuridica della Università degli Studi di Camerino* 23, 1957, pp. 1–216.

Rigo, Angelo. "Giudici del Procurator e Donne 'Malmaritate': Interventi della Giustizia Secolare in Materia Matrimoniale a Venezia in Epoca Tridentina." *Atti dell'Istituto Veneto di Scienze, Lettere ed Arti* 151 (1992–93).

Romano, Dennis. "Gender and the Urban Geography of Renaissance Venice." *Journal of Social History* 23, no. 2 (1989): 339–53.

———. *Housecraft and Statecraft: Domestic Service in Renaissance Venice, 1400–1600.* Baltimore, 1996.

———. *Patricians and Popolani: The Social Foundations of the Venetian Renaissance State.* Baltimore, 1987.

———. "The Regulation of Domestic Service in Renaissance Venice." *Sixteenth Century Journal* 22, no. 4 (1991): 661–77.

Rosenthal, Margaret F. *The Honest Courtesan: Veronica Franco, Citizen and Writer in Sixteenth-Century Venice.* Chicago, 1992.

———. "Venetian Women and Their Discontents." In *Sexuality and Gender in Early Modern Europe: Institutions, Texts, Images,* ed. James Grantham Turner. Cambridge, U.K., 1993.

Rowlands, Marie B. "Recusant Women, 1560–1640." In *Women in English Society, 1500–1800,* ed. Mary Prior. London, 1985.

Ruggiero, Guido. *Binding Passions: Tales of Magic, Marriage, and Power at the End of the Renaissance.* New York, 1993.

———. *The Boundaries of Eros: Sex Crime and Sexuality in Renaissance Venice.* Oxford, 1985.

———. "Più che la vita è caro: Onore, matrimonio, e reputazione femminile nel tardo rinascimento." *Quaderni Storici* 66, no. 3 (1987): 753–75.

———. *Violence in Early Renaissance Venice.* New Brunswick, N.J., 1980.

———. "Vizi e virtù nel rinascimento." *Storia Dossier: Storia* 4, no. 25 (special issue, *La storia della prostituzione,* ed. G. Ruggiero) (1989): 25–39.

Sagredo. *Sulle Consorterie delle Arti Edificative.* Venice, 1856.

Scarabello, Giovanni. "Devianza sessuale ed interventi di giustizia a Venezia nella prima metà del XVI secolo." In *Tiziano e Venezia.* Vicenza, 1980.

———. "La Pena del carcere: Aspetti della condizione carceraria a Venezia nei secoli xvi–xviii: L'assistenza e l'associanismo." In *Stato, società, e giustizia nella Repubblica veneta* (sec. 15–18), ed. Gaetano Cozzi. Rome, 1986.

———. "Le strutture assistenziali." In *Storia di Venezia: Dalle origini alla caduta della Serenissima,* vol. 6, *Dal rinascimento al barocco,* ed. Gaetano Cozzi and Paolo Prodi. Rome, 1994.

Schutte, Anne Jacobson. "Irene di Spilimbergo: The Image of a Creative Woman in Late Renaissance Italy." *Renaissance Quarterly* 44, no. 1 (1991): 42–61.

Scott, Joan W. "Experience." In *Feminists Theorize the Political,* ed. Judith Butler and Joan W. Scott. New York, 1992.

———. " 'L'ouvrière! Mot impie, sordide . . .': Women Workers in the Discourse of French Political Economy, 1840–1860." In Joan W. Scott, *Gender and the Politics of History.* New York, 1988.

Scott, Joan W., and Louise A. Tilly. *Women, Work, and Family.* New York, 1978.

Scully, Sally. "Marriage or a Career?: Witchcraft as an Alternative in Seventeenth-Century Venice." *Journal of Social History* 28, no.4 (1995): 857–76.

Sella, Domenico. "Coping with Famine: The Changing Demography of an Italian Village in the 1590s." *Sixteenth Century Journal* 22, no. 2 (1991): 185–97.

———. "Crisis and Transformation in Venetian Trade." In *Crisis and Change in the Venetian Economy in the Sixteenth and Seventeenth Centuries,* ed. Brian Pullan. London, 1968.

———. "L'Economia." In *Storia di Venezia,* vol. 6, *Dal rinascimento al barocco,* ed. Gaetano Cozzi and Paolo Prodi. Rome, 1994.

————. "Household, Land Tenure, and Occupation in North Italy in the Late Sixteenth Century." *Journal of European Economic History* 16, no. 3 (1987): 487–509.

————. "The Rise and Fall of the Venetian Woolen Industry." In *Crisis and Change in the Venetian Economy,* ed. Brian Pullan. New York, 1968.

Sewell, William. *Structure and Mobility: The Men and Women of Marseille, 1820–1870.* Cambridge, U.K., 1985.

Shorter, Edward. *The Making of the Modern Family.* New York, 1977.

Starn, Randolph, and Loren Partridge. *Arts of Power: Three Halls of State in Italy, 1300–1600.* Berkeley, 1992.

Stone, Lawrence. *The Family, Sex, and Marriage in England, 1500–1800.* New York, 1977.

Strocchia, Sharon. "Remembering the Family: Women, Kin, and Commemorative Masses in Renaissance Florence." *Renaissance Quarterly* 42, no. 4 (1989): 635–55.

Stuard, Susan Mosher. "To Town to Serve: Urban Domestic Slavery in Medieval Ragusa." *Women and Work in Preindustrial Europe,* ed. Barbara A. Hanawalt. Bloomington, Ind., 1986.

Thomas, Keith. *Religion and the Decline of Magic.* New York, 1971.

Tilly, Charles. "On Uprooting, Kinship, and the Auspices of Migration." *International Journal of Comparative Sociology* 8, no. 2 (1967): 143–64.

Tilly, Louise. "Demographic History Faces the Family: Europe since 1500." *Family History,* special issue, *Family History at the Crossroads,* ed. Tamara Hareven and Andrejs Plakans. Princeton, 1987.

Todd, Barbara J. "The Remarrying Widow: A Stereotype Reconsidered." In *Women in English Society, 1500–1800,* ed. Mary Prior. London, 1985.

Trexler, Richard. "The Foundlings of Florence, 1395–1455." *History of Childhood Quarterly* 1 (1974): 259–84.

————. "Infanticide in Florence: New Sources and First Results." *History of Childhood Quarterly* 1 (1974): 96–116.

————. "La Prostitution florentine au XVe siècle: patronages et clienteles." *Annales: ESC* 36, 1981, pp. 983–1015.

Trocchi, Cecilia Gatto. *Magia e medicina popolare in Italia.* Rome, 1982.

Tucci, Ugo. "The Psychology of the Venetian Merchant in the Sixteenth Century." In *Renaissance Venice,* ed. John Hale. London, 1973.

Ulvioni, Paolo. *Il gran castigo di Dio: Carestia ed epidemie a Venezia e nella Terraferma, 1628–1632.* Padua, 1989.

Urban, Lina. *Locande a Venezia: Dal xiii al xix secolo.* Venice, 1989.

Walker, Jonathan. "Bravi and Venetian Nobles, c. 1550–1650," *Studi Veneziani* 26 (1998): 85–113.

Weissman, Ronald F. E. "The Importance of Being Ambiguous: Social Relations, Individualism, and Identity in Renaissance Florence." In *Urban Life in the*

Renaissance, ed. Susan Zimmerman and Ronald F. E. Weissman. Newark, Del., 1989.

———. "Reconstructing Renaissance Sociology: The 'Chicago School' and the Study of Renaissance Society." In *Persons in Groups: Social Behavior as Identity Formation in Medieval and Renaissance Europe.* Papers of the Sixteenth Annual Conference of the Center for Medieval and Early Renaissance Studies, ed. Richard C. Trexler. Binghamton, N.Y., 1985.

Wiesner, Merry E. "Early Modern Midwifery: A Case Study." In *Women and Work in Preindustrial Europe,* ed. Barbara A. Hanawalt. Bloomington, Ind., 1986.

———. "Spinsters and Seamstresses: Women in Cloth and Clothing Production." In *Rewriting the Renaissance,* ed. Margaret W. Ferguson, Maureen Quilligan, and Nancy J. Vickers. Chicago, 1986.

———. *Women and Gender in Early Modern Europe.* Cambridge, U.K., 1993.

———. "Women's Response to the Reformation." In *The German People and the Reformation,* ed. R. Po-Chia Hsia. Ithaca, N.Y., 1988.

———. "Women's Work in the Changing City Economy, 1500–1650." In *Connecting Spheres: Women in the Western World, 1500 to the Present,* ed. Marilyn J. Boxer and Jean H. Quataert. New York, 1987.

———. *Working Women in Renaissance Germany.* New York, 1986.

Woolf, S. J. "Venice and the Terraferma: Problems of the Change from Commercial to Landed Activities." In *Crisis and Change in the Venetian Economy in the Sixteenth and Seventeenth Centuries,* ed. Brian Pullan. London, 1968.

Wrightson, Keith. "Infanticide in Early Seventeenth-Century England." *Local Population Studies* 15 (1975): 10–21.

Wrigley, E. A., and R. S. Schofield. *The Population History of England, 1541–1871: A Reconstruction.* Cambridge, Mass., 1981.

Zago, Roberto. *I Nicolotti.* Padua, 1982.

Zanelli, Guglielmo. *Traghetti veneziani: La gondola al servizio della città.* Venice, 1997.

Zannini, Andrea. "Un ceto di funzionari amministrativi: I cittadini originari veneziani, 1569–1730." *Studi Veneziani* n.s. 23 (1992): 131–45.

Zell, Michael. "Families and Households in Staplehurst, 1563–64." *Local Population Studies* 33 (1984): 54–58.

Zingarelli, Nicola, with Miro Dogliotti and Luigi Rosiello, eds. *Lo Zingarelli, 1998: Vocabolario della lingua italiana.* Milan, 1998.

Zorattini, Pier Cesare Ioly. *Processi del S. Uffizio di Venezia contro Ebrei e Giudaizzanti.* Florence, 1982.

Index

Library of Congress Cataloging-in-Publication Data

Chojnacka, Monica.
Working women of early modern Venice /
by Monica Chojnacka.
    p. cm. — (The Johns Hopkins University studies
in historical and political science 118th ser., 3)
Includes bibliographical references and index.
ISBN 0-8018-6485-2 (hardcover : alk. paper)
1. Women—Employment—Italy—Venice—History.
2. Women employees—Italy—Venice—History.
3. Women—Italy—Venice—History.   I. Title.
II. Series.
HD6155.V45 C47 2001
331.4′0945′31—dc21
00-009273